Strange Encounters

Strange Encounters examines the relationship between strangers, embodiment and community. It challenges the assumption that the stranger is simply *anybody* we do not recognise and instead proposes that *some bodies* are already recognised as stranger than other bodies.

In this fascinating new book Sara Ahmed analyses a diverse range of texts which produce the figure of 'the stranger', showing that it has both been expelled as the origin of danger – as in neighbourhood watch – or celebrated as the origin of difference – as in multiculturalism. However, the author argues that both of these standpoints are problematic as they involve 'stranger fetishism'; they assume that the stranger 'has a life of its own'.

Using feminist and post-colonial theory, this book examines the impact of multiculturalism, migration and globalisation on embodiment and community. It also considers the ethical and political implications of its critique of stranger fetishism for post-colonial feminism.

Sara Ahmed is a lecturer in the Institute of Women's Studies, Lancaster University. She is currently Co-Director of the Institute with Jackie Stacey.

D1566035

Transformations: Thinking Through Feminism
Edited by:
Maureen McNeil
Institute of Women's Studies, Lancaster University
Lynne Pearce
Department of English, Lancaster University
Beverley Skeggs
Department of Sociology, Manchester University

Other books in the series include:

Strange Encounters

Embodied Others in Post-Coloniality

Sara Ahmed

London and New York

First published 2000
by Routledge
11 New Fetter Lane, London EC4P 4EE

Simultaneously published in the USA and Canada
by Routledge
29 West 35th Street, New York, NY 10001

Routledge is an imprint of the Taylor & Francis Group

Typeset in Garamond by Taylor & Francis Books Ltd

British Library Cataloguing in Publication Data
A catalogue record for this book is available from the British Library

Library of Congress Cataloguing in Publication Data
Ahmed, Sara.
Strange encounters: embodied others in post-coloniality / Sara
Ahmed.
p. cm. – (Transformations)
Includes bibliographical references and index.
1. Intercultural communication. 2. Strangers. 3. Immigrants. 4.
Minorities. 5. Feminist theory. I Title. II. Series.
HM1211.A35 2000
303.48'2–dc21   00–028076

ISBN 0–415–20184–5 (hbk)
ISBN 0–415–20185–3 (pbk)

For Erin and Charlotte

Contents

Series editors' preface

Sara Ahmed's *Strange Encounters* is an important contribution to the Transformations series. In tackling difficult but pressing issues associated with notions of 'strangers', 'embodiment' and 'community' in the contemporary Western world, Ahmed mobilises feminist and post-colonial theory astutely and critically. Analysing the production of 'the stranger', she identifies the fetishisation of this figure in a variety of contemporary sites including: 'neighbourhood watch', discourses of multiculturalism, and some postmodernist celebrations of hybridity. Ahmed contends that the agency of the Western self and nation is constructed, mobilised and legitimised through such fetishisation.

We welcome *Strange Encounters* as a valuable study in its own right and as path-setting for the Transformations series. This volume signals to us and, we anticipate, to other readers, a critical openness which we hope will characterise the series. Sara Ahmed draws on and continues some interesting recent feminist research trajectories in post-colonial studies and in cultural studies of the body. However, she does not simply carry on in the streams of this feminist work. Instead, her research poses critical questions about these emerging traditions: has post-colonial feminism concentrated on the question of 'otherness', whilst neglecting the question of 'strangeness'? Has the feminist attention to the body been decontextualised and separated from the study of migration, multiculturalism and globalisation? Our expectation is that the Transformations series will continue in this mode: extending, whilst critically reflecting on, key developments in feminist thinking and research.

This volume, like the series as a whole, attempts to *think through feminism* in challenging ways. One dimension of this is the use of feminist theory to conceptualise issues that are pressing or neglected. In Sara Ahmed's case, this meant examining the cultivation of fears and desires around the figure of the stranger in the West and investigating the political significance of such cultivation. Although migration, othering and otherness, globalisation and sexual and racial violence (to name but a few relevant topics) have all come under the scrutiny of feminists and other critical scholars, strangerness has had limited attention. Unfortunately, as Ahmed contends, universalising has been a feature of the previous critical forays into this field (Kristeva 1991; Bauman 1993).

Strange Encounters is a critical text which points to the need for transformation in established Western practices and thinking around strangerness, but also in some alternative (including feminist) conceptions of strangerness. It is, nevertheless, an optimistic book, which exudes enthusiasm for new forms of post-colonial feminist ethics and politics. In this sense, it sets the tone for the Transformations series as one in which contributors think through feminism critically and optimistically for the twenty-first century.

Maureen McNeil
Lynne Pearce

Acknowledgements

I would like to thank all my colleagues at the Institute for Women's Studies, Lancaster University, especially Maureen McNeil, Imogen Tyler and Jackie Stacey. Thanks to Janet Hartley, Sandra Irving and Cathie Holt for your support and for not minding too much about my nasty habit of stealing pens! A big cheers to all the students who have taken WS301: Gender, Race and Colonialism, as well as to my research students, for always surprising me with unexpected questions. My gratitude to all those who took the time to read parts of this book and for being friendly in your criticisms, including Claudia Castañeda, Josie Dolan, Anne-Marie Fortier, Jane Kilby, Elena Loizidou, Mimi Sheller, Beverley Skeggs, Jackie Stacey and Imogen Tyler. Thanks to Debra Ferreday for helping me to edit the final manuscript. My appreciation goes to Maureen McNeil, Lynne Pearce and Beverley Skeggs for their help and advice as series editors, and to Mari Shullaw, for being patient with my impatience. I was very lucky to complete this book while on sabbatical in Australia. Can I express my gratitude to all those in the Department of Social Inquiry, Adelaide University, who made this possible, to the Institute for Women's Studies, Lancaster University, who allowed me to stay away for so long, and to Fiona Nicoll and Aileen Moreton-Robinson for shared beers and conversation during my time in Adelaide.

A big thanks to all my sisters: Tanya, Tamina, Shana and Alisa. As always, my gratitude to my mother for years of love and sharing, despite the physical distance between us (and for overcoming your technophobia and going on-line so we could communicate more easily!). Thanks also to my father and Jill for their support. In fond memory of Jackie Fisher, my grandmother, who sadly passed away while I was writing this book. My appreciation to Jen and Don Spooner, Caroline and Neil Barratt, as well as Julie Fisher and David Scott, for shared dinners and chats while I've been living in England. For all the friendships that now litter these pages, and to all of you who've laughed with me and even at me, I am deeply grateful. A big cheers to: Bruce Bennett, Fred Botting, Peter Buse, Josie Dolan, Elena Loizidou, Simon O'Sullivan, Lorna Stevens, Núria Triana Toribio, Imogen Tyler, Anna Weaver, Clare Whatling and Anne Wilbourne. And my thanks and love go to Simon Spooner.

While this book was in press, we were all shocked and distressed by the murder of one of our final year undergraduates, Lorraine Price. I would also like to dedicate this book to the memory of Lorraine, and to all her peers who graduated in July 2000, whose lives have been so deeply affected by this tragic event.

A shorter version of Chapter 2 appeared as 'Embodying Strangers' in Avril Horner and Angela Keane (eds), *Body Matters*, Manchester: Manchester University Press (2000). An extended version of Chapter 3 was published as, 'Who Knows? Knowing Strangers and Strangerness', *Australian Feminist Studies* 15, 31: 49–68 (2000). Another version of Chapter 4 was published as 'Home and Away: Narratives of Migration and Estrangement' in *International Journal of Cultural Studies* 2, 3: 329–347 (1999). Short segments from chapter 6 have been published in two papers: 'Phantasies of Becoming (the Other)', *European Journal of Cultural Studies* 2, 1: 47–63 (1999); ' "*She'll wake up one of these days and find she's turned into a Nigger*": Passing Through Hybridity', *Theory. Culture and Society* 16, 2: 87–106 (1999). I gratefully acknowledge permission to reprint copyright material.

Introduction

Stranger fetishism and post-coloniality

I look up 'Global Books in Print'. Taking an easy route, I type in two words, 'strange' and 'encounters'. A number of book titles flash up on the screen. I examine them with nervous attention, worried that it has all been done before. But no, the sub-titles indicate a difference: here the named encounters are with UFOs, Aliens, Abductions. I sit back on my chair with a haughty relief. I am not interested in *that* kind of encounter. I smile, not bothering to write down the reference details of these alien books.

But then each time I return to my title, I think alien thoughts. I wonder at the conditions of possibility for the writing of these other 'strange encounters', as encounters with aliens, those who are beyond the very category of 'the human'. It seems symptomatic that the strange encounter is written as the encounter with the one who is, quite literally, not from this planet.

The alien, on the one hand, is so over-represented in popular culture that it has become quite recognisable. We recognise aliens on our screens: the green almost-flesh, the shape of the head, the protruding eyes. I can doodle on a piece of paper and draw an alien. It appears as if by magic. On the other hand, the absence and presence of the alien pushes us to recognise the limits of representation as that which exceeds 'our' knowledge. There is always the possibility that we might not recognise an alien if we see one: aliens may be alien to the very cultural imagination which allows them to appear as 'little green men'. The figure of the alien reminds us that what is 'beyond the limit' is subject to representation: indeed, what is beyond representation is also, at the same time, over-represented. What is over-represented and familiar in its very alien-ness cannot be reduced or *found* in such representational forms. Such a double and contradictory existence of aliens in and beyond representation invites us to ask questions about the very relationship between the categories of alien and human: What techniques are available to allow us to differentiate aliens from humans? How do such techniques of differentiation serve to constitute the very category of 'the human'? To what extent does the familiarity of the alien form involve the designation of 'the beyond' as that which is already contained within?

Indeed, the detection of alien forms becomes a mechanism for the reassertion of a most human 'we': we must be able to tell (see, smell, touch) the difference. Aliens may get inside our heads: they may infiltrate us; they may even *appear as (like) humans*. How can we tell the difference between a human being and an alien who passes as human? How can we prevent ourselves from becoming alien? Can we become aliens in order to know them better? The fantasy of aliens who are too close to home expands rather than threatens our knowledge: the possibility that aliens could be nearby requires that we invent new ways of telling the difference, new forms of detection, better practices of surveillance. In the *X Files*, we watch surgeons operating on aliens with a sense of anticipation: what can we tell from the insides of aliens? How can we get underneath their skin? How can we penetrate into the being of alien forms?

The alien then is not simply the one whom we have failed to identify ('unidentified flying objects'), but is the one whom we have already identified in the event of being named as alien: the alien recuperates all that is beyond the human into the singularity of a given form. The alien hence comes to be a fetish: it becomes abstracted from the relations which allow it to appear in the present and hence *reappears* no matter where we look. Through seeing aliens, here and elsewhere, we imagine we can tell the difference, a difference that is registered on the green slime, that is almost, but not quite, skin. Encounters with aliens are bodily encounters, encounters in which slime and skin slide off one another: we are already touched by alien forms (we are touched, in our very withdrawal from the slime of alien skin). Our disgust at the abjection of alien forms allows us to contain ourselves. We shiver and tremble and pull our hands away: it is a close encounter.

On the one hand, we could consider the over-representation of alien forms as a discourse of 'alien danger': the alien represents the danger of the unknown. We recuperate all that is dangerous about the unknown into the singularity of the alien form: danger is not only projected onto the outside, *but the outside is contained within a figure we imagine we have already faced*. But, on the other hand, the alien is a source of fascination and desire: making friends with aliens, eating with aliens, or even eating one (up), might enable us to transcend the very limits and frailties of an all-too-human form. Or, by allowing some aliens to co-exist 'with us', we might expand our community: we might prove our advancement into or beyond the human; we might demonstrate our willingness to accept difference and to make it our own. Being hospitable to aliens might, in this way, allow us to become human. It could even allow us to become alien, to gain access to alien worlds, previously uncharted by other humans. Perhaps this is how we can read the fantastic narrative of the film *Close Encounters of the Third Kind*, where the decoding of an alien language into the simplicity of a musical rhythm allows a cultural transaction between aliens and humans, in the form of trading stolen human bodies for one that *willingly* enters the alien world. What is at stake in the *ambivalence* of such relationships between human and alien is not whether aliens are represented as good or bad, or as 'beyond' or 'within' the human, but how they function to establish and define the boundaries of who 'we' are in their very proximity, in the very intimacy of the relationship between (alien) slime and (human) skin.

Of course, not all aliens hesitate at the borders of the human. To be an alien in a particular nation, is to hesitate at a different border: the alien here is the one who does not belong in a nation space, and who is already defined as such by the Law. The alien is hence only a category within a given community of citizens or subjects: as the outsider inside, the alien takes on a spatial function, establishing relations of proximity and distance within the home(land). Aliens allow the demarcation of spaces of belonging: by coming too close to home, they establish the very necessity of policing the borders of knowable and inhabitable terrains. The techniques for differentiating between citizens and aliens, as well as between humans and aliens, allows the familiar to be established as the familial.

This book, while it takes as its point of entry a rather different set of encounters, is nevertheless an attempt to work through the familiarity of alien forms ('strangers'). Through strange encounters, the figure of the 'stranger' is produced, not as that which we fail to recognise, but as that which we have already recognised as 'a stranger'. In the gesture of recognising the one that we do not know, the one that is different from 'us', we flesh out the beyond, and give it a face and form. It is this 'fleshing out' of strangers in encounters with embodied others that I examine. The alien stranger is hence, not beyond human, but a mechanism *for allowing us to face that which we have already designated as the beyond.* So we imagine, here, now, that we are facing an alien stranger: it allows us to share a fantasy that, in the co-presence of strange and alien bodies, we will prevail.

Stranger fetishism

At the same time, this is *not* a book about strangers (or aliens). Rather, it is a book that attempts to question the assumption that we can have an ontology of strangers, that it is possible to simply *be a stranger*, or *to face a stranger* in the street. To avoid such an ontology, we must refuse to take for granted the stranger's status as a figure. The stranger is clearly figured in a variety of discourses, including the crime prevention and personal safety discourse of 'stranger danger' (see Chapter 1). In such a discourse, which is clearly a field of knowledge that marks out what is safe as well as what is dangerous, the stranger is always a figure, stalking the streets: there are some-bodies who simply are strangers, and who pose danger in their very co-presence in a given street. The assumption that we can tell the difference between strangers and neighbours which is central to, for example, neighbourhood watch programmes, functions to conceal forms of social difference. By defining 'us' against any-body who is a stranger, what is concealed is that some-bodies are already recognised as stranger and more dangerous than other bodies (see also Chapter 2).

However, as I will argue throughout the book, the problems implicit in discourses such as 'stranger danger' – where it is assumed that being a stranger is a matter of inhabiting a certain body – are not resolved by simply welcoming 'the stranger'. Such a gesture still takes for granted the status of the stranger as a figure with both linguistic and bodily integrity. Hence, I examine how multiculturalism can function to assimilate 'the stranger' as a figure of the unassimilable (see Chapter 5). While 'stranger danger' discourse may work by expelling the stranger as the *origin of danger*, multicultural discourse may operate by welcoming the stranger as the *origin of difference*. I suggest that it is the processes of expelling *or* welcoming the one who is recognised as a stranger that produce the figure of the stranger in the first place. That figure is also taken for granted in ethnographic discourses which seek to transform the being of strangers into knowledge (see Chapter 3), and consumerist discourses which invite the consumer to become the stranger or inhabit the bodies of strangers by wearing certain products (see Chapter 6). The stranger does not have to be recognised as 'beyond' or outside the 'we' in order to be fixed within the contours of a given form: indeed, it is the very gesture of getting closer to 'strangers' that allows the figure to take its shape.

In this book, I also challenge the turn towards the stranger in some recent postmodern theory. The figure of the stranger has been taken to represent all that was excluded or delegitimated in modernity with its belief in order, sameness and totality (Bauman 1993, 1995). The figure of the stranger has become crucial: no longer seen as a threat to community, the stranger becomes a reminder of the differences we must celebrate. For example, Zygmunt Bauman calls for postmodern strangerhood 'to be protected and lovingly preserved' (1997: 54). However, in *Strange Encounters* this idea that we should simply love the stranger as a basis for an ethics of alterity (see Chapter 7), or a non-universalist form of political activism (see Chapter 8), is questioned. While such theoretical moves may challenge the discourse of 'stranger danger' by refusing to recognise the stranger as dangerous, they also take for granted the stranger's status as a figure that contains or *has* meaning. It is this very granting of figurability that functions to conceal the histories of determination which were already concealed in the discourses of stranger danger.

In other words, the turn to the stranger as a figure who should be welcomed does question the discourses of 'stranger danger', *but only insofar as it keeps in place the fetishism upon which those discourses rely*. Such a fetishism can be described as a fetishism of figures. Indeed, the Marxist model of commodity fetishism might help us to understand how a fetishism of figures might function.[1] The classical Marxist account of commodity fetishism considers the 'enigmatic' form of the commodity as a *substitution*; the social relations of labour become displaced onto the commodity form (Marx 1976: 164).

While this is clearly a theory of objectification, it also allows us to consider the relationship between object fetishism and a fetishism of figures. When Marx makes his (problematic) analogy between primitive religion and commodification, he considers how the 'products of the brain', 'appear as autonomous *figures* endowed with a life of their own' (1976: 164; emphasis added). The analogy suggests that the process of fetishisation involves, not only the displacement of social relations onto an object, but the transformation of fantasies into figures.[2] We could bring the two processes together and suggest that fetishism involves the displacement of social relations of labour *through the transformation of objects into figures*. What is at stake is the 'cutting off' of figures from the social and material relations which overdetermine their existence, and the consequent perception that such figures have a 'life of their own'. Stranger fetishism is a fetishism of figures:[3] *it invests the figure of the stranger with a life of its own insofar as it cuts 'the stranger' off from the histories of its determination*. We need to consider, then, what are the social relationships (involving both fantasy and materiality) that are concealed in stranger fetishism, even if we no longer use the version of determination that is exercised in Marxist theory.

In the theoretical celebration of 'the stranger' as a figure that is paradigmatic of postmodernism, there is an investment in strangerhood as an ontological condition, and in the stranger, as *having a life of its own*. Michael Dillon suggests that, 'the stranger by *his or her very nature* is outwith the settled modes of questioning, and the received understandings of truth and identity' (1999: 121; emphasis added). Here, strangers are assumed to have a nature. Although that nature is no longer represented as dangerous, this argument still ontologises the stranger, turns the stranger into something that simply *is*. The investment in the figure of the stranger involves making claims about the stranger's being. As a result, Dillon defines the figure of 'the stranger' only as having effects, rather than as an effect in itself (= stranger fetishism).

What are the effects of ontologising the stranger? What forms of difference are concealed in that act of fetishisation? The problems of ontologising 'the stranger' as a way of being in the world are clear in Bülent Diken's *Strangers, Ambivalence and Social Theory* (1998). Diken takes up the figure of the stranger as the one who is excluded from forms of belonging and identity, particularly within the context of discourses of nationhood. He defines the stranger as the one who inhabits a space of ambivalence, in which one is not quite 'us' or 'them' (Diken 1998: 11). Diken then names who is included within the category of 'the stranger': 'I want to view immigrants, foreigners, refugees etc. all as "strangers" ' (1998: 123). This extraordinary statement highlights the problems with granting the stranger the status of a figure which has a referent in the world: it functions to elide the substantive differences between ways of being displaced from 'home'. 'The stranger', when used in this way, works to conceal differences; it allows different forms of displacement to be gathered together in the singularity of a given name.

Such an erasure of differences is implicated in any attempt to define the stranger as the one who leaves home and moves to a different place (see Chapter 4). Within this model, all forms of movement, travel and displacement are assumed to lead to the same place: the place of the stranger.[4]

Diken then suggests that everybody is a stranger: 'almost all people are in one way or another displaced, or become immigrants, because of globalisation, increasing mobility, urbanization, tourism etc.' (1998: 124). Here, strangerness is not simply ontologised, *but it is universalised as that which 'we' have in common*, in the presumed universality of homelessness. The effects of stranger fetishism are clear: the figure of the stranger assumes a life of its own only insofar as it is cut off from the histories of its determination, and hence only insofar *as it erases the very forms of difference that render impossible the formation of an inclusive community*.

Not surprisingly then, Diken concludes his book with the following statement, 'with the stranger, we find ourselves' (1998: 334). Diken is clearly borrowing from Julia Kristeva, who calls for us to follow the lead of psychoanalysis in a 'journey into the strangeness of the other and of oneself, toward an ethics of respect for the irreconcilable. How could one tolerate the stranger if one did not know one was a stranger to oneself?' (1991: 182). The journey towards the stranger becomes a form of self-discovery, in which the stranger functions yet again to establish and define the 'I'. This 'I' translates swiftly into a 'we' (I am the stranger, we are all strangers). I would argue, in contrast, that we need to understand how identity is established through strange encounters without producing a universe of strangers. While identity itself may operate through the designation of others as strangers, rendering strangers internal rather than external to identity, to conclude simply that we are all strangers to ourselves is to avoid dealing with the political processes whereby some others are designated as *stranger than other others*. This book will pose the question: how can we understand the relationship between identity and strangerness in lived embodiment without creating a new 'community of strangers'?

Encounters

I suggest that we can only avoid stranger fetishism — that is, avoid welcoming or expelling the stranger as a figure which has linguistic and bodily integrity — by examining the social relationships that are concealed by this very fetishism. That is, we need to consider how the stranger is an effect of processes of inclusion and exclusion, or incorporation and expulsion, that constitute the boundaries of bodies and communities, including communities of living (dwelling and travel), as well as epistemic communities.

I describe such processes in terms of encounters in order to show how they are determined, but not fully determined. The term encounter suggests a meeting, but a meeting which involves surprise and conflict. We can ask:

how does identity itself become instituted through encounters with others that surprise, that shift the boundaries of the familiar, of what we assume that we know? Identity itself is constituted in the 'more than one' of the encounter: the designation of an 'I' or 'we' requires an encounter with others. These others cannot be simply relegated to the outside: given that the subject comes into existence as an entity only through encounters with others, then the subject's existence cannot be separated from the others who are encountered. As such, the encounter itself is ontologically prior to the question of ontology (the question of the being who encounters).

At one level, we can think about encounters as face-to-face meetings. Such face-to-face meetings can be thought of as 'eye-to-eye', involving a visual economy of recognition (see Chapter 1), and as 'skin-to-skin', involving an economy of touch (see Chapter 2). In face-to-face meetings, where at least two subjects get close enough to see and touch each other, there is a necessary movement in time and space. The face to face requires that at least two subjects *approach* each other. The encounter, as a face to face, can only be thought of as a discrete event when the temporal and spatial function of this approach is negated. An emphasis on encounters involves a radical rethinking of what it might mean to face (up to) others (see Chapter 7). The face-to-face encounter is mediated precisely by that which allows the face to appear in the present. The face-to-face is hence not simply about two persons facing each other – the face to face cannot be thought of as a coupling. This encounter is mediated; it presupposes other faces, other encounters of facing, other bodies, other spaces, and other times. To talk about the importance of encounters to identity is to remind ourselves of the processes that are already at stake in the coming together of (at least) two subjects. Thinking of encounters as 'face-to-face' meetings also suggests that identity does not simply happen in the privatised realm of the subject's relation to itself. Rather, in daily meetings with others, subjects are perpetually reconstituted: the work of identity formation is never over, but can be understood as the sliding across of subjects in their meetings with others.

However, meetings do not have to involve the face-to-face encounter of at least two subjects. Meetings do not even presuppose the category of the human person. More generally, a meeting suggests *a coming together of at least two elements*. For example, we can think of reading as a meeting between reader and text. In this context, to talk of encounters as constitutive of identity (that which makes a given thing a thing) is to suggest that there is always more than one in the demarcation of 'the one': there is always a relationship to a reader, who is not inside or outside the text, in the determination of the text as such. To make the encounter prior to the form of the text (what the text would be within itself) is, not only to refuse to assume that the text or reader have an independent existence, but also to suggest that it is through being read that the text comes to life as text, that the text comes to be thinkable as having an existence in the first place. A thesis on the priority of encounters over identity suggests that it is only through meeting with an-other that the identity of a given person *comes to be inhabited as living*.

If encounters are meetings, then they also involve surprise. The more-than-one of such meetings that allow the 'one' to be faced and to face others, is not a meeting between already constituted subjects who know each other: rather, the encounter is premised on the absence of a knowledge that would allow one to control the encounter, or to predict its outcome. As a result, encounters constitute the space of the familial (by allowing the 'I' or the 'we' to define itself in relation to others who are already faced), but in doing so, they shift the boundaries of what is familiar. Encounters involve both fixation, and the impossibility of fixation. So, for example, when we face others, we seek to recognise who they are, by reading the signs on their body, or by reading their body *as* a sign. As I will argue, such acts of reading constitute 'the subject' in relation to 'the stranger', who is recognised as 'out of place' in a given place. The surprising nature of encounters can be understood in relation to the structural possibility that *we may not be able to read the bodies of others*. However, each time we are faced by an other whom we cannot recognise, we seek to find other ways of achieving recognition, not only by re-reading the body of *this* other who is faced, but by telling the difference between this other, and other others. The encounters we might yet have with other others hence surprise the subject, but they also *reopen the prior histories of encounter that violate and fix others in regimes of difference* (see Chapter 6).

Encounters are meetings, then, which are not simply in the present: each encounter reopens past encounters. Encounters involve, not only the surprise of being faced by an other who cannot be located in the present, they also involve conflict. The face-to-face meeting is not between two subjects who are equal and in harmony; the meeting is antagonistic. The coming together of others that allows the 'one' to exist takes place given that there is an asymmetry of power. The relationship between the encounter and forms of social antagonism requires that we consider the relationship between the particular – this encounter – and the general. At one level, we can think of this relationship as determined by that which must already have taken place to allow the particular encounter to take place, that is, the social processes that are at stake in the coming together of (at least) two subjects. However, this would presuppose that the particular is an *outcome* of the general, and would assume that both are already determined at different times and places. I want to consider how the particular encounter both informs and is informed by the general: encounters between embodied subjects always hesitate between the domain of the particular – the face to face of this encounter – and the general – the framing of the encounter by broader relationships of power and antagonism. The particular encounter hence always carries *traces* of those broader relationships. Differences, as markers of power, are not determined in the 'space' of the particular *or* the general, but in the very determination of their historical relation (a determination that is never final or complete, as it involves strange encounters).

It will be my argument that differences can be understood through thinking about the role of everyday encounters in the forming of social space (see Chapter 1) as well as bodily space (see Chapter 2). Such differences are not then to be found *on the bodies of others* (see Chapter 7), but are determined through encounters between others: they are impossible to grasp in the present. We can return now to my argument about stranger fetishism. To say that stranger fetishism functions to conceal forms of difference is to suggest that the figure of the stranger only appears *by being cut off from such encounters between embodied others*. For example, if we were to describe the subaltern woman *as* the stranger then we would erase the particularity of her embodiment. This is not to say that difference can be found on her body: this difference can be encountered only in relationship to other encounters, that are determined elsewhere (that is, they are not simply in the present), such as those that are determined by the international and gendered division of labour. She can only become the stranger *by a forgetting of how her embodiment carries traces of these labouring formations* (see my reading of the short story, 'Douloti the Bountiful' in Chapter 7).

The face to face of this encounter cannot, then, be detached or isolated from such broader relations of antagonism: to do so, would be to forget how the possibility or impossibility of some face-to-face encounters is already determined. It is here that my thesis on the priority of encounters over identity meets its limits: we must pose the question of historicity, which is forgotten by the very designation of 'the encounter' as such.

Post-coloniality

To the extent that historicity poses itself as a question, then it also reveals its own impossibility as an answer. That is, we cannot assume that history is something that can be simply missing from the abstraction of the encounter from the broader social relationships that make encounters possible: to do so would turn history into another fetish, into an object that could be absent or present. Rather, the question of history can only be posed partially: it is a question that allows us to think about how the relationship between particular encounters and more general processes requires an impure or *failed theory*. That is, although the relationship between the particular and the general may be determined, it is not fully determined, which means that we must give up the assumption that it can be translated into a meta-discourse (such as History). Such a meta-discourse would both explain and not explain the relation: for example, we could say that the relationship between the particular and general is History, but to name that relationship as History would be to describe both everything and nothing. Rather than saying that History determines the relationship between this and that, we can ask, 'how is the relationship between this and that determined?' as a historical question, a question that henceforth cannot be answered in a total or exhaustive manner. An historical approach to the relationship between particular encounters and more general processes requires that we give up any totalising thesis about what does and does not determine each encounter as such. Indeed, rethinking the primacy of the encounter over ontology is also a means by which we can introduce historicity, as the very absence of any totality that governs the encounter.

It is here that I want to introduce post-coloniality as *a failed historicity*: a historicity that admits of its own failure in grasping that which has been, as the impossibility of grasping the present. Post-colonialism has already been accused of its failure as a history: for example, critics have argued that it is too totalising and universalising to grasp the multiplicity of colonial histories, and that it is bound up with an inadequate temporality in the very assumption of the 'post' (McClintock 1992; Ahmad 1992, 1995).[5] One of the key arguments is that the term 'post-colonial' is problematic precisely because it makes colonialism the marker of historical difference. As Anne McClintock states, 'If the theory promises a decentering of history in hybridity, syncretism, multi-dimensional time and so forth, the *singularity* of the term effects a recentering of global history around the single rubric of European time' (1992: 86).

Aijaz Ahmad's critique of post-colonialism's emphasis on the centrality of colonialism as a marker of time involves a recentring on capitalist modernity as the primary engine in determining historical change. He implies that colonialism is almost incidental to this history insofar as modernisation took place whether or not particular nation-states were colonised by the Europeans (Ahmad 1995: 7). He argues that the primary determination of history is capitalist modernity which then, 'takes the colonial form in particular places and at particular times' (ibid.). To some extent, I seek to contest such a position by arguing that colonialism is structural rather than incidental to any understanding of the constitution of both modernity and postmodernity (if we can define the latter, very inadequately, as the relative globalisation of modernity). To make such an argument is not to say that we can only understand such historical transitions in terms of colonialism – I am not seeking to reverse the terms of Ahmad's version of Marxism, by making colonialism primary and capitalist modernity, secondary. What is crucial is that the colonial project was not *external* to the constitution of the modernity of European nations: rather, the identity of these nations became predicated on their relationship to the colonised others. This is one of the significant theoretical contributions made by those working on post-colonialism, and its implications are far reaching.

Others critics of post-colonialism have suggested that it (conservatively) assumes that colonialism has been overcome in the present (Shohat 1992: 104). I would agree with this critique, if post-colonialism was being used literally to refer to a time after colonialism. However, my understanding of post-coloniality is different. In some sense, the impossibility of post-colonialism describing the past or the present is my starting point. When post-colonialism is assumed to be referential – we are in a post-colonial time or place – then it does become deeply conservative: it assumes that 'we' have overcome the legacies of colonialism, and that this overcoming is what binds 'us' together. For me, post-colonialism is about rethinking *how* colonialism operated in different times in ways that permeate all aspects of social life, in the colonised and colonising nations. It is hence about the complexity of the relationship between the past and present, between the histories of European colonisation and contemporary forms of globalisation. That complexity cannot be reduced by either a notion that the present has broken from the past (a narrative that assumes that decolonisation[6] meant the end of colonialism) or that the present is simply continuous with the past (a narrative that assumes colonialism is a trans-historical phenomenon that is not affected by local contexts or other forms of social change). To this extent, post-coloniality allows us to investigate how colonial encounters are both determining, and yet not fully determining, of social and material existence.

It is in this very precise sense that I understand post-colonialism as a failed historicity: it re-examines the centrality of colonialism to a past that henceforth cannot be understood as a totality, or as a shared history. It is the very argument that colonialism is central to the historical constitution of modernity (an apparently simple argument, but one that must nevertheless be repeated) that also suggests history is not the continuous line of the emergence of a people, but a series of discontinuous encounters between nations, cultures, others and other others. History can no longer be understood as that which determines each encounter. Rather, historicity involves the history of such encounters that are unavailable in the form of a totality.

My analysis of strange encounters begins with the failed historicisation of post-coloniality.[7] Indeed, post-colonialism as a body of knowledge, has come into existence through a prior theorisation of colonialism as an encounter between cultures, and cultural difference as a form of encounter (Hulme 1986; Greenblatt 1993; Bailyn and Morgan 1991). Colonialism as an encounter involves, not only the territorial domination of one culture by another, but also forms of discursive appropriation: other cultures become appropriated into the imaginary globality of the colonising nation. The encounters that characterise colonialism are not simply one-sided or monological: encounters involve at least two cultures who, in their meeting, transform the conditions of the encounter itself. In Mary Louise Pratt's work, the encounter becomes theorised in terms of the contact zone as, 'an attempt to involve the spatial and temporal co-presence of subjects previously separated by geographic and historical disjunctures' (Pratt 1992: 7). Here, the encounter involves both a temporal and spatial dislocation that transforms both the colonising and colonised subjects: in other words, colonial encounters involve a necessarily unequal and asymmetrical dialogue between once distant cultures that transforms each one.

However, one problem with Pratt's model of the 'contact zone' is the use of a linear narrative that assumes a transition from distance to proximity. I want to suggest that colonial encounters involve a much more complex relationship between proximity and distance. Take, for example, Michel de Certeau's analysis of travel writing and colonial encounters (1986: 67). According to de Certeau, the travel account involves a search outward for the strange and works through the rhetorical device of distanciation (the 'appearance' of monsters and marvels, the documenting of cannibalism and polygamy). The homeward journey *almost* returns us to the beginning: the writing always returns home, but with a difference. The one who moves through space, or gets closer to the stranger, returns home as almost the savage, as contaminated by the inbetween of the narrative. In his reading, the relationship between travel and writing determines rather than is determined by a spatialising operation whereby the cultural fields of familiar and strange are precariously established.

Narratives which construct 'the strange culture' as their object (distance), are also contaminated by that very object (proximity). Colonial encounters do not just involve a transition from distance to proximity: they involve, at one and the same time, social and spatial relations of distance and proximity. Others become strangers (the ones who are distant), and 'other cultures' become 'strange cultures' (the ones who are distant), only through coming *too close to home*, that is, through the proximity of the encounter or 'facing' itself. There is hence an intimate relationship between colonial encounters, spatial dislocation and hybridity. Colonial encounters disrupt the identity of the 'two' cultures who meet through the very process of hybridisation – the meeting of the 'two' that transforms each 'one'. But just as the conditions of meeting are not equal, so too hybridisation involves differentiation (the two do not co-mingle to produce one). How others are constituted and transformed through such encounters is dependent upon relationships of force.

Indeed, another of the main critiques of post-colonial theory has been its failure to account for the structural conditions in which 'local encounters' with hybridity and difference take place. Ahmad (1995), Juan (1998) and Dirlik (1997) argue that post-colonial theory is complicit with global capitalism insofar as it emphasises play, hybridity and inbetweenness. Juan, for example, argues that 'post-coloniality can be interpreted as a refurbishing of the liberal individualist ethos geared to the "free play" of the market' (1998: 10), while Ahmad suggests that, 'the underlying logic of this celebratory mode is that of the limitless freedom of a globalised marketplace' (1995: 17). Dirlik bases the entire thesis of his book, *The Post-colonial Aura*, on the assumption that post-colonial theory is a *symptom* of global capitalism, given its emphasis on hybridity and inbetweeness at the expense of power, ideology and structure (1997: 65–66). To some extent, I share a suspicion of some of the post-colonial work that emphasises how hybridity involves the transgression and destabilisation of identity.[8] In Chapter 3 and

Chapter 6, I suggest that hybridisation can become a mechanism for the reconstitution of dominant identities precisely insofar as the hybrid subject – who becomes other through knowledge and consumption – remains defined against the 'native subject' who, paradoxically, is also represented as *being* the stranger. However, both Juan's and Ahmad's critiques involve making sweeping claims that underestimate the rigour of post-colonial critics such as Gayatri Spivak, whose work attends to the complexity of the institutional conditions of global capitalism (and who defines these conditions not simply in terms of class, but also in terms of race and gender).[9] What post-colonialism can allow us to examine is *how* forms of hybridisation, and border crossings, are a means by which contemporary relationships of power are structured. In other words, the encounters in global capitalism may involve the restructuring of power relations *through* (rather than despite) the very forms of play, hybridity and movement discussed by some post-colonial critics.[10]

In *Strange Encounters*, I examine the ways in which contemporary discourses of globalisation and multiculturalism involve the reproduction of the figure of the stranger, and the enforcement of boundaries, through the very emphasis on becoming, hybridity and inbetweenness. If we are to think of post-coloniality as that which is yet to come (we need to think the impossibility of the 'post' if we are to make the 'post' possible), then we need to pay attention to *how* and *where* colonialism persists after so-called decolonisation. That is, we need to pay attention to the *shifting conditions* in which encounters between others, and between other others, take place. From Chapter 4 onwards, I attend to the effects of globalisation, migration and multiculturalism on the relationship between communities and strangers. With the transnational movement of bodies, objects and capital, one could argue that the stranger is always in proximity; that the stranger has come closer to home. However, to say that the stranger is *now* close by would be to assume that the stranger was distant in the past. As my analysis of stranger fetishism suggests, the 'stranger' only becomes a figure through proximity: the stranger's body cannot be reified as the distant body. It is our task to think through the different *modes* of proximity we may have to strangers in contemporary contexts without assuming that the stranger was distant in the past. We need to ask how contemporary modes of proximity *reopen prior histories of encounter*. In *Strange Encounters*, I analyse globalisation, migration and multiculturalism as particular modes of proximity, which produce the figure of 'the stranger' in different ways and which, in doing so, reopen such prior histories of encounter *as* the historical (that is, partial) determination of regimes of difference.

An analysis of strange encounters allows us to address how the encounters that produce 'the stranger' as a figure that has linguistic and bodily integrity are determined. In other words, it is such encounters between embodied others, *impossible to grasp in the present*, which are concealed by stranger fetishism. It is here that we can begin to pose the relationship between stranger fetishism and post-coloniality. In this book, post-coloniality is not stabilised as 'the context' in which strange encounters take place: rather, it is my interest in the *complexity* of the relationship between histories of colonialism and contemporary modes of encounter that is signalled by my use of the term 'post-coloniality'. As a result, the encounters between embodied others that are concealed by stranger fetishism can only be partly understood in terms of post-coloniality. My consideration of the relationship between stranger fetishism and post-coloniality *is also a thesis about how post-coloniality is impossible to grasp in the present.*

Encounters as method and structure

Strange encounters also provide the methodological framework for this book. While the chapters share a concern with stranger fetishism, they also represent fragments or moments of encounter in my own life world. The various readings I offer in the book come in part from my encounters within the academy, for example, my encounters with post-colonialism and with feminism. My concern with the ways in which stranger fetishism operates to conceal forms of difference has been shaped by my intellectual and political encounter with black and post-colonial feminisms, which have paid attention to how differences are always articulated in relationship to each other (hooks 1992; McClintock 1995). But there are other encounters at stake in my choice of different texts; these encounters were themselves shaped by my everyday dwelling (where I live) and travel (where I move). Hence, in the first chapter, I read texts that I first encountered in my local habitat – Lancaster, in the north of England. But, as someone who has travelled, and who has lived in Australia, and who has family connections with Pakistan as well as Britain, I also include readings of texts from other contexts including: political representations of multiculturalism in Australia; feminist ethnographies from Australia; and short stories by South Asian women in Britain and the subcontinent. These different texts reflect my multiple encounters in different local spaces of inhabitance.

One of my arguments is that the relationship between 'the local' and the 'global' is a site of differentiation (I would not talk of globalisation as such, but uneven processes whereby certain locales are constituted as 'the global'). Partly my concern is with the implications of the way in which people, images and objects move across national borders, *as well as the way in which others fail to move.* Some of the texts I encounter, then, are texts that have already moved away from their local space of production and, at least in some cases, have already been elevated into 'the global': for example, images from Boots's *Global Collection* (see Chapter 6) and The Body Shop (see Chapter 8); American stories of racial discovery, both autobiographical and cinematic (see Chapter 6); and documents on women produced by the United Nations (see Chapter 8). In the case of the latter, it is through my encounters with the internet that I came to have access to the texts that I read as constituting (rather than describing) the global. In other words, my encounters with the very texts I read as encounters presuppose the movement and border crossings that I read *within the texts*.

In some ways, then, *Strange Encounters* is the story of my own encounters as a particular, located subject who both dwells and travels in certain places, and who has access to forms of 'nomadic global citizenship' (see Chapter 4) that enable some movements and disallow others. Where possible, I have attempted to write these encounters into my readings of the texts, as a way of avoiding textual fetishism (where one invests meaning in a text by cutting it off from the history of its production and consumption), and as a way of drawing attention to the differences between the texts that I read, at different times and places.

The emphasis on reading (texts) as a form of strange encounter allows us to understand how such encounters are always mediated and partial. Encounters involve the production of meaning as a form of sociality. That is, meanings are produced precisely in the intimacy of the 'more than one': as I suggested earlier in this introduction, by 'coming together' at a particular time and place, the reader and the text generate certain possibilities and foreclose others. Texts of course are not simply written or visual documents: as I argue in the final chapter, there is an intimate relationship between writing and acting, between forms of construction and ways of doing. As a result, the encounters that shape this work are not simply about how and where the stranger is produced as a figure (stranger fetishism), but also *how that figure is put to work, and made to work*, in particular times and places. Indeed, it is precisely the differential relationships of labour that are concealed in stranger fetishism.

The book is structured through different encounters. In Part I, I examine how the stranger becomes a figure and fetish, through modes of recognition and knowledge, as well as forms of embodiment. Chapter 1 considers how 'the stranger' is already recognised as 'the body out of place' and as the origin of danger in neighbourhood watch programmes as well as crime prevention discourses in the United Kingdom. Here, I am interested in local spaces of inhabitance – neighbourhoods – and the relationship between dwelling, strangers and the legitimation of certain ways of moving within space. In Chapter 2, I describe how the recognition of strangers involves the demarcation, not only of social space, but also bodily space. Rather than assuming the stranger is the one who inhabits a strange body, I examine the way strange bodies are produced through tactile encounters with other bodies: differences are not marked *on* the stranger's body, but come to materialise in the relationship of touch between bodies. One of the arguments that runs through these opening chapters is that an emphasis on the dialectic between the self and other is insufficient: it is the very acts and gestures whereby subjects differentiate *between* others (for example, between familiar and strange others) that constitute the permeability of both social and bodily space. In the concluding chapter to this part, I address the relationship between strangers and community more explicitly, by considering how 'the stranger' is produced through knowledge, rather than as a failure of knowledge. I suggest that it is by 'knowing strangers' that the 'we' of the epistemic community is established, even though that 'we' is called into question by the very proximity of 'the strangers' through which it comes to know.

In Part II, I complicate the terms of my analysis by thinking through what happens when our 'homes' are destabilised by the proximity of strangers, that is, when the stranger can no longer be recognised as 'outside' the community, or as 'an outsider' within the community. In Chapter 4, I discuss how the very concept of 'home' is exercised in narratives of migration. I examine how migrant communities are formed in the absence of 'a common terrain' by considering the processes of *estrangement*. This chapter challenges the association between home and stasis, and the assumption that migration is necessarily a movement *away* from home. In the following chapter, I analyse the discourse of nationhood more closely. Rather than simply assuming that 'the stranger' is the one who hesitates at the border of the nation, and who is expelled as the undesirable, I examine multicultural discourses to see how national identity can be established through welcoming (some) strangers. By reading some political documents produced in Australia, I consider how multiculturalism also comes to differentiate between some others and stranger others, such that the stranger is assimilated within the nation, only insofar as she or he becomes 'a native' underneath the appearance of difference. What is crucial then, is that the difference of 'strangers' is claimed as that which makes the nation be itself, rather than being seen as that which threatens the nation. And in Chapter 6, I examine how stranger fetishism is rehearsed in individuated narratives of 'going strange' or 'going native': it is through (rather than despite) the assumption that difference is a style that can be assumed by the subject, that difference becomes fixed onto the bodies of strangers. That is, strangers appear as having 'a life of their own' (being strange) in order to enable the consumer to take on their difference, that is, to take on their style (going strange).

In the final Part, I consider some of the ethical and political implications of my critique of stranger fetishism, whether that fetishism operates by welcoming or expelling the figure of the stranger. In Chapter 7, I begin with a critique of the celebration of otherness in ethical philosophy, in particular, in Levinasian ethics. I introduce a model of difference as economy in order to think through the finite and particular circumstance in which I face up to others. I suggest that an ethics that responds to each other *as if they were other in the same way* is inadequate. Rather than just thinking of ethics as hospitality to strangers, I argue that the ethical demand is to work with that which has been already assimilated, in order to work with that which fails to be assimilated (that which cannot be found in the figure of 'the stranger'). I consider, within the impossible context of post-coloniality, how I can respond more ethically to the work of Mahasweta Devi, as translated by Gayatri Spivak.

Finally, in Chapter 8, I demonstrate how a refusal of stranger fetishism might allow us to theorise differently how transnational feminism can move across spaces. Arguing against universalism and cultural relativism, I analyse how women already encounter each other across the globe, in ways that involve differentiation and antagonism, by examining the production of the signifier 'global woman' in cultural practices and in 'global institutions' such as the United Nations. My model of strange encounters as a form of political activism and collective work suggests that we need to find ways of re-encountering these encounters so that they no longer hold other others in place. Alliances then are not guaranteed by the pre-existing form of a social group or community, whether that form is understood as commonality (a community of friends) or uncommonality (a community of strangers). Collectivities are formed through the *very work that has to be done* in order to get closer to other others. Such a transnational feminism would interrupt, in the work that it does in making a community, the very forms of stranger fetishism that are discussed in this book.

Part I

Encountering the stranger

1   Recognising strangers

I turn around as you pass me. You are a stranger. I have not seen you before. No, perhaps I have. You are very familiar. You shuffle along the foot path, head down, a grey mac shimmering around your feet. You look dirty. There are scars and marks on your hands. You don't return my stare. I think I can smell you as you pass. I think I can hear you muttering. I know you already. And I hold myself together and breathe a sigh of relief as you turn the corner. I want you not to be in my face. I cast you aside with a triumph of one who knows this street. It is not the street where you live.

How do you recognise a stranger? To ask such a question, is to challenge the assumption that the stranger is the one we simply fail to recognise, that the stranger is simply *any-body* whom we do not know. It is to suggest that the stranger is *some-body* whom we have *already recognised* in the very moment in which they are 'seen' or 'faced' as a stranger. The figure of the stranger is far from simply being strange; it is a figure that is painfully familiar in that very strange(r)ness.[1] The stranger has already come too close; the stranger is 'in my face'. The stranger then is not simply the one whom we have not yet encountered, but the one whom we have already encountered, or already faced. The stranger comes to be faced as a form of recognition: we recognise somebody *as a stranger*, rather than simply failing to recognise them.

How does this recognition take place? How can we tell the difference between strangers and other others? In this chapter, I will argue that there are techniques that allow us to differentiate between those who are strangers and those who belong in a given space (such as neighbours or fellow inhabitants). Such techniques involve ways of reading the bodies of others we come to face. Strangers are not simply those who are not known in this dwelling, but those who are, in their very proximity, *already recognised as not belonging*, as being out of place. Such a recognition of those who are out of place allows both the demarcation and enforcement of the boundaries of 'this place', as where 'we' dwell. The enforcement of boundaries requires that some-body – here locatable in the dirty figure of the stranger – has already crossed the line, has already come too close: in Alfred Schutz's terms, the stranger is always approaching (1944: 499). The recognition of strangers is a means by which inhabitable or bounded spaces are produced ('this street'), not simply as the place or locality of residence, but as the very living form of a community.

In this chapter, I analyse how the discourse of stranger danger produces the stranger as a figure – a shape that appears to have linguistic and bodily integrity – which comes then to embody that which must be expelled from the purified space of the community, the purified life of the good citizen, and the purified body of 'the child'. Such an approach to 'the stranger' considers how encounters between others involve the production and over-representation of the stranger as a figure of the unknowable. That is, such encounters allow the stranger to appear, to take form, *by recuperating all that is unknowable into a figure that we imagine we might face here, now, in the street.*

On recognition

To recognise means: to know again, to acknowledge and to admit. How do we know the stranger *again*? The recognisability of strangers is determinate in the social demarcation of spaces of belonging: the stranger is 'known again' as that which has already contaminated such spaces as a threat to both property and person: 'many residents are concerned about the strangers with whom they must share the public space, including wandering homeless people, aggressive beggars, muggers, anonymous black youths, and drug addicts' (Anderson 1990: 238). Recognising strangers is here embedded in a discourse of survival: it is a question of how to survive the proximity of strangers who are already figurable, *who have already taken shape*, in the everyday encounters we have with others.

A consideration of the production of the stranger's figure through modes of recognition requires that we begin with an analysis of the function of local encounters in public life. As Erving Goffman suggests, 'public life' refers to the realm of activity generated by face-to-face interactions that are organised by norms of co-mingling (1972: ix). Such an approach does not take for granted the realm of the public as a physical space that is already deter-mined, but considers how 'the public' comes to be lived through local encounters, through the very gestures and habits of meeting up with others. How do such meetings, such face-to-face encounters, involve modes of recognition that produce the stranger as a figure?

Louis Althusser's thesis of subjectivity as determined through acts of misrecognition evokes the function of public life. Althusser writes:

ideology 'acts' or 'functions' in such a way that it 'recruits' subjects among the individuals (it recruits them all), or 'transforms' the individuals into subjects (it transforms them all) by that very precise operation which I have called *interpellation* or hailing, and which can be imagined along the lines of the most commonplace everyday police (or other) hailing: 'Hey, you there!'

(1971: 162–163)

All individuals are transformed into subjects through the ideological function of interpellation, which is imagined as a commonplace everyday police (or other) hailing. The recognition of the other as 'you there' is a misrecognition which produces the 'you' as a subject, and as subject to the very law implicated in recognition (the subject is suspect in such encounters). Althusser's thesis is clearly to be understood as a universal theory of how subjects come into being as such. However, we might note the following. First, the constitution of the subject through hailing implies that subjectivity is predicated upon an elided 'inter-subjectivity' (see Ahmed 1998a: 143). Second, the function of the act of hailing an-other, 'hey you', opens out the possibility *that subjects become differentiated at the very same moment that they are constituted as such*. If we think of the constitution of subjects as implicated in the uncertainties of public life, then we could imagine how such differentiation might work: the address of the policeman shifts according to whether individuals are already recognisable as, 'wandering homeless people, aggressive beggars, muggers, anonymous black youths, and drug addicts' (Anderson 1990: 238). Hailing as a form of recognition which constitutes the subject it recognises (= misrecognition) might function to differentiate *between* subjects, for example, by hailing differently those who seem to belong and those who might already be assigned a place – out of place – as 'suspect'.

Such an over-reading of Althusser's dramatisation of interpellation through commonplace hailing suggests that the subject is not simply constituted in the present as such. Rather, inter-subjective encounters in public life continually reinterpellate subjects into differentiated economies of names and signs, where they are assigned different value in social spaces. Noticeably, the use of the narrative of the police hailing associates the constitution of subjects with their subjection to a discourse of criminality, which defines the one who is hailed as a threat to property ('Hey, you there'). If we consider how hailing constitutes the subject, then we can also think about how hailing constitutes the stranger in a relationship precisely to the Law of the subject (the stranger is constituted as the unlawful entry into the nation space, the stranger hence allows Law to mark out its terrain). To this extent, the act of hailing or recognising some-body as a stranger serves to constitute the lawful subject, the one who has the right to dwell, and the stranger at the very same time. It is not that the 'you' is or can be simply a stranger, but that to address some-body as a stranger constitutes the 'you' as the stranger in relation to the one who dwells (the friend and neighbour). In this sense, the (mis)recognition of strangers serves to differentiate between the familiar and the strange, a differentiation that allows the figure of the stranger to appear. The failure embedded in such misrecognition – rather than the failure of recognition – determines the impossibility of reducing the other to the figure of the stranger: as I will argue in Chapter 2, the singularity of the figure conceals the different histories of lived embodiment which mark some bodies as stranger than others.

By analysing recognition in this way, I am suggesting that the (lawful) subject is not simply constituted by being recognised by the other, which is the primary post-Hegelian model of recognition (see Taylor 1994). Rather, I am suggesting that it is the recognition of others that is central to the constitution of the subject. The very act through which the subject differentiates between others is the moment that the subject comes to inhabit or dwell in the world. The subject is not, then, simply differentiated from the (its) other, but comes into being by learning how to differentiate between others. This recognition operates as *a visual economy*: it involves ways of *seeing the difference* between familiar and strange others as they are (re)presented to the subject. As a mode of subject constitution, recognition involves differentiating between others on the basis of how they 'appear'.[2]

Given the way in which the recognition of strangers operates to produce who 'we' are, we can see that strangers already 'fit' within the 'cognitive, moral or aesthetic map of the world', rather than being, as Zygmunt Bauman argues, 'the people who do not fit' (1997: 46). There are established ways of dealing with 'the strangers' who are already encountered and recognised in public life. The recognisability of strangers involves, not only techniques for differentiating strange from familiar (ways of seeing), but also ways of living: there are, in Alfred Schutz's terms, 'standardized situations' in which we might encounter strangers and which allow us to negotiate our way past them (1944: 499). Goffman's work on bodily stigma, for example, attends to how the bodies of others that are marked as different, such as disabled bodies, are read in ways which allow the subject to keep their distance (1984: 12). Social encounters involve rules and procedures for 'dealing with' the bodies that are read as strange (Morris 1996: 72–74).

Encounters between embodied others hence involve *spatial negotiations* with those who are already recognised as either familiar or strange. For Schutz, the stranger is always approaching – coming closer to those who are at home (1944: 499). In the sociological analysis of strangers offered by Simmel, the stranger is understood, paradoxically, as both near and far (1991: 146). In the next section, I consider how the determination of social space and imagined forms of belonging takes place through the differentiation between strangers and neighbours in relationships of proximity and distance.

Neighbourhoods and dwelling

How do you recognise who is a stranger in your neighbourhood? To rephrase my original question in this way is to point to the relation between the recognition of strangers and one's habitat or dwelling: others are recognised as strangers by those who inhabit a given space, who 'make it' their own. As Michael Dillon argues, 'with the delimitation of any place of dwelling, the constitution of a people, a nation, a state, or a democracy necessarily specifies who is *estranged from* that identity, place or regime' (1999: 119; emphasis added). At one level, this seems to suggest the relativisability of the condition of strangers: any-one can be a stranger if they leave home (the house, the neighbourhood, the region, the nation).[3] However, in this section I want to argue that forms of dwelling cannot be equated in order to allow such a relativisation. Some homes and neighbourhoods are privileged such that they define the terrain of the inhabitable world. The recognition of strangers brings into play relations of social and political antagonism that *mark some others as stranger than other others*.

How do neighbourhoods become imagined? In the work of Howard Hallman, neighbourhoods are understood as arising from the 'natural human trait' of being neighbourly, which combines a concern with others and a concern for self (1984: 11). According to Hallman, the neighbourhood is an organic community that grows, 'naturally wherever people live close to one another' (1984: 11). It is both a limited territory – a physical space with clear boundaries – and a social community where 'residents do things together' (1984: 13).The simple fact of living nearby gives neighbours a common social bond. However, according to Hallman, some neighbourhoods are closer and hence better than others. He argues that neighbourhoods are more likely to be successful as communities when people live near 'like people': 'people with similarities tend to achieve closer neighbour relationships' (1984: 24). Hallman defines a close neighbourhood through an analogy with a healthy body, 'with wounds healed, illness cured, and wellness maintained' (1984: 256).

The analogy between the ideal neighbourhood and a healthy body serves to define the ideal neighbourhood as fully integrated, homogeneous, and sealed: it is like a body that is fully contained by the skin (see Chapter 2). This implies that a good or healthy neighbourhood does not leak outside itself, and hence does not let outsiders (or foreign agents/viruses) in. The model of the neighbourhood as an organic community – where a sense of community arises from the simple fact of shared residence – defines social health in terms of the production of purified spaces and the expulsion of difference through ways of living together. Matthew Crenson's consideration of neighbourhood politics hence concludes, 'social homogeneity and solidarity ... may contribute to the defensive capabilities of neighbourhoods, and in fact it may take an external attack upon some of these homogenous neighbourhoods to activate the latent sense of fellow feeling along local residents' (1983: 257). Likewise, David Morris and Karl Hess describe neighbourhoods as protective and defensive, like 'tiny underdeveloped nations' (1975: 16).

Neighbourhoods become imagined as organic and pure spaces through the social perception of the danger posed by outsiders to moral and social health or well-being. So although neighbourhoods have been represented as organic and pure communities, there is also an assumption that those communities will fail (to be). A failed community is hence one which has weak or negative connections: where neighbours appear as if they are strangers to each other. The neighbour who is also a stranger – who only passes as a neighbour – is hence the danger that may always threaten the community from within. As David Sibley argues, 'the resistance to a different sort of person moving into a neighbourhood stems from feelings of anxiety, nervousness or fear. Who is felt to belong and not to belong contributes to an important way of shaping social space' (1995: 3). However, the failure of the community should not just be understood in terms of failed communities. *It is the very potential of the community to fail which is required for the constitution of the community.* It is the enforcement of the boundaries between those who are already recognised as out of place (even other fellow residents) that allows those boundaries to be established. The 'ideal' community has to be worked towards and that labour requires failure as its moment of constitution (to this extent, then, the organic community is a fantasy that *requires* its own negation).

It is symptomatic then of the very nature of neighbourhood that it enters public discourse as a site of *crisis*: it is only by attending to the trauma of neighbourhoods which fail that the ideal of the healthy neighbourhood can be maintained as a possibility (which is then, endlessly deferred as 'the real', as well as endlessly kept in place as 'the ideal', by that very language of crisis). Such failed communities are the source of fascination: they demonstrate the need to regulate social spaces. On British television in 1998, there were a number of programmes dedicated to 'neighbours from hell', neighbours who are dirty, who make too much noise, who steal, and who are 'at war' with each other. On *Panorama*'s 'Neighbours from Hell' (30 March 1998), urinating in the street becomes the ultimate expression of the anti-sociability of stranger neighbours. The passing of bodily fluids in public spaces becomes symptomatic of the failure to pass as neighbours. In the United Kingdom, new powers of eviction for local councils give further power to the community to reassert itself against these stranger neighbours. The imaginary community of the neighbourhood hence requires enforcement through Law.

The enforcement of the boundaries which allow neighbourhoods to be imagined as pure and organic spaces can be understood as central to neighbourhood watch schemes. Such schemes began in the United States in the 1970s, and in the United Kingdom in 1982. The National Neighbourhood Watch Association in the United Kingdom (NNWA) describes it as, 'the best known and most effective example of the police and community working together in partnership to prevent crime, build safer communities and improve quality of life'. In the United Kingdom, there are currently over 161,000 schemes and over 10 million people involved. Neighbourhood Watch brings together the creation of an ideal community as one 'which cares' and the production of safer spaces through the discourse of 'crime prevention'. Its main motto is, 'Crime cannot survive in a community that cares – Neighbourhood Watch works'. In other words, crime only exists when communities fail, when communities do not care. Marginalised or under-valued spaces where there is a high rate of crime against property are hence immediately understood in terms of *a failure to care.*

Neighbourhood Watch schemes are more common in middle-class areas, where residents are more likely to want to co-operate with the police, and where there is more 'property' with value to protect (Hill 1994: 150). The value attached to certain spaces of belonging is enforced or 'watched' through schemes that allow middle-class spaces to become valued: the subject who watches out for crime, is also *maintaining the value of her or his neighbourhood.* The link here between value of spaces, the protection of property, and the maintenance of social privilege helps us to theorise how the defence of social boundaries against unwelcome intrusions and intruders produces certain categories of strangers – those who don't belong in the leafy suburbs – that are socially legitimated and enforced. In Elijah Anderson's work, there is a discussion of how the concern with safety amongst residents means that, 'they join their diverse counterparts in local struggles to fight crime and otherwise preserve the ideal character for the neighbourhood, forming town watches and shoring up municipal codes that might discourage undesirables and encourage others more to their liking' (1990: 4). The production of safe spaces that have value or 'ideal character' involves the expulsion of unlike and undesirable 'characters'. In Anderson's work, these characters have *already* materialised or taken the form of, 'wandering homeless people, aggressive beggars, muggers, anonymous black youths, and drug addicts' (1990: 238).

How does neighbourhood watch work to produce such safe spaces? The literature produced on the Neighbourhood Watch schemes by the Home Office in the United Kingdom certainly links the designation of value to social spaces with the detection of strange events, and the expulsion of strangers. There is a double emphasis on the improvement of community living and on security and crime prevention. So Neighbourhood Watch schemes are described as both providing 'the eyes and ears of the police' and as providing, 'the soul and heart of the community' (Home Office 1997). The NWS link the production of safe spaces with the organic growth of a healthy social body: 'Neighbourhood Watch is not just about reducing burglary figures – it's about creating communities who care. It brings local people together and can make a real contribution to improving their lives. The activity of Watch members can foster a new community spirit and a belief in the community's ability to tackle problems. At the same time, you

feel secure, knowing your neighbours are keeping an eye on your property'
(1997). There is a constant shift between an emphasis on a caring community and a safe one: a safe community moreover is one in which you feel safe
as your property is being 'watched' by your neighbours. A link is established
here between safety (in which safety is associated with property), a discourse
on good neighbourliness (looking out for each other) and the production of
community as purified space ('a new community spirit'). Hence, 'it is widely
accepted that within every community, there is the potential for crime
prevention. Neighbourhood Watch is a way of tapping into this and of
drawing a community together'. Neighbourhood Watch hence constitutes
the neighbourhood as a community through the protection of the property
of nearby others from the threat posed by the very proximity of distant
others.

In an earlier Neighbourhood Watch pamphlet (Home Office 1992), the
reader is addressed more directly, 'Deciding to join your local group means
you have made a positive commitment to act against crime in your
community. You have also become one of the largest and most successful
grass-roots movements in the country.' Here, the reader is praised for her or
his community spirit: not only are you a good neighbour – willing to look
out for your neighbours – but you are also a good citizen, who has displayed
a positive commitment to 'act against crime in the community'. Neighbourhood watch purifies the space of the community *through purifying the life
of the good citizen*, whose life becomes heroic, dedicated to fighting against
crime and disorder. Significantly, then, the praise given to the reader/citizen
involves a form of reward/recognition: 'You can also get lower insurance
premiums from some Insurance companies' (1992). The reward demonstrates the value given to social spaces where subjects watch out for the
extraordinary sounds and signs of crime, or the sounds and signs of that
which is suspect and suspicious.

But how does Neighbourhood Watch involve techniques of differentiating between the ordinary life of the purified neighbourhood and the
extraordinary events that threaten to contaminate that space? The Home
Office pamphlet is cautious, 'Sometimes it is hard to tell if you are
witnessing a crime or not. You must rely on common sense. ... You may also
become suspicious if you notice something out of the ordinary. Don't be
afraid to call your local police station to report the incident' (1992). Here,
common sense should tell the good citizen what they are witnessing.
Whatever happens, the good citizen must be a witness: a witness to an event
that might or might not be a crime, an *event that unfolds before the patient eye
and ear*. The last sentence moves from the importance of differentiating
between extraordinary events through common sense (is it a crime?), to the
differentiation between ordinary and extraordinary. Here, you might be
made suspicious by *some-thing* out of the ordinary. The good citizen is a
citizen who *suspects rather than is suspect*, who watches out for departures from
ordinary life in the imagined space of the neighbourhood. The good citizen

hence watches out for the one who loiters, acts suspiciously, looks out of place. As a Chief Inspector explains in a letter to *The Independent*, 'Neighbourhood Watch is about looking after your property and that of your neighbours, taking sensible crime prevention action *and reporting suspicious persons to the police*' (Scougal 1996, emphasis added). According to the leaflet given by the Divisional Commander to Neighbourhood Watch coordinators, Neighbourhood Watch 'rests on the concept of good neighbourliness', which means that, 'Neighbours are encouraged to report suspicious persons and unusual events to the police'. With such an exercise in good neighbourliness and good citizenship, the neighbourhood comes to police itself: not only is it 'the heart and soul of the community', but in being the 'heart and soul of the community', it is also *the ears and eyes of the police*'.

The signifier 'suspicious' does an enormous amount of work in Neighbourhood Watch discourse precisely insofar as it is *empty*. The good citizen is not given any information about how to tell what or who is suspicious in the first place. It is my argument that the very failure to provide us with techniques for telling the difference is itself a technique of knowledge. It is the technique of *common sense* that is produced through Neighbourhood Watch discourse. Common sense not only defines what 'we' should take for granted (that is, what is normalised and already known as 'the given'), but it also involves the normalisation of ways of 'sensing' the difference between common and uncommon. That is, information is not given about how to tell the difference between normal and suspicious, because that difference is already 'sensed' through a prior history of making sense *as* the making of 'the common'. The good citizen knows what they are looking for, because they know what is common, and so what departs from the common: 'You must rely on common sense' (1992). Neighbourhood watch is hence about *making* the common: it makes the community ('the heart and soul of the community') insofar as it looks out for and hears the threat to the common posed by those who are uncommon, or those who are 'out of place' in 'this place' ('the eyes and ears of the police').

In this way, the 'suspicious person' and 'the stranger' are intimately linked: they are both emptied of any content, or any direct relationship to a referent, precisely as they are tied to a (missing) history of seeing and hearing others: *they are both already seen and heard as 'the uncommon' which allows 'the common' to take its shape*. The failure to name those who inhabit the signifier 'suspicious' hence produces the figure of the unspecified stranger, a figure that is required by the making or sensing of 'the common', of what 'we' are, as a form of distinction or value (property). Neighbourhood Watch can be characterised as a form of humanism. Such a humanism – Neighbourhood Watch is 'about creating communities who care' (1992) – conceals the exclusions that operate to allow the definition and policing of the 'we' of the good neighbourhood. The definition and enforcement of the good 'we' operates through the recognition of others as strangers: by seeing those who do not belong simply as 'strangers' (that is, by not naming *who* are the ones who do not belong in the community), forms of social exclusion are both concealed and revealed (what is concealed is the brute fact of the matter – only some others are recognisable as 'the stranger', the one who is out of place). In this sense, the policing of valued spaces allows the legitimation of social exclusion by being tied to a heroic 'we' who takes shape against the figure of the unspecified stranger. The production of the stranger as a figure that has linguistic and bodily integrity conceals how strangers are always already specified or differentiated. Neighbourhood Watch becomes definable as a mechanism for ensuring, not only that certain spaces maintain their (property) value, but that *certain lives become valued over other lives*. The recognition of strangers within the neighbourhood does not mean that anybody can be a stranger, depending on her or his location in the world: rather, some-bodies are more recognisable as strangers than other-bodies precisely because they are already read and valued in the demarcation of social spaces.

What is also significant about the Neighbourhood Watch concern with seeing and hearing the difference (becoming the eyes and ears of the police), is that it involves the production of a model of 'good citizenship'. The discourse on good citizenship involves an individualising of responsibility for crime (Stanko 1997). This model of the good citizen, which Stanko's work suggests is very much gendered as masculine, takes such responsibility in part through a form of self-policing by, in some sense, *becoming the police*. Certainly in post-Foucauldian work on surveillance, the emphasis is on the shift from public forms of monitoring – where the subject is watched by an anonymous and partially unseen and partially seen Other – to self-monitoring, when *the subject adopts the gaze of the other* (Foucault 1975). My analysis of Neighbourhood Watch might complicate this model of displacement from the gaze of the other to the gaze of the self. The 'eye' of the good citizen is certainly the site of labour – it is this 'eye' that is doing the work. However, that 'eye' does not simply return to the body, as that which must be transformed and regulated as 'the seen', but looks elsewhere, to and at others. In other words, 'the good citizen' is one who watches (out for) suspicious persons and strangers, and who in that very act, becomes aligned, not only with the police (and hence the Law), but with the imagined community itself whose boundaries are protected *in the very labour of his look*.

Furthermore, self-policing communities are inscribed as moral communities, those that care. Caring evokes a figure of who must be cared for, who must be protected from the risks of crime and the danger of strangers. So Neighbourhood Watch 'reassures vulnerable members of the community that you are keeping a neighbourly eye on them' (1992). The construction of the figure of the vulnerable member/body alongside the heroic good citizen provides the moral justification for the injunction to watch; it detaches 'watching out for' from 'busybodying' (1992) by redefining it as 'watching out on behalf of'. The discourse of vulnerability allows self-policing to be readable as the protection of others: the risk posed by suspects and strangers is a risk posed to the vulnerable bodies of children, the elderly and women. The figuring of the good citizen is built on the image of the strong citizen: in this sense, the good citizen is figurable primarily as white, masculine and middle-class, the heroic subject who can protect the vulnerable bodies of 'weaker others': 'crime cannot survive in a community that cares – Neighbourhood Watch Works' (NNWA).

The 1997 pamphlet also describes the newer scheme 'Street Watch' (there are currently over 20,000 in operation in the United Kingdom) which, 'covers many different activities, ranging from providing transport or escort services for elderly people, to walking a specific route regularly, keeping an eye out for trouble and reporting it to the police'. Here, the good citizen is valued not only for his heart, eyes and ears, but also his feet.[4] He takes specific routes, but most importantly, according to the Home Secretary responsible for the introduction of the scheme, Michael Howard, he is 'walking with purpose' (Bennetto 1995). Street Watch is described as 'patrolling with a purpose'.

We can consider here Hallman's definition of who and what must be watched in his work on neighbourhoods: 'people who seem to have no purpose in the neighbourhood' (Hallman 1984: 159). Strangers are suspicious because they 'have no purpose', that is, they have no legitimate function within the space which could justify their existence or intrusion. Strangers are hence recognisable precisely insofar as they *do not enter into the exchanges of capital that transforms spaces into places*. Strangers are constructed as an illegitimate presence in the neighbourhood: they have no purpose, and hence they must be suspect. You can recognise the stranger through their loitering gait: strangers loiter, they do not enter the legitimate exchanges of capital that might justify their presence. In contrast, the street watcher is constructed as a heroic figure whose purpose is the very detection of those who are without a legitimate purpose, of those whose purpose can hence only be explained as suspicious, as criminal, as a crime (Young 1996: 5). The stranger's presence on the street is a crime (waiting to happen). The proximity of such loitering strangers in the purified space of the good neighbourhood hence requires that the heroic citizen take a specific route: those who are recognisable as strangers, *whose lack of purpose conceals the purpose of crime*, need to be expelled through purposeful patrolling in order that the value of property can be protected.

Such a construction of the good citizen through the figure of the loitering stranger is clearly subject to forms of social differentiation: in one reading, the good citizen is structured around the body of the dominant (white, middle-class) man, who protects the vulnerable bodies of women and children from the threat of marginalised (black, working-class) men. However, these differences are concealed by the very modes of recognition: the figure of the stranger appears as 'the stranger' precisely by being cut off from these histories of determination (= stranger fetishism). That is, the recognition of strangers involves the differentiation between some others and other others at the same time as it conceals that very act of differentiation. What is significant about Neighbourhood Watch is precisely the way in which it links the formation of community with safety and the detection of crime: such links produce the figure of the stranger as a *visible danger* to the 'we' of the community, and hence as the necessary condition for making what 'we' have in common.

Stranger danger

If the construction and enforcement of purified spaces of belonging takes place through the production of the figures of the good citizen, the vulnerable body and the loitering stranger, then how is this linked to the social perception of danger? In this section, I examine the discourse of stranger danger as a way of analysing how strangers are already recognised as posing danger to property and person, not just in particular valued dwellings and neighbourhoods, but also in public life as such. I want to consider, not only how the construction of stranger danger is tied to valued and devalued spaces, but also how strangers are read as posing danger *wherever* they are: the projection of danger onto the figure of the stranger allows the definition of the subject-at-home, and home as inhabitable space, as inherently safe and valuable. One *knows again* those whom one does not know by assuming they are the *origin* of danger.

Partly, this concern with public life involves a consideration of urban space and cities as 'a world of strangers' (Lofland 1973). Lofland suggests that cities, in particular public spaces within cities (such as streets and leisure spaces), involve perpetual encounters between people who are not personally known to each other, although they may be known through forms of visual identification and recognition (1973: 15–16). As a result, he argues that cities involve particular kinds of social and spatial encounters. I would not want to refute the premise that there are different kinds of spaces that involve different kinds of encounters between others (such as urban and rural spaces, or such as different forms of the public within urban spaces). However, Lofland's account does involve a form of spatial determinism – these spaces determine these encounters between others – which shifts quickly into a form of cultural determinism – cultures have different spaces and therefore involve different encounters between others.[5] What I am interested in is how the very encounters that take place between others involve the forming of both cultural and spatial boundaries: that is, how the (mis)recognition of others as strangers is what allows the demarcation of given spaces within 'the pubic domain', but also the legitimation of certain forms of mobility or movement within the public, and the delegitimation of others.

I am positing here a relationship between dwelling and movement:[6] spaces are claimed, or 'owned' not so much by inhabiting what is already there, but by moving within, or passing through, different spaces which are only given value as places (with boundaries) through the movement or 'passing through' itself. The relationship between movement, occupation and ownership is well documented in feminist work: for example, women's restricted movement within public spaces is a result, not only of the fear of crime, but of the regulation of femininity, in which 'being seen' in certain spaces becomes a sign of irresponsibility (Stanko 1997: 489). Women's movements are regulated by a desire for 'safe-keeping': respectability becomes measured by the visible signs of a desire to 'stay safe'. In this sense, movement becomes a form of subject constitution: *where* 'one' goes or does not go determines *what* one 'is', or where one is seen to be, determines what one is seen to be.

Elijah Anderson's work on how communities are established through the concern with safety examines how the fear of crime becomes a fear of strangers. Such a fear produces a way of inhabiting the world, as well as moving through it. He writes, 'Many worry about a figure lurking in the shadows, hiding in a doorway or behind a clump of bushes, ready to pounce on the unsuspecting victim' (Anderson 1990: 5). The danger posed by the stranger is imagined as partly concealed: the stranger always lurks in dark spaces. While the victim is unsuspecting, the safe subject must be suspecting: the safe subject suspects that the suspect is around the corner, always hidden to the gaze, to the watchful eye. The danger of the stranger is hence always there in the imagined future of the subject who is safely at home, the stranger is always lurking as the threat of that-which-might-yet-be. Safety hence requires that the subject must become familiar with the terrain: the safe subject must become 'street wise' and 'alive to dangerous situations' (Anderson 1990: 6). Certain lives become liveable as both safe and valuable insofar as they are *alive to* the danger of strangers.

The discourse of personal safety is not about the production of safe and purified spaces from which strangers are expelled (such as 'the home'), but also defines ways of moving through spaces that are already dangerous given the possibility that strangers are close by, waiting in the shadows of the streets (where good citizens walk only with purpose, living their legitimated lives). The possibility of personal safety for mobile subjects hence requires 'collective definitions' of that which is 'safe, harmless, trustworthy' and that which is 'bad, dangerous and hostile' (Anderson 1990: 216). Such collective definitions provide the subject with the knowledge required to move within the world, allowing the subject to differentiate between familiar and strange, safe and dangerous, as well as to differentiate between different kinds of strangers ('characters').

Clearly, discourses of personal safety involve forms of self-governance that differentiate between subjects. As much feminist research has suggested, safety for women is often constructed in terms of not entering public spaces, or staying within the home (see Stanko 1990). Safety for men also involves forms of self-governance, not in terms of refusing to enter the public space, but in terms of *how* one enters that space. So at one level, the discourse of personal safety presumes a vulnerable citizen who is gendered as feminine, at another level, it legislates for a form of mobile and masculine subjectivity that is not only a safe form of subjectivity, but also one that is heroic. Such a mobile subject, who can 'avoid' the danger of strangers in public spaces is constructed as 'street wise'. This subject's mobility is legitimated as a form of dwelling: first, in relation to the vulnerable bodies that stay within the home; and second, in relation to the strangers whose passing though public spaces is delegitimated as the 'origin' of danger (the movement of strangers is hence not a form of dwelling; it does not lead to the legitimated occupation of space).

The knowledges embedded in street wisdom are linked by Anderson to a kind of 'field research' (Anderson 1990: 216). The wise subject, the one who knows where and where not to walk, how and how not to move, who and who not to talk to, has an expertise that can be understood as both *bodily and cultural capital*. It is such wise subjects who will prevail in a world of strangers and dangers: 'To prevail means simply to get safely to one's destination, and the ones who are most successful are those who are "streetwise" ' (Anderson 1990: 231). In this sense, the discourse of stranger danger involves techniques of knowledge that allow wise subjects to prevail: to arrive at their destination, to leave and return home and still maintain a safe distance between themselves and dangerous strangers. Community is not just established through the designation of pure and safe spaces, but becomes established *as a way of moving through space*. Becoming street wise defines the subject in terms of the collective: the wise subject has collective knowledge about what is, 'safe, harmless, trustworthy' and what is 'bad, dangerous and hostile' that gives that subject the ability to move safely in a world of strangers and dangers. The stranger is here produced as a figure of danger that grants the wise subject and community, those who already claim both knowledge and capital, the ability to prevail.

The discourse of stranger danger also involves the figuring, not only of the wiser subject who can move through dangerous places (a mobile subject who is racialised, classed and gendered), but also the vulnerable body, the one who is most at risk. Here, 'the child' becomes a figure of vulnerability, the purified body that is most endangered by the contaminating desires of strangers. Indeed, it is the literature on child protection that has familiarised 'stranger danger' as the mechanism for ensuring personal safety. One double page of the Home Office leaflet on crime prevention in the United Kingdom is hence dedicated to 'your family' and, 'to keeping your children safe' (the ideal reader/subject/citizen is always a parent, bound to Law and duty through the demands of parenthood). The pamphlet advises, 'Do not talk to strangers. Most well-meaning adults will not approach a child who is on his own, unless he is obviously distressed or in need. Tell your children never to talk to strangers, and to politely ignore any approach from a stranger. Get them to tell you if a stranger tries to talk to them.' Immediately, strangers are differentiated from 'well-meaning' adults, who would not approach children. Indeed, the child itself must become 'street wise': one colouring-in book produced by the Lancashire Constabulary in the United Kingdom is entitled, 'Operation Streetwise workbook' and aims 'to provide children with an exciting opportunity to learn and practice personal safety skills'. Here, growing up is narrated in terms of acquiring the wisdom to deal with danger that already stalks in the figure of the stranger.[7]

The figure of the child comes to perform a certain role within the narrative of crime prevention and stranger danger: the innocence of the child is what is most at risk from the proximity of strangers. The child comes to embody, in a narrative that is both nostalgic (returning to an imagined past) and fearful (projecting an unimaginable future), all that could be stolen or lost by the proximity of strangers. The child's innocence and purity becomes a matter of social and national responsibility: through figuring the stranger as too close to the child, the stranger becomes recognisable as an attack on the moral purity of nation space itself. It is over the bodies of children that the moral campaign against strangers is waged.

In recent debates in the press, the paedophile is hence represented as the ultimate stranger that communities must have the power to evict. A change in the law in 1997 allowed the British police force to inform members of the community when a paedophile is in their midst, on a 'need to know' basis. Community action groups, as well as some local councils, have redefined the need to know as *a right to know*: arguing that paedophiles should not be allowed into communities as they pose a risk to children, 'Recent moves include attempts by some councils to ban paedophiles from their communities altogether, and campaigns to keep them in prison longer' (Hilpern 1997). The construction of sex offenders against children as monsters who do not belong in a community is clear in the following statement from John O'Sullivan, from the pressure group, *Parents Against Child Abuse*: 'If there is a wild lion loose in the street, the police would tell us. A paedophile in the neighbourhood is the same. They might not rip the flesh, but they are just as damaging to the mind of a child. We need to know who they are.' The number of vigilante attacks on suspected paedophiles in Britain in the 1990s suggests what this knowledge will be used for.

Significantly, then, the paedophile comes to embody the most dangerous stranger as he poses the greatest risk to the vulnerable and pure body of the child. The community comes together through the recognition of such dangerous strangers: they must expel him, he who is the wild animal, the lion, at loose in the street. The monstrosity of such recognisable strangers is figured through the tearing of the skin of the child. The monsters who must be excluded to keep children safe, prey on children: they require the heroic action of the moral community that cares. The imaginary community is constructed as a safe community where children's bodies are not vulnerable: the moral community itself becomes the child, pure, innocent and free. The recognition of dangerous strangers allows the enforcement of the boundaries of such communities: a definition of the purity of the 'we' against the monstrous 'it'.

Sally Engle Merry's *Urban Danger: Life in a Neighbourhood of Strangers*, discusses how the fear of crime 'focuses on the threat of the violent attack by a stranger' (Merry 1981: 6). Such a fear means that the familiar is already designated as safe: one is safe at home, unless there is an intrusion from a stranger. One could comment here how such a reduction of danger to the stranger conceals the danger that may be embedded in the familiar: much feminist work, for example, demonstrates how the perception of the rapist as a stranger conceals how most sexual attacks are committed by friends or family. As Elizabeth Stanko argues, 'Danger many of us believe arises from the random action of strangers who are, we further assume, usually men of colour. Yet according to most people's experiences ... danger and violence arise within our interpersonal relationships' (1990: 3). The projection of danger onto the figure of the stranger allows violence to be figured as exceptional and extraordinary – as coming from outside the protective walls of the home, family, community or nation. As a result, the discourse of stranger danger involves *a refusal to recognise how violence is structured by, and legitimated through, the formation of home and community as such.*

The stranger is here figured as the violent monster whose elimination would mean safety for women and children. Such a figuration allows the home to be imagined as a safe haven: an imagining that cannot deal with the violence that is instituted through the social relations within the home. As Merry argues, 'Violence at the hand of the stranger is usually perceived as dangerous, but an assault in the context of a fight with a known enemy or neighbour is rarely viewed in this way' (Merry 1981: 14). The notion of violence as domestic, while now recognised through Law as a result of years of feminist campaigning, remains a difficult one for the social imaginary: the violent husband is then read as a monster underneath, as a stranger passing as husband, rather than as a husband exercising the power that is already legitimated through hegemonic forms of masculinity. According to stranger danger discourse, the stranger husband has intruded into the ideal home: he is not understood as an element *in the ordinary production of domestic space*, and in the formation of relations of power and exchange within that space.

The ultimate violent strangers are hence figured as immigrants: they are the outsiders in the nation space whose 'behaviour seems unpredictable and beyond control' (Merry 1981: 125). Cultural difference becomes the text upon which the fear of crime is written: 'cultural difference exacerbates feelings of danger. Encounters with culturally alien people are defined by anxiety and uncertainty, which inhibits social interaction and reinforces social boundaries' (Merry 1981: 125). The projection of danger onto that which is already recognisable as different – as different from the familiar space of home and homeland – hence allows violence to take place: it becomes a mechanism for the enforcement of boundary lines that almost secure the home-nation as safe haven. On the one hand, the fear of crime embedded in the discourse of stranger danger allows the protection of domestic, social and national space from the outsider inside, the stranger neighbour, by projecting danger onto the outsider. On the other hand, the stranger only appears as a figure of danger by coming too close to home: the boundary line is always crossed, both 'justifying' the fear and legitimating the enforcement. In doing so, the discourse of stranger danger, not only allows the abdication of any social and political responsibility for the violence that takes place within legitimated spaces, and which is sanctioned through Law, but also becomes a mechanism for the justification of acts of violence against those who are already recognised as strangers.

In this chapter, I have examined how 'the stranger' is produced as a figure precisely by being associated with a danger to the purified space of the community, the purified life of the good citizen, and the purified body of 'the child'. Rather than assuming that the stranger is any-body we don't recognise, I have argued that strangers are those that are already recognised through techniques for differentiating between the familiar and strange in discourses such as Neighbourhood Watch and crime prevention. The 'knowing again' of strangers defines the stranger as a danger to both moral health and well-being. The knowing again of strangers as the danger of the unknown is a means by which the 'we' of the community is established, enforced and legitimated.

2   Embodying strangers

The AA subway train to Harlem. I clutch my mother's sleeve, her arms full
of shopping bags, christmas-heavy. The wet smell of winter clothes, the
train's lurching. My mother spots an almost seat, pushes my little snow-
suited body down. On one side of me a man reading a paper. On the other, a
woman in a fur hat staring at me. Her mouth twitches as she stares and
then her gaze drops down, pulling mine with it. Her leather-gloved hand
plucks at the line where my new blue snowpants and her sleek fur coat
meet. She jerks her coat close to her. I look. I do not see whatever terrible
thing she is seeing on the seat between us – probably a roach. But she has
communicated her horror to me. It must be something very bad from the
way she's looking, so I pull my snowsuit closer to me away from it, too.
When I look up the woman is still staring at me, her nose holes and eyes
huge. And suddenly I realise there is nothing crawling up the seat between
us; it is me she doesn't want her coat to touch. The fur brushes my face as
she stands with a shudder and holds on to a strap in the speeding train.
Born and bred a New York City child, I quickly slide over to make room for
my mother to sit down. No word has been spoken. I'm afraid to say anything to my mother because I don't know what I have done. I look at the
side of my snow pants secretly. Is there something on them? Something's
going on here I do not understand, but I will never forget it. Her eyes. The
flared nostrils. The hate.

(Lorde 1984: 147–148)

How do strange encounters, encounters in which some-thing that cannot be
named is passed between subjects, serve to embody the subject? How do
encounters with the one whom we already recognise as a stranger take place
at the level of the body? To what extent do strange encounters involve, not
just reading the stranger's body, but defining the contours or boundaries of
the body-at-home, through the very gestures that enable a withdrawal from
the stranger's co-presence in a given social space?

In the above encounter, recalled as memory, Audre Lorde ends with 'the
hate'. It is an encounter in which some-thing has passed, but something she
fails to understand. What passes is hence not spoken; it is not a transparent
form of communication. The sense that some-thing is wrong is communi-

cated, not through words, or even sounds that are voiced, but through the body of another, 'her nose holes and eyes huge'. What is the woman's body saying? How do we read her body? The woman's bodily gestures express her hate, her fear, her disgust. The strange encounter is played out *on* the body, and is played out *with* the emotions.

This bodily encounter, while ending with 'the hate', also ends with the reconstitution of bodily space. The bodies that come together, that almost touch and co-mingle, slide away from each other, becoming relived in their apartness. The particular bodies that move apart allow the redefinition of social as well as bodily integrity: black bodies are expelled from the white social body despite the threat of further discomfort (the woman now must stand in order that she can keep her place, that is, in order to keep Audre at a distance). The emotion of 'hate' aligns the particular white body with the bodily form of the community – such an emotion functions to substantiate the threat of invasion and contamination in the dirty bodies of strangers. The gestures that allow the white body to withdraw from the stranger's body hence reduce that body to dirt, to 'matter out of place' (Douglas 1996: 36), such that the stranger becomes recognised *as the body out of place*. Through such strange encounters, bodies are both de-formed and re-formed, they take form through and against other bodily forms.

Does Audre's narrative of the encounter involve her self-designation as the body out of place? Certainly, her perception of the cause of the woman's bodily gestures is a misperception that creates an object. The object – the roach – comes to stand for, or stand in for, the cause of 'the hate'. The roach crawls up between them; the roach, as the carrier of dirt, divides the two bodies, forcing them to move apart. Audre pulls her snowsuit, 'away from it too'. But the 'it' that divides them is not the roach. Audre comes to realise that, 'it is me she doesn't want her coat to touch'. What the woman's clothes must not touch is not a roach that crawls between them, but Audre herself. Audre becomes the 'it' that stands between the possibility of their clothes touching. She becomes the roach – the impossible and phobic object – that threatens to crawl from one to the other: 'I don't know what I have done. I look at the side of my snow pants secretly. Is there something on them?' The stranger's lived embodiment hesitates on the question, 'am I the roach?' or, 'am I the dirt that forces me away?'

In this chapter, I will address the role of such 'eye-to-eye' (Lorde 1984) or 'skin-to-skin' encounters in the formation of bodily and social space. As I argued in the introduction to this book, the word 'encounter' suggests a meeting, but a meeting which involves surprise. How does embodiment take shape through encounters with others that surprise, that both establish and shift the boundaries of the familiar, of what is already recognisable or known? By opening with a scene from Audre Lorde's *Sister Outsider*, I have already pointed to how 'the encounter' is mediated through a range of different kinds of texts or, more precisely, different forms of writing. In *Sister Outsider*, Lorde uses the poetics of remembering to dramatise the operation of racism on her body, in the violence of its particularity. At the same time, we must remind ourselves as readers, that the recalled encounter between herself and an-other is written, and that it functions as an aspect of an argument within a text that shifts between academic, personal and political modes of address. The encounter is lived and written, but it fails to be an event, or even a text, that is simply in the present. The encounter is already recalled and relived in the metonymic slide between different encounters: not only do we have the (re)narrativised encounter between Audre and the white woman, but also we have encounters between Audre's past and present self, between an apparently intimate self and a public life, between the writer and her subject, and between the reader (myself as reader) and the text.

A concern with strange encounters involves a concern with the dialogical production of different bodies and texts. While Audre Lorde's text allows me to address what is at stake in such strange encounters – to dramatise that there is always *some-body* at stake – it does not provide the only means by which I ask the impossible question, 'what about the stranger's body?' The ethics of my own encounter with *Sister Outsider* demands a more responsible reading, a reading which admits to its limits, its partiality and its fragility. I hence do not use the text as an example that simply holds my argument together, as the object of my writing. I move towards and away from her text, *only ever sliding across it*: my encounter with this text allows me to re-encounter different kinds of bodies and texts. Quite clearly, I am touched by Audre Lorde's story – 'being touched' is a way of understanding how encounters always involve, not only a meeting of bodies, but between bodies and texts (the face to face of intimate readings), in which the subject is moved from her place (see Chapter 7).

My concern with the embodied nature of strange encounters requires that we first ask the question, 'what is the body?' I will argue that there is no body as such that is given in the world: bodies materialise in a complex set of temporal and spatial relations to other bodies, including bodies that are recognised as familiar, familial and friendly, and those that are considered strange. My argument will challenge some psychoanalytical and feminist approaches to embodiment by thinking through the function of cultural difference and social antagonism in marking out the boundaries of bodies.

Bodies

Within feminist theory, 'bodies' certainly have become a privileged focus of attention. Partly, this attention can be explained by the feminist recognition that women's marginalisation from philosophical discourses and the public sphere has been produced through the association between masculinity and reason and femininity and the body. The feminist concern with revaluing the body, and undermining such mind/body dualism, has led to an acknowl-edgment that bodies are not simply given (as 'nature'), that bodies are differentiated, and that subjectivity and identity cannot be separated from specific forms of embodiment (Bordo 1993). A philosophy that refuses to privilege mind over body, and that assumes that the body cannot be transcended as such, is a philosophy which emphasises contingency, locatedness, the irreducibility of difference, and the worldliness of being. However, despite many appeals to the differentiated body within feminist philosophy, I think there has been less substantive analysis of how 'bodies' come to be lived through being differentiated from other bodies, whereby differences in 'other bodies' already mark 'the body' as such.

Indeed, Kathryn Bond Stockton has argued that 'the body' has achieved an onto-theological status in feminist theory (1994). She suggests that the assumption that 'the body' is already determined, partly in the sense that it is already gendered, reflects an epistemic reliance on the body as in some way prior to, or at least irreducible to, the contingency of linguistic and social relations. I do not go along altogether with her argument as it clearly misses the point that the concern with the body as already determined constitutes an important aspect of a feminist critique of Cartesianism and ideality in general (that the subject gains its identity and distinction from the exclusion of the material, that is, the divisible realm of bodily experience). However, it is interesting to reconsider the status of 'the body' in some recent feminist writings. For while the reflection is on bodies that are clearly differentiated (for example, bodies that are sexed or sexy), the body has also become somewhat of an abstraction, that is, a way of signalling a certain kind of feminist rhetoric as much as the means through which a feminist critique of traditional philosophy proceeds. Take some recent titles of feminist publications: *Bodies that Matter* (Butler 1993), *The Bodies of Women* (Diprose 1994), *Volatile Bodies* (Grosz 1994), *Sexy Bodies* (Grosz and Probyn 1995), *Flexible Bodies* (Martin 1995) and *Imaginary Bodies* (Gatens 1996). Bodies are clearly a matter for feminism, and quite rightly so, but is there something more at stake in the rendering of bodies as objects-in-themselves for feminist analysis?

The appeal to the body as already determined and as differentiated in terms of gender and sexuality, and also race and class, does not always involve in practice an analysis of the particularity of bodies or of subjectivity in general. I admit that it is easy simply to point out that *appeals* to difference do not always involve an *analysis* of difference (those moments where, often in brackets, a theorist will add – and also, race, class, disability etc.). But the appeal to the differentiated body as a rhetorical ploy that does not operate beyond that level has structural implications for the bodies that are discussed and reinscribed in feminist discourse. For example, in Elizabeth Grosz's *Volatile Bodies*, there is little mention of the racialised nature of the multiple and differentiated bodies she dedicates her text to, except in the following quote:

The more or less permanent etching of even the civilised body by discursive systems is perhaps easier to read if the civilized body is decontextualised, stripped of clothing and adornment, behaviourally displayed in its nakedness. The naked European/American/African/Asian/Australian body (and clearly even within these categories there is enormous cultural variation) is still marked by its disciplinary history, by its habitual practices of movement, by the corporeal commitments it has undertaken in day-to-day life. It is in no sense a natural body, for it is as culturally, racially, sexually, possibly even as class distinctive, as it would be clothed.

(Grosz 1994: 142)

Here, Grosz introduces race as a signifier of difference ('European/American /African/Asian/Australian') in order to illustrate her point that there is no natural or indeed real body, that the body is always clothed, that is, always inscribed within particular cultural formations. Race becomes a means by which Grosz illustrates a philosophical shift in thinking about bodies. It appears then (and also disappears) as a *figure* for the differentiated body. In this sense, race is made present only through an act of negation: it is included as a vehicle for the re-presentation of a philosophy of difference rather than as a constitutive and positive term of analysis. This metaphoric reliance on race to signify the differentiated body has quite clear theoretical and political implications. It means that a philosophy of the differentiated body – a philosophy of difference – does not necessarily involve, in practice, a recognition of the violent collision between regimes of difference. A philosophy of difference *can* involve a universalism; a speaking from the place of (for example) the white subject, who reincorporates difference as a sign of its own fractured and multiple coming-into-being.

In order to avoid reading the differentiated body through the figure of race, we need to think through the questions: How do 'bodies' become marked by differences? How do bodies come to be lived precisely through being differentiated from other bodies, whereby the differences in other bodies make a difference to such lived embodiment? Such questions require that we consider how the very materialisation of bodies in time and space involves techniques and practices of differentiation. To differentiate between the familiar and the strange is to mark out the inside and outside of bodily space (to establish the skin as a boundary line). What is required is, not only an analysis of body images or representations of bodily difference, but also an analysis of how bodily habits and gestures serve to constitute bodily matter and form. Judith Butler's consideration of 'bodies that matter' defines 'materialisation', as the production of an 'effect of boundary, fixity and surface' (1993: 9). To examine the function of cultural difference and social antagonism in the constitution of bodily matters is not to read differences on the surface of the body (the body as text), but to account for the very effect of the surface, and to account for how bodies come to take certain shapes over others, and in relation to others.

At one level, psychoanalysis seems to provide us with such a model of embodiment. In Lacanian psychoanalysis, for example, the child's accession into the realm of subjectivity takes place through the process of assuming a body image. In 'The Mirror Stage as Formative of the Function of the I', the child sees itself in the mirror, and misrecognises the image as itself. This act, 'rebounds in the case of the child in a series of gestures in which he experiences in play the relation between the movements assumed in the image and the reflected environment – the child's own body, and the persons and things' (Lacan 1977: 1). This play with an image structures the relation of the child to its body and to others, in the form of an identification, that is, in 'the transformation that takes place in the subject when he assumes an image' (Lacan 1977: 2). These processes of identification provide the child with an 'imaginary anatomy'. Lacan's approach allows us to consider how the form of bodies is not given or pre-determined, but involves a temporal and spatial process of misrecognition and projection, whereby the body becomes distinguished from others (the marking out of an inside and outside). The body materialises – takes shape and form – through phantasy (flesh and image are here mutually implicated).

Frantz Fanon takes up the Lacanian model of the mirror stage in an interesting footnote in *Black Skin, White Masks*. He suggests that there is a racialised dynamic to the assumption of the body image: 'When one has grasped the mechanism described by Lacan, one can have no further doubt that the real Other for the white man is and will continue to be the black man. And conversely. Only for the white man The Other is perceived on the level of the body image, absolutely as not-self – that is, the unidentifiable, the unassimilable' (Fanon 1975: 114). Fanon is clearly using the Lacanian theory as a general theory of the psychic mechanisms which institute subjectivity, which he then redefines as already racialised. That is, the encounter through which the subject assumes a body image and comes to be distinguishable from the Other is a racial encounter. The theory of identification which is articulated by Lacan as a *general* theory of the subject (he writes that the 'drama' of the mirror stage will 'mark with its rigid structure the subject's entire mental development' (1977: 4)) is immediately differentiated and divided. The relation of the 'I' to the 'not-I' is determined, not simply by the psychic processes of misrecognition and projection, but by the racialising of the ego (white) in relation to the materiality of other bodies (black).

Lacan's theory defines both the subject and its other in terms of the relation between the play of the assumed image and 'the reflected environment' which includes the child's own body, 'persons and things' (1977: 1). The dialectic of self-othering defined here is abstract: the other is simply that which the mirror presents as beyond the spatial form of the child's body image, which is to say, *any-beyond, to any-body*. Where Fanon's theory is implicitly challenging the Lacanian model of identification as constituting the subject (and its impossibility) in general, is through the implication that both the embodied subject and the persons and things that are excluded from it are *already* particular and *already* framed and constituted in a broader sociality. The *primary* identification does not then simply take place as such (that act which, according to Lacan, 'rebounds ... in a series of gestures' (1977: 1)). *When assuming a body image, subjects 'take on' the burden of particular bodily others which both precede them and are reinvented by them.* The imaginary relation of the child's body, persons and things hence already carries traces of social antagonism and conflict which differentiate bodies from each other. Fanon's reworking of Lacan implies that the self–other dynamic cannot be abstracted, as it is contingent on bodily differences that are themselves inflected by histories of particular bodily others.

An analysis of strange encounters as bodily encounters suggests that the marking out of the boundary lines between bodies, through the assumption of a bodily image, involves practices and techniques of differentiation. That is, bodies become differentiated not only *from each other* or *the other*, but also through differentiating *between others*, who have a different function in establishing the permeability of bodily space. Here, there is no generalisable other that serves to establish the illusion of bodily integrity; rather the body becomes imagined through being related to, and separated from, particular bodily others. Difference is not simply found in the body, but is established as a relation between bodies: *this suggests that the particular body carries traces of the differences that are registered in the bodies of others.* In the next section of this chapter, I consider how different bodies come to be lived through the establishment of boundaries and contours between the inside and the outside, in which the very habits and gestures of marking out bodily space involve differentiating 'others' into familiar (assimilable, touchable) and strange (unassimilable, untouchable). As I will suggest, such a consideration requires that we begin to think through the skin, rather than taking 'the body' as our point of entry.

Bodies with skins

Why is it necessary to think through the skin in a consideration of how strange encounters take place at the level of the body? If we address the role of skin in marking out bodily spaces, then we can refuse to accept that the contours or boundaries of bodies are given. A consideration of the subject as 'skinned' is not then a question of thinking about bodies as having inherent ends or limits (bodies do not necessarily end at their skins). The skin is not simply invested with meaning as a visual signifier of difference (the skin as coloured, the skin as wrinkled, and so on). It is not simply implicated in the (scopophilic) logic of fetishism where the visual object, the object which *can* be seen, becomes the scene of the play of differences. The skin is also a border or boundary, supposedly holding or containing the subject within a certain contour, keeping the subject inside, and the other outside; or in Frantz Fanon's terms, the skin becomes *a seal* (1975: 9). But, as a border or a frame, the skin performs that peculiar destabilising logic, calling into question the exclusion of the other from the subject and risking the subject's becoming (or falling into) the other. Hence, Jean-Luc Nancy discusses the skin as an *exposure* to the other, as always passing from one to the other (1994: 30). The skin may open out a moment of undecidability which is at once a rupture or breakage, where the subject risks its interiority, where it meets and leaks into the world at large.

The skin is not simply matter in place, but rather involves a process of materialisation; it is the effect of surface, boundary and fixity (Butler 1993: 9). The skin allows us to consider how boundary-formation, the marking out of the lines of a body, involves an affectivity which already crosses the line. For if the skin is a border, then it is *a border that feels*. In the work of Jennifer Biddle, for example, the skin, 'as the outer covering of the material body', is where the intensity of emotions such as shame are registered (1997: 228). So while the skin appears to be the matter which separates the body, it rather allows us to think of how the materialisation of bodies involves, not containment, but an affective opening out of bodies to other bodies, in the sense that the skin registers how bodies are touched by others. Sue Cataldi's concern with skin as an 'ambiguous, shifting border' centres on the question of how our skin 'paradoxically protects us from others and exposes us to them. How we touch and how we are touched affects us' (1993: 145). The skin provides a way of thinking about how the boundary between bodies is formed only through being traversed, or called into question, by the affecting of one by an other.

But is there danger that we might fetishise the skin as having a peculiar form and logic of its own, just as 'the body' can become fetishised as the lost object of philosophical discourse? I do not want to suggest here that the skin contains a logic which provides us with the means of rearticulating the relation of self and other *in general*. Rather, I want to think of how the skin, as the border that feels, functions as a mechanism for social differentiation. Take Anthony Smith's description of the skin in *The Body*:

> The only unprotected tissue which has the living body on one side and the outside world on the other is the skin. Taken as a whole it is the body's largest organ; it is enormously versatile; it keeps out foreign agents; it keeps in body fluids.
>
> (1974: 482)

Here, 'the skin' marks and polices the difference between inside and outside. It is a boundary that guarantees a separation. Its task is to ward off the danger of the foreigner, to keep out the other, to protect the self from the unruliness of others. Its task is not simply one of policing the outside. Its task is also, at one and the same time, to keep in, that is, to prevent the inside from becoming outside and to prevent the self from becoming other.

This construction of the skin as a mechanism for keeping out foreign agents might suggest a relationship between the individual body and the body-politic. The individual body is *like* the body politic; a mechanism for ensuring the integrity of the body by warding off foreigners. However, we need to question the status of this analogy. What is the relationship between the individual body and the body politic? In Moira Gatens's work, the construction of the body politic is modelled on a particular construction of the human body. The human body appears unmarked, but it is marked by privilege; it is, for example, a white, male, middle-class, heterosexual body. The unmarked body is the body that appears contained, enclosed and separate. We can consider such an unmarked body as a body which is *at-home* or *in-place*. Bodies that are marked as different from the human body, bodies that are (although in different ways) out of place, are hence excluded from the body politic: 'Slaves, foreigners, women, the conquered, children, and the working class, have all been excluded from political participation, at one time or another, by their bodily specificity' (Gatens 1991: 82).

The relationship between the integrity of the 'human body' and the body politic is not best expressed through analogy. Rather, there is a metonymic relation between the apparently unmarked body and the body politic; a relation of proximity or closeness. This suggests that the forming of the boundaries of 'unmarked' bodies – bodies-at-home or bodies-in-place – has an intimate connection to the forming of social space – homeland. The containment of certain bodies in their skin (bodily space) is a mechanism for the containment of social space. We can recall here how the white woman's refusal to touch the black child does not simply *stand for* the expulsion of blackness from white social space, but actually re-forms that social space through re-forming the apartness of the white body. The re-forming of bodily and social space involves a process of *making the skin crawl*; the threat posed by strange bodies to bodily and social integrity is registered on the skin.

The metonymic relation between the individual body-at-home – the body that appears not to be marked by difference – and the body politic, suggests an intimate connection between the particular body and sociality, or the imaginary social body. The particular body is often discussed in terms of the body one inhabits, that is, the personal body, or *my* body: 'Perhaps we need a moratorium on saying "the body". For it's also possible to abstract the "body". I see nothing in particular. To write "my body" plunges me into lived experience, particularity. ... To say "the body" lifts me away from what has given me primary perspective' (Rich 1986: 215). Here, the particular body is the body that I experience as lived, and is defined against any abstract or general notion of 'the body'. There is an equation here between lived experience, the privatised realm of 'the my', and particularity. I would suggest that 'my body' is possible in its particularity only through encountering other bodies, 'your body', 'her body' and so on. In other words, we need an understanding of embodiment as lived experience which moves beyond the privatised realm of 'my body'. Such an understanding of embodiment can be theorised in terms of *inter-embodiment*, whereby the lived experience of embodiment is always already *the social experience of dwelling with other bodies*. Or, as Gail Weiss puts it, 'To be embodied is to be capable of being affected by other bodies' (1999: 162).

Such an approach would appear to borrow heavily from the phenomenological tradition in which 'this body' no longer belongs to me, but opens out into a fleshy world of other bodies (Merleau-Ponty 1968; Vasseleu 1998). Merleau-Ponty theorises the fleshiness of such intercorporeality through considering the reversibility of touch:

> While each monocular vision, each touching with one sole hand has its own visible, its tactile, each is bound to every other vision, to every other touch; it is bound in such a way as to make up with them the experience of one sole body before one sole world, through a possibility for reversion, reconversion of its language into theirs, transfer and reversal. .... Now why would this generality, which constitutes the unity of my body, not open it to other bodies? The handshake too is reversible; I can feel myself touched as well and at the same time as touching.
>
> (1968: 142)

Merleau-Ponty suggests that the very experiences that make the body 'my body', as if it were a 'sole body before a sole world' are the very same experiences that open my body to other bodies, in the simultaneous mutuality of touch and being touched, and seen and being seen. In this sense, 'my body' does not belong to me: embodiment is what opens out the intimacy of 'myself' with others. The relationship between bodies is characterised by a 'with' that precedes, or is the condition of possibility for, the apartness of 'my body'. This 'with' is the fleshiness of the world that inhabits us and is inhabited by us – flesh, not understood simply as matter, but as the very sensibility of the seen, and the very sight of the sensible.

While I find these arguments powerful and suggestive, they remain limited insofar as they remain tied to a general theory of inter-embodiment which transforms 'my body' into 'our body': '*my body* is at once phenomenal body and objective body. ... It is thus, and not as the bearer of a knowing subject, that *our body* commands the visible for us' (Merleau-Ponty 1968: 136; emphasis added).[1] This curious conjoining of signifiers, 'our body', with its plural pronoun and singular noun is suggestive: it suggests that many inhabit, and are inhabited by, the body, as that which exceeds the singularity of 'me' yet also includes that me in the sense that it is lived through or as it. Rather than simply pluralising the body (there are many bodies), this approach emphasises *the singular form of the plural*: that is, sociality becomes the fleshy form (body) of many bodily forms (our). However, I want to consider the sociality of such inter-embodiment as the impossibility of any such 'our'. What I am interested in, then, is not simply how touch opens bodies to other bodies (touchability as exposure, sociality as body) but how, in that very opening, touch differentiates between bodies, a differentiation, which complicates the corporeal generosity that allows us to move easily from 'my body' to 'our body'.

Rosalind Diprose takes from the phenomenological approach, the basis for a theory of corporeal generosity in which bodies 'borrow' from other bodies ways of inhabiting the world: 'the self is produced, maintained and transformed through the socially mediated inter-body transfer of movements and gestures and body bits and pieces. Just as through the look and the touch of *the other's body*, I feel *my difference*, it is from the same body that I borrow my habits and hence my identity without either body being reducible to the other or to itself' (1996: 258; emphasis added). The relationship that is posited here, as the basis of a generous corporeality, is between 'my difference' and 'the other's body', which *together* form an 'inter-body' that is not reducible to one body or the other. Although this inter-body is not simply the coming together of my difference, that is *my body as difference* with the other's body (my difference is not mine; it is taken from the other's body), it nevertheless positions both bodies *together*. They are together precisely insofar as they are not one. Corporeal generosity, the giving between bodies, does not lead to two bodies which are positioned in the same way, but it does lead to a new form of inclusivity, in which what is shared is the very failure to be self-identical or proper ('our bodies' is hence possible given the very impossibility of having a body that belongs to me or to you – 'me' and 'you' are aligned here as impossible gifts to the other). My body is *with* the other's body, insofar as each other's body makes the other's body.

In contrast, I want to consider inter-embodiment as a site of differentiation rather than inclusion: in such an approach 'my body' and 'the other's body' would not be structurally equivalent (even as impossible bodies), but in a relation of asymmetry and potential violence. Beyond this, inter-embodiment would not just involve the inter-bodily transfer between my body and the other's body: rather, it would involve different modes of transfer between 'this body' and other bodily others. We need to complicate what it means to be 'with', such that 'with-ness' is a site, not of shared co-habitance, but of differentiation (= sociality as differentiation). In other words, in the inter-bodily movements that allow bodies to be formed (as well as de-formed), *bodies are touched by some bodies differently from other bodies*. Not only could we ask the question, 'which bodies are touched by which bodies?', but we could also ask about the different ways in which bodies 'touch' other bodies, and how those differences are ways of forming the bodies of others. We could differentiate, for example, between the caress, the shake, the beating, and so on (see also Chapter 7), in terms of the affect they have on the living out of one's bodily relation to others. We could consider how some forms of touch have been means of subjugating others, or of forming the other as a place of vulnerability and fear (colonial and sexual histories of touch as appropriation, violation and possession). We could also begin to deal with the relationship of touch implicit in the very fear of touching some others: such a refusal of touch is also a means of forming and de-forming some bodies in relationship to other bodies. I am calling here for a phenomenological analysis of corporeal generosity to be supplemented by an understanding of the *economies of touch*.

We can return to my notion of the metonymic relation between particular bodies and sociality, as well as between the body-at-home and the body-politic. We can theorise that relation in terms of touch – touch operates precisely as a *fleshy metonymy*. There is a relation of closeness and proximity between particular bodies and the 'body' of the social in that each comes into a precarious being only through being touched by the other. However, the particular body is touched by the social body in a much stronger sense. For what is meant by the social body is *precisely the effect of being with some others over other others*. The social body is also an imaginary body that is created through the relations of touch between bodies recognisable as friendly and strange; who one allows near, who is further away, and so on. Bodies with skins, while they are already touched in the sense of being exposed to others, are touched differently by near and far others, and *it is this differentiation between others that constitutes the permeability of bodily boundaries*. The differenti-ated relation between 'this body' and 'other bodies', or between 'this' or 'that' other body, can be understood as the metonymic slide of touch; through touch, bodies slide into each other, in such a way that aligns some bodies with other bodies, engendering the perpetual re-forming and de-forming of both bodily and social space.

Strange encounters are hence tactile as well as visual: just as some others are 'seen' and recognised as stranger than other others (as I suggested in Chapter 1, recognition involves a visual economy), so too some skins are touched as stranger than other skins. It is in this specific sense that touch is economic. Rather than thinking of skin as always exposed and touchable, we can think about how different ways of touching allow for different configurations of bodily and social space. Friendship and familial relation involve the ritualisation of certain forms of touch, while the recognition of an-other as a stranger might involve a refusal to get too close through touch.[2] But the stranger's body cannot be reified as the untouchable. For example, although the white woman refuses to touch Audre's clothes which have been touched by Audre's skin, she is still touched by Audre; her bodily gestures express precisely the horror of being touched. In other words, to withdraw from a relation of physical proximity to bodies recognised as strange is precisely to be touched by those bodies, in such a way that the subject is moved from its place. In this sense, the stranger is always in proximity: a body that is out of place because it has come too close. The contours of bodies – the skin – are de-formed and re-formed precisely through being touched by bodies that are recognisable as strange and untouchable.

In Paul Schilder's *The Image and Appearance of the Human Body*, there is a recognition that bodily contours – or the postural model of the body – are always shrinking and expanding in the bodily encounter with other bodies (1970: 210). The permeability of bodily space is produced through the connectedness between bodies: 'A body is necessarily a body amongst other bodies' (Schilder 1970: 281). However, different forms of connection have different effects on that permeability: 'There is no doubt that the far distant body will offer less possibility of interplay' (Schilder 1970: 235). Bodies that are close by may be taken in by, or incorporated into, the body image, hence expanding the contours of the body, while bodies that are further away, are less likely to offer this expanded sense of the body. We could perhaps even suggest that further away bodies – and this sense of distance is irreducible to physical distance – may serve to contract or shrink bodily space, producing discomfort and resistance.[3]

We can build on Schilder's work by considering how familiar bodies can be incorporated through a sense of community – being together as like bodies – while strange bodies are expelled from bodily space – moving apart as unlike bodies. Both incorporation and expulsion serve to re-form the contours of the body, suggesting that the skin, not only registers familiarity and strangeness, but is touched by both differently, *in such a way that the skin becomes the locus for social differentiation*. As such, 'like bodies' and 'unlike bodies' do not precede the tactile encounters of incorporation or expulsion: rather, likeness and unlikeness as 'characteristics' of bodies are produced through these encounters. As bodies move towards and away from each other, in relationships of proximity and distance, both bodily space (the shape of the skin) and social space (the skin of the community) expand and contract. Rosalind Diprose suggests that 'the ease of an encounter with another is limited by the extent to which you already have gestures in common. Faced with a stranger, with a different cultural history and hence a different corporeal schema, one's own lived body may exhibit intolerance or resistance to the encounter' (1994: 122). Although I would question the assumption that the stranger is the one who 'has' difference *on* her body, Diprose does draw our attention to how encounters with others who are already recognised as strange(rs), as out of place in this place, involve forms of discomfort and resistance, that are felt on the skin.

Strange bodies

How do the processes of incorporation and expulsion produce assimilable and unassimilable bodies? In this section, I want to consider how 'strange bodies' or bodies that cannot be assimilated into a given social space are, in some sense, already read and recognisable through the histories of determination in which such bodies are associated with dirt and danger. Such histories of determination that define the parameters of the bodies that are marked as different from the familiar body – the body which is mere home for the white masculine thinker and viewer – inform the strange bodily encounters that take place between subjects, though in such a way that the encounters are not fully determined.

How does the reconfiguration of bodily space through strange encounters evoke such histories of the stranger's body, the body which is already recognisable as strange? In order to deal with such a difficult question, I will firstly examine Kristeva's theories of abjection, as a model which gives primacy to the bodily encounter with dirt and filth. In *Powers of Horror: An Essay on Abjection*, Kristeva argues that, 'There looms, within abjection, one of those violent, dark revolts of being, directed against a threat that seems to emanate from an exorbitant outside or inside; ejected beyond the scope of the possible, the tolerable, the thinkable' (1982: 1). The abject relates to what is revolting, to what threatens the boundaries of both thought and identity: 'The abject has only one quality of the object – that of being opposed to *I*' (Kristeva 1982: 1). At one level, the abject is a jettisoned object that is excluded, or cast out, from the domain of the thinking subject. The abject is expelled – like vomit – and the process of expulsion serves to establish the boundary line of the subject. At the same time, the abject holds an uncanny fascination for the subject, demanding its attention and desire: 'from its place of banishment, the abject does not cease challenging its master' (Kristeva 1982: 2). The abject both establishes and undermines the border between inside and outside: 'It is as if the skin, a fragile container, no longer guaranteed the integrity of "one's own and clean self" ' (Kristeva 1982: 53).

Kristeva's approach to abjection emphasises the physicality of emotions that threaten to pulverise the subject and cross the boundary line. Such physicality is directed towards filth, defilement and pollution, though these are not themselves abject. Rather, they define the crisis posed by abjection insofar as they threaten to undermine the integrity of the subject by passing between the inside and outside. The abject is not reducible to a particular object or body: the abject relates precisely to the border which becomes the object (Kristeva 1982: 4). In the encounter between the white woman and Audre, when the white woman withdraws with horror and disgust at the black body, the border that is threatened by their skin and clothes touching is itself turned into an object of abjection: the roach. It is through a complex sliding of signifiers and bodies, that the roach becomes the black body, and the black body becomes the border which is hence transformed into an object of abjection (rather than an abject object). To this extent, black lived embodiment is, as Frantz Fanon has argued, 'sealed into that crushing objecthood' (1975: 77).

The relation between the physical emotions of horror and disgust, the function and effect of dirt and pollution, and the production of strange bodies as objects, is determined through the 'border': strange bodies threaten to traverse the border that establishes the 'clean body' of the white subject. It is the function and effect of the border – which we can again theorise in terms of the skin – that allows us to think about how the bodily exchange between subjects reopen the histories of encounter that both substantiate and subjugate strange bodies, here constructed as black bodies. However, the association of strange bodies with the border that establishes the inside and outside – and here we can think of both bodily and social space – requires a more proper historicisation than Kristeva's psychoanalytics of abjection will allow. We need to ask: how is it that some bodies are recognised as stranger than others and come to be liveable as unliveable, as the impossible object that both establishes and confounds the border (to return to the stranger's question, 'am I the dirt that forces me to move away?'). What is required is not simply a psychoanalytical approach to how identity *as such* gets established and contested, *but how bodies are differentiated through the metonymic association of some bodies (and not others) with the border that confounds identity.*

In *Bodies that Matter*, Judith Butler considers how abjection functions to produce a domain of unthinkable and unliveable bodies. She writes, 'This exclusionary matrix by which subjects are formed thus requires the simultaneous production of a domain of abject beings, those who are not yet "subjects", but who form the constitutive outside to the domain of the subject' (Butler 1993: 3). Such a domain of abject beings inhabit the 'unliveable' and 'uninhabitable' zones of social life. The unliveable and uninhabitable zones of social life are, at the same time, 'densely populated by those who do not enjoy the status of the subject' (Butler 1993: 3). How can bodies populate zones which are uninhabitable? The marking out of the border which defines the subject – the constitutive outside – is the condition of possibility for the subject, the process through which it can come into being. *This* subject is precisely the subject who determines the formation of home – the space one inhabits as liveable – and whose access to subjectivity is determined through being at home – the centre from which other beings are expelled. The subject who can act and move in the world with ease – the white, masculine, heterosexual, subject – does so through expelling those other beings from this zone of the living (although the expulsion always leaves its trace). One does not then live *in* abjection: abject bodies are precisely the bodies that are not inhabited, are not liveable as such, or indeed, are not at home.

To account for strange bodies is to account for the historical determination of his white body as the body which becomes home: *the body that comes to matter through the reduction of other bodies to matter out of place* (= strange bodies). However, we need a model of how his body is determined as (at) home, without assuming a structural equivalence between those others who are expelled from the domain of the liveable. There are different forms of expulsion, all of which also involve prior acts of incorporation. We need to examine how the processes of 'taking in' and 'expelling' (which involve the transformation of the border into an object) allow some bodies to be lived as (at) home.

Strange bodies do not exist as such, as they can only be assimilated as the unassimilable within the home of the white masculine subject: his being is here *and* there, secured as a dwelling that allows him to occupy and move within space. And yet, strange bodies are also over-represented and perpetually encountered as the impossible border that both establishes and threatens his identity and home: 'A fear of difference is projected onto the objects and spaces comprising the home or locality which can be polluted by the presence of non-conforming people, activities or artefacts' (Sibley 1995: 38). The different value given to homes or localities discussed in Chapter 1, slides into the different value given to bodies: the most privileged white masculine body is at home in the spaces which themselves are privileged (his body = his home = the world). In some sense, the domain of the white masculine subject is established by the equation of his body with home as such: his body transcends itself to become simply where he lives (= the knowable, inhabitable world).

The histories of determination of 'strange bodies' as an impossible object that establishes the domain of the privileged subject (his bodily world), also produce such bodies as dangerous, uncontrollable, dirty, engulfing and *over-reaching space itself*. In Stallybrass and White's *The Poetics and Politics of Transgression*, for example, there is an examination of how marginalised bodies are associated with the grotesque, and are seen as being multiple and bulging (1986: 9). Strange bodies are also represented as bodies that are incomplete, that threaten to leak and contaminate, and that have open orifices (Stallybrass and White 1986: 9). The over-representation of strange bodies as grotesque already positions the bodies of those that are not yet subjects, as out of place precisely in their refusal to be contained by place. The threat of contamination posed by strange bodies is precisely that those bodies already exceed the place in which they come to be encountered as such.

This exceeding of the out-of-place-ness of strange bodies opens out the temporality of the bodily encounter: rather than simply understanding strange bodies as produced in the present encounter with an-other we recognise as strange, we can now theorise that such encounters slide not only through space (bodily space leaks into social space), but also through time (the present encounter reopens past encounters). The over-determination of the local encounter by the historical and social production of ideal, contained and closed bodies suggests that strange bodies remain threatening: they not only make possible the designation of the body-at-home, but also, at the same time, confirm the impossibility of such a body being at home, in the present, as such. The strange body can only become a material 'thing' that touches the body-at-home, or a figure that can be faced in the street, through a radical forgetting of the histories of labour and production that allow such a body to appear in the present. The strange body becomes a fetish which both conceals and reveals the body-at-home's reliance on strangers to secure his being – his place – his presence – in the world.

This production of unliveable or unassimilable strange bodies involves contingent and over-determined regimes of difference that are concealed in the very forms of stranger fetishism (the production of the stranger as a figure with bodily integrity). In the encounter discussed in this chapter, the strange body becomes the black body, a strange body in relation to the liveable domain of the white female subject. The antagonism between white and black femininities is here determined through a bodily encounter: an encounter which involves the refusal to share social space, to touch each other, a refusal of co-habitation that contains the black body *as body*, and allows the white body to move away, even away from itself. Other forms of power differentiation intersect in the recognition of bodily strangerness: while the white female body can become lived as the body-at-home by the withdrawal from proximity to the strange black body, the white female body becomes uninhabitable and unliveable in relation to the formation of the masculine body. What is required is precisely an analysis of how abjection – the unstable constitution of the domain of the liveable – brings into play multiple forms of social antagonism. The relationship between the processes of incorporation and expulsion which produce the abject and the marking of, and withdrawal from, particular bodily others as strange bodies, is hence *contingent* rather than necessary: there is a metonymic sliding across different borders, objects and bodies within such strange encounters.

Strange bodies are precisely those bodies that are temporarily assimilated *as* the unassimilable within the encounter: they function as the border that defines both the space into which the familiar body – the body which is unmarked by strangeness as its mark of privilege – cannot cross, and the space in which such a body constitutes itself as (at) home. The strange body is constructed through a process of incorporation and expulsion – a movement between inside and outside, which renders that the stranger's body has already touched the surface of the skin that appears to contain the body-at-home. The economy of xenophobia – the production of the stranger's body as an impossible and phobic object – involves, not just reading the stranger's body as dirt and filth, but the re-forming of the contours of the body-at-home, through the very affective gestures which enable the withdrawal from co-habitation with strangers in a given social space. The withdrawal remains registered on the skin, on the border that feels.

3 Knowing strangers

[H]ave you not observed that it is characteristic of a well-bred dog to behave with the utmost gentleness to those it is used to and knows, but to be
savage to strangers ... it is a trait that shows real discrimination and a truly
philosophical nature ... for the dog distinguishes the sight of a friend and
foe simply by knowing one and not knowing the other.

(Plato 1970: 111)

How do you know the difference between a friend and a stranger? How do
you know a stranger? Such questions challenge the assumption that the
stranger is the one who is precisely *not* the object of knowledge. For in such
a question, knowledge is staged as constitutive, not only of what is familiar,
what is already known or indeed knowable, but also of what is strange, and
who is the stranger. As I argued in the previous two chapters, the stranger is
not *any-body* that we have failed to recognise, but *some-body* that we have
already recognised *as* a stranger, as 'a body out of place'. Hence, the stranger
is some-body we know as not knowing, rather than some-body we simply do
not know. The stranger is produced as a category within knowledge, rather
than coming into being in an absence of knowledge. The implications of
such a rethinking of the relationship between knowledge and strangers are
far reaching: it suggests that knowledge is bound up with the formation of a
community, that is, with the formation of a 'we' that knows through (rather
than against) 'the stranger'.

In the above quotation, knowing the difference between friend and
enemy, or between friend and stranger,[1] reflects 'a truly philosophical
nature'. So we might guess that philosophers have good noses. And we
might guess that having a good nose means being able to smell the
difference. Smelling the difference is here a way of knowing that establishes
the border between the familiar and the strange: do you smell like a friend
or stranger? Should the philosopher let you in? I can just see it: philosophers
and guard dogs at the door, busy, smelling, smelling you as you all come in.
You might get a gentle lick from the philosopher's tongue if you smell
familiar, and you might get bitten if you don't: the philosopher's teeth may
bite deeply into your already scarred not-quite-human flesh. You may of

course want to refuse the choice of being licked or bitten (at least by a philosopher), but you may have resigned any right of refusal by simply being-Here.

Smelling the difference involves a practice of differentiation: those we know we treat with kindness, we let you in, we allow a relation of proximity or closeness. Those we don't know turn us into the savages. The knowing of one from the other is here determinate in the constitution of Law as savagery: as the cutting off of the stranger, as the determination of the standard of 'letting in' or 'keeping out'. And so Plato narcissistically admires the guard dog's nose (in the end, it must be a question of him, in front of a mirror, admiring his own nose): 'it is a trait that shows real discrimination and a truly philosophical nature ... for the dog distinguishes the sight of a friend and foe simply by knowing one and not knowing the other. And the creature that distinguishes between the familiar and the unfamiliar on the grounds of knowledge or ignorance must be gifted with a real love of knowledge' (1970: 11). And then, 'is not philosophy *the same thing* as the love of knowledge' (Plato 1970: 111).

The same thing. Philosophy is a thing that is the same as loving knowledge: a love of knowledge which is the same thing as telling the difference between what you know and don't know, which is the same thing as smelling the difference between the friend and the foe. These slips from one 'same thing' to another are the gift of a philosophical community: a community of those whose epistemic privilege is a form of loving, a loving of the 'same thing', and an expulsion of strangeness from the thing itself (the thing which is, in the end, the philosopher's most elegant nose). But the difference which is cast as strange, the smell then of strangeness itself, is only smellable from within that nose. The stranger is here the condition of possibility for the philosopher's narcissism, for the love which lets him caress his nose through which he always smells himself as the one he knows or who knows. He loves himself, and the 'same-thing-ness' of himself, only by first smelling the stranger, which makes him, if you like, sneeze the stranger out of the philosophical body. The stranger is both within and without the same thing: as the border that determines the necessity and impossibility of the difference between one and an-other.

In other words, the stranger is produced as a figure that is distinct from the (philosophical) body, only through a process of expulsion: the stranger 'comes to be' as an entity precisely by a prior inhabiting of that philosophical body, or the body of the community 'that knows'. So while it is the love of knowledge that creates the spatial distinction between friend and stranger (perhaps another way of talking about Orientalism), that love also causes the philosopher to sneeze 'the stranger' out of the philosophical body; it threatens the integrity of the philosophical body. The sneeze which allows the figure of the stranger to take shape, as if it were 'outside' of the knowledge, can be understood, not as a form of purification (where there is no *trace* of the stranger left in the body), but as a form of contamination.

Knowing strangers, in this sense, is about telling the difference between what one knows and does not know, in such a way that this difference is already called into question.

In the quotation above, the stranger is already known precisely insofar as it is known as an enemy (see Chapter 1). What I will examine in this chapter, through exploring the relationship between ethnography and translation, is how knowledge is *accumulated* about 'the stranger' that both confirms and threatens the difference between the one 'who knows' and the one who is known. The stranger is not necessarily known as an enemy, but may come to be known as a stranger, once she or he has become a friend. The stranger is hence both familiar and strange, both within and without 'our field of knowledge'. This consideration of the relation between knowledge and the stranger (in which I will suggest that knowledge allows the stranger to enter the epistemic community *as a figure*) will shift the debate in post-colonial theory, feminist theory and postmodern ethnography from the question of 'the other' as such. As I will discuss in more detail later, the fascination with otherness has allowed us to hesitate on questions such as 'who speaks', where the question of speaking has taken on 'a life of [its] own' (Marx 1976: 164), becoming abstracted from the conditions of knowing and labour which allow for the very possibility of speaking or listening. In other words, if we consider the production of 'the stranger' through relationships of knowledge (rather than simply speech), we can draw attention to the processes of inclusion and exclusion, or incorporation and expulsion, that are concealed in stranger fetishism.

Ethnography and strangers

In order to examine the production of 'strangers' in knowledge, I will examine the role of ethnography which has, in relationship to the emergence of the discipline of anthropology, been predicated on a model of translating 'strange cultures'. To talk about ethnography as the translation of a strange culture might appear to equate ethnography and anthropology. So why is this chapter not framed as a critique of anthropology? There are a number of reasons for this decision. First, I want to consider *techniques* of knowing implicit in the notion of 'fieldwork' that cannot be reduced to the discipline of anthropology. Second, I do not want to reify the link between anthropology and 'strange cultures', not only because anthropology can return home (see Jackson 1987), but also because the notion of strange cultures as radically exterior to the culture of the ethnographer must be criticised (hence sociological ethnography is also an encounter with strangerness). Third, the discipline of anthropology has self-reflexively considered its relation to 'the Other' and how it constructs rather than describes the Other (for examples, see Asad 1973; McGrane 1989; Fabian 1992; Trouillot 1991; Clifford 1986). While my work involves a critique of some of that recent literature (for example, the postmodern model of ethnography as collaboration), I am also aware that I cannot exhaust the complex and multi-fold ways anthropology has articulated its relation to its Other.

One of the central models for the production of ethnographic knowledge has been cultural translation: the translation of a strange culture into the language of ethnography, the language of the one who knows. A classical formulation is offered by Lienhardt: 'The problem of describing to others how members of a remote tribe think then begins to appear largely as one of translation, of making the coherence primitive thought has in the languages it really uses, as clear as possible in our own' (1956: 97). Here, translation is a question of making the strange appear *within* the familial as clearly as possible. The process is one of exchange, of moving strangeness from one system of meaning to another without altering its coherence. Strangeness could only be thought in terms of the primitive: translation is a translation of the primitive which is itself a residual trace of that which was prior to 'our own'. The exchange hence is spatial and temporal: from one culture to another, and from (our) past to the present.

Vincent Crapanzano reconsiders the metaphor of translation in an article that appears in the collection, *Writing Cultures*, one of the (if you can forgive the irony) classical articulations of a postmodern ethnography (see also Asad 1986). First, Crapanzano cites Benjamin's consideration of all translation as a provisional way of coming to terms with the foreignness of languages (Crapanzano 1986: 51). The phrase, 'coming to terms' demands our close attention. Coming to terms can suggest 'dealing with', coping with. However, the phrase could also work to suggest, 'coming (into) the terms of': in other words, translating as re-terming. The double meaning of the term, 'coming to terms', is suggestive: the event of dealing with foreignness could be rearticulated as a re-terming of the foreign such that the foreign becomes the familiar. In other words, ethnographic translation produces knowledge of the foreign through a radical *de-terming* of the foreign. Ethnographic knowledge would not be knowledge of the stranger, but knowledge of the familiar: knowledge which creates the stranger in the familial in order then to destroy it. If the 'coming to terms with' is provisional, then creating strangerness involves acts of violence that can be endlessly repeated.

How does Crapanzano translate Benjamin on translation into ethnography? Of course, we begin with the assumption of analogy. He writes, '*Like* translation, ethnography is also a somewhat provisional way of coming to terms with the foreignness of language – of cultures and societies. The ethnographer does not translate texts the way the translator does. He must first produce them' (Crapanzano 1986: 51; emphasis added). Here, the analogy has its limits. The limits of the analogy between translation and ethnography resides in the different status of the text: in ethnography the text has to be produced before any 'coming to terms with' can take place. We can relate this to Todorov's model of the ethnographic as the accumulation of documents (1984: 240). The ethnographer creates the writing (about the strange culture) in order then to translate or re-term: the act of violence is here an act that not only presupposes creation (the strange is created in order to be destroyed), but is an act of creation in and of itself. The ethnographer creates and destroys at the same time in the very accumulation of documents (the authorisation of knowledge as writing).

The stranger comes to appear as a figure of speech at the same time as it is rendered impossible. The Stranger hence becomes a figure for that which has been made impossible by the necessity of translation. Crapanzano concludes that the ethnographer, 'Like Benjamin's translator ... aims at a solution to the very problem of foreignness, and like the translator (a point missed by Benjamin) he must also communicate the very foreignness that his interpretations (the translator's translations) deny, at least in their claim to universality. He must render the foreign familial and preserve its very foreignness at the same time' (1986: 52). The task of the ethnographer is hence not only to write about the strange, but to write about strange cultures for other ethnographers (it is their ear which must be the text's proper destination). The writing has an *institutional home*, so to speak, and hence the writing of strangerness must *return home*. But the need to resolve foreignness is set against a need to preserve it: we must translate the foreign into terms we understand, but in such a way that it can still live in the writing *as* the foreign. The doubling of the assertion and disavowal of foreignness and strangeness is symptomatic: knowledge both creates and destroys the stranger (the document) and yet re-creates the strange as a spectre of itself: as that which is then known in terms of (coming to the terms of) the not-quite-strange or not-quite-familiar. The knowing of strangers is, in this way, linked to the production of hybridity.

We can compare the model of ethnography as translation with the model of the ethnographer as the professional stranger offered by Michael Agar. On the surface, this model appears very different. It is the ethnographer who is the stranger coming into a space where others are familiar with each other. Does this suggest the relativisability of the very condition of strangerness? Agar writes, 'Ethnography is really quite an arrogant enterprise. In a short period of time, an ethnographer moves in among a group of strangers to study and describe their beliefs, document their social life, write about their subsistence strategies, and generally explore their territory right down to their recipes for the evening meal' (1980: 41). Quite clearly from this statement of the ethnographic project there is no renunciation of authority (however much the ethnographer admits to the arrogance of the enterprise). The ethnographer moves among, studies, describes, documents, writes and, importantly, explores their territory. Ethnography is maintained as an exploratory and accumulative discourse: we get closer to the object, in order to gain more knowledge.

Agar's representation of the ethnographer as the professional stranger does not lead to a relativisation of strangerness. On the contrary, the objects of the ethnographic exploration remain the strangers. What we have instead is the creation of another epistemic distinction: the ethnographer turns strangerness into a profession, into a technique for the accumulation of knowledge. Those Agar writes about writing about are named simply as 'a group of strangers' (1980: 41). The distinction is now between strangers (objects of knowledge) and the professional stranger (the subject of knowledge). Such a distinction suggests that ethnography can occupy the position of the strangers in order to accumulate documents, without simply becoming the stranger. The desire to tell the difference is here a desire to know the strangers, to get closer to them through exercising various techniques of observation and writing (so that we can even cook and eat their food). Professional strangers constitute the stranger as an unknowing other (the one who simply *is* a stranger rather than *takes on* strangerness through knowledge). Knowing strangers is here knowing strangers as unknowing. Ethnography defines itself as the professionalisation of strangerness: *the transformation of the stranger from an ontological lack to an epistemic privilege.*

Feminist knowledge and strangers

So if the ethnographic techniques for the accumulation of documents about groups of strangers involve the designating of strangerness as an ontological lack which can be transformed only through those documents into knowledge, then what are the implications for feminist ethnography? Does the feminist challenge to such ethnographic techniques produce a structurally different kind of knowledge? What I want to do here is bring the concern with research methodologies that is clear in feminist ethnography into contact with some of the questions concerning representation raised by feminist post-colonial theory. I will suggest that such a contact can only be productive: it will shift the terms of reference for both sets of approaches.

The central question for post-colonial feminism has been, 'who is speaking here?' Indeed, the question, 'who is speaking here?' has become familiar. The question does not demand to know the particularity of the 'who' that is speaking. The question, as it has gained our critical attention, calls for us to refuse any such particularism and to grant the 'who' a tenuous existence as marking only a position from which a speech *can be* made. This question has become a reminder of the relations of force and authorisation that institute the very possibility of speech: some speak precisely because they are in the position to be heard, to command our attention. Gayatri Spivak has asked the question powerfully, 'does the subaltern woman speak?' Her reply has been as powerful: 'she does not' (1988). Some, such as Benita Parry (1987), have responded negatively to such an assertion, suggesting that it forecloses the possibility of subaltern agency. However, Spivak's assertion is a challenge to the condition of subalternity itself: what constitutes the position of the subaltern is precisely the impossibility of being heard (1996: 289). In other words, the question becomes not so much, 'who speaks?', but 'who hears?'

The question, 'who is speaking here?', has also been addressed to feminism itself. There has been a suggestion that certain privileged white women have themselves spoken for the subaltern woman and have hence been implicated in this politics of not-hearing (Mohanty 1991).[2] The question, 'who is speaking here?' reminds us that feminism is implicated in the relations of force and authorisation that structure the very possibility of the one speaking and the other being spoken for. While the question of 'who speaks?' remains an important and necessary one, it is also in need of supplementation. This chapter has already posed an alternative question, 'who knows?' It is this question that brings the ethnographic desire to know more about strangers into contact with the post-colonial concern with the politics of representing others. The question, reformulated as an epistemological one is, 'who is knowing, here?' Such a shift opens out the contexts in which speaking and hearing take place: we need to ask, what knowledges are *already* in place which allow one to speak for, about or to a 'group of strangers'? (Agar 1980: 41). In other words, we need to move our attention from the production of otherness to the (re)production of strangerness.

The shift implicit in the question, 'who knows?', echoes the shift in Gayatri Spivak's work. In an interview, Spivak suggests that to always return to the question of speaking is to conceal the structuration of speech by labour. She asks instead, 'who works *for* whom?' (1996: 296). It is my argument that considering the epistemic dimensions of speaking will demonstrate the links between representation and broader relationships of production: in other words, labouring formations are at work in the assumption that the subaltern woman can be known. An epistemological dimension is implicit in both questions, 'who speaks?' and 'who works?', suggesting a mutually constitutive and over-determined relation between speaking, knowledge and work. We can ask the provocative question: *how does the act of speaking already know 'the stranger' as within or without a given community?*

In order to address the implications of such a shift for both feminist post-colonial theory and feminist ethnography I want to consider what has become known in Australia as 'the Bell debate'. The Bell debate is a debate about a white Australian feminist, Diane Bell, and an article in which she, alongside her 'co-author'[3] Topsy Napurrula Nelson, an Indigenous woman, speaks out about the rape of Indigenous women by Indigenous men. Her/their first article, published by *Women's Studies International Forum*, was entitled, 'Speaking About Rape is Everyone's Business' (Bell and Nelson 1989). The title itself confirms the position: everyone must speak out about rape: everyone has the right to speak out about rape, as rape is a fundamental violation of the rights of women. While I am not able to address here the issue of rights and universalism (see Ahmed 1998a), we might consider how the 'everyone' might operate as a general term to conceal who might come to speak about rape. It is the concealed relation between the 'everyone' and the 'I' claimed elsewhere by Bell (in a later article, Bell writes, 'Speaking out, speaking of, speaking with, speaking about, speaking for ... *What did I say*' (1996: 107; emphasis added)) that may partly explain the controversy.

Following the publication of the article in 1989, as Bell puts it, all 'hell broke loose' (1996: 108):

> In February 1990, a letter bearing no signatures to validate the names typed at the bottom of the second page, and no address, was sent to colleagues and *WSIF*, but was not sent directly to me (although my address was on the article).[4] It accused me of creating divisions within the 'Aboriginal community', appropriating Topsy Napurrula Nelson's voice by citing her as a co-author rather than 'informant', of exhibiting white imperialism, of exercising middle-class privilege.
>
> (Bell 1996: 108)

The debate at one level can be read as a debate as to who has the right to speak for Indigenous women (see Moreton-Robinson 1998, forthcoming). Does the white woman who speaks out about the rape of Indigenous women necessarily speak *for* those women? Is the event of her speaking inevitably a form of imperialism? What else can we say about the relationship between her speaking and the position of Indigenous women in the debate? How is it that she came to speak in the first place? What alternatives would there be to her speaking, and to what extent does her speaking involve hearing? As Anna Yeatman summarises, 'This debate signals an emergent politics of voice and representation within Australian feminism, where, in this instance, Aboriginal women are contesting the historically established dominance of white settler women in Australian feminism' (1993: 239).

To question Bell's discourse of speaking with (Topsy Napurrula Nelson) as a form of speaking for is to pose a challenge to some of the developments in what has been termed the new reflexive ethnography or postmodern ethnography. For here, there has been a counter-move to define the 'native informant' as a 'co-author' and to admit to the plurality of the ethnographic document. Sally McBeth in 'Myths of Objectivity and the Collaborative Process in Life History Research' argues that, 'Current ethnographic writing is seeking new ways to adequately represent the authority of "informants" and to explore methodologies that more adequately legitimise the expertise of the members of the culture being investigated' (1993: 145). This exploration of new methodologies is described by McBeth as 'dispersed authority' (1993: 161), which moves from the traditional ethnographic objectivity to an 'informed intersubjectivity' predicated on listening and collaboration (1993: 146). The informant is 'an equal partner' (McBeth 1993: 162).

Such a democratisation of ethnography has been constructed as intrinsically postmodern. James Clifford, for example, argues that in postmodernism: 'Anthropology no longer speaks with automatic authority for others defined as unable to speak for themselves' (1986: 10). The postmodern ethnographic text is dialogical rather than monological, partial rather than apparently total: it is a text in which, 'Many voices clamour for expression' and in which informants are 'co-authors' (Clifford 1986: 15, 17). To argue that there has been such a shift in the relation between ethnography and authority is *to presuppose the possibility of overcoming the relations of force and authorisation that are already implicated in the ethnographic desire to document the lives of strangers.*

To return to the Bell debate, we can see that the question of whether Topsy Napurrula Nelson has spoken is a difficult one. One can take Bell's point that to assume Nelson hasn't spoken – or that she cannot speak – would be to deny Nelson agency. Bell even suggests that Huggins *et al.* are being racist insofar as they assume that Nelson was not 'really' involved in the production of the article (1991b: 509). But that rather misses the point. What is at issue is not whether Nelson has a voice, but whether or not her voice can be heard *within* the article itself. The article was published in an international women's studies journal, in English. It fulfils some very specific formal and scholarly requirements in terms of language and argument. Within the original article, the two 'I's' are separated, and have a different function and effect within the text itself. Nelson's writing is italicised, and separated off from the main body of the text, which develops the over-arching framework and argument. What Huggins *et al.* are suggesting is that the white feminist anthropologist cannot simply 'give voice' to those already known as strangers 'in the field', by including the voice of an Indigenous woman within such a text, however much the act of inclusion is signalled by the italicisation.

Bell places much emphasis on the fact that the article is authorised by Nelson as well, given that Nelson made a significant contribution to it in terms of making Bell's own knowledge possible. That is, the co-authorship signals Bell's debt to Nelson, a debt that would not have been made transparent if she had only been named as chief informant. Again, I think this is problematic as it represents debt to the informant as an exception to anthropological practice. One could argue that anthropology is precisely in debt to the strangers through which it has come to know: it knows only through them, and through the transformation of their being into knowledge. But to say that ethnographers should rename their informants as co-authors would be to conceal how this debt also involves forms of appropriation and translation: it would conceal that the ones who are known have not authorised the forms of writing and knowledge produced by ethnographers, but have been authorised by it. To say that Nelson was not a co-author in any 'equal' sense of the term, is to point to the way in which Bell's debt to her informants does not mean an overcoming of the power relations that allow the ethnographer to transform others into strangers, in order to mark out 'a field (of knowledge)'.

The redefinition of the 'informant' as an 'equal partner' hence works to conceal the power relations that still allow the gathering together of a document. In other words, the narrative of overcoming the relations of authorisation in traditional ethnography constitutes another form of authorisation. This suggests that (rather ironically given that she writes against postmodernism as a radical feminist), Bell is implicated in the postmodern fantasy that it is the 'I' of the ethnographer who can undo the power relations that allowed the 'I' to appear. Such a fantasy allows the ethnographer to be praised for her or his ability to listen well. So it remains the ethnographer who is praised: praised for the giving up of her or his authority. The event of recognition demonstrates that the ethnographic document *still returns home in postmodernism*, but that the returning home is *concealed* in the fantasy of being-together-as-strangers. When Jackie Huggins *et al.* (1991), followed by Anna Yeatman (1993: 239), rename Topsy Napurrula Nelson as a 'native informant' rather than as a co-author, they are writing against this assumption that a plural text can overcome the relations of force and authorisation embedded in the desire to know (more) about strangers.

In critiquing such a narrativisation of overcoming within reflexive and postmodern ethnography, I support the claims made by feminist critics such as Kamala Visweswaran who argues that, 'dispensing authority represents anthropology's last grasp of the "other" ' (1994: 32) and Judith Stacey, who suggests that an emphasis on antagonism, 'undermine(s) these anthropological pretensions to alliance and collaboration with the Other' (1988: 25). However, as Stacey argues, such a challenge is also a challenge to feminist ethnography which has valued empathy and identification between women as researchers and researched (1988: 25). We have the ironic situation whereby the critique of postmodernism parallels the critique of the work of radical feminists such as Diane Bell.[5] Importantly, the challenge to notions of reciprocity and collaboration in both postmodern and feminist ethnographic research can be made through a post-colonial feminist emphasis on the power differences *between* women.

So, at one level, to question Diane Bell's shift from the 'everyone' to the 'I' in speaking about the rape of Indigenous women is to provide an important critique of the assumption that the 'I' can itself overcome the power relations that allow it to appear. However, at the same time, I would argue that to define such a debate as simply about a battle over representation and voice – as Anna Yeatman does – is insufficient: the debate is not simply about the question of who is speaking and who is being spoken for.[6] Rather, the contestability of Bell's claims must be linked to the relations of production that surround the text, 'Speaking about Rape is Everyone's Business'. In other words, we need to ask: how is it that Diane Bell came close enough to Topsy Napurrula Nelson to allow her to speak about/for/with/to her in the context of 'everyone's business'? We need to take on board the implications of Nelson's own contributions to the Bell debate.

Diane Bell cites Nelson's contribution to dramatise how the reactions against the article serve to render Nelson voiceless (as they serve to deflect attention away from the immediate political issue of sexual violence against Indigenous women), and calls for a model of 'actual friendship and personal trust' as the basis for 'cross-cultural collaboration' (1996: 110). In a seemingly analogous manner, Topsy Napurrula Nelson writes:

> I had no Aborigine to write this down. Diane is like a sister, a best friend. She wrote all this down for me. That's OK – women to women; it doesn't matter black or white. I want these things written down and read again later. I was telling Diane to write this story for me.
>
> (1990: 507)

Does the coincidence of these representations suggest that a radical feminist ethnography could take friendship as its epistemic basis: that the ethnographic desire to know the stranger could be rearticulated as the transformation of strangers into friends? While Nelson's description of her friendship with Bell appears to be close to Bell's own call for friendship as the basis for cross-cultural collaboration or dialogue, I think there are important differences. Bell calls for friendship *in general*, as a new agenda for research that can overcome the barriers of strangeness. In contrast, Nelson is describing a *particular* friendship that exists which led her to want Bell to write 'this story for (her)'. In other words, Bell's call remains a call which is motivated by the demands of feminist research: the call situates her as an ethnographer who poses general questions about what to do and how to work. Bell writes about how Nelson and she, 'had worked together', but does not name the kind of work that enables this 'togetherness'. However, the work is named as prior and constitutive of her theoretical approach: the trust that she achieves through their work becomes the basis for an approach to feminism that emphasises relationality rather than boundary maintenance (Bell 1996: 110). What is the connection between becoming friends, the working relation of ethnography, and the theoretical reflection on how to do feminism across different cultural spaces?

The incommensurate ways in which friendship is constructed in their texts demonstrates that trust and friendship – getting closer or intimacy – does not overcome the distance and the division between the ethnographer and the one who is constructed as a 'past stranger'. Bell's gaining of Nelson's trust is hence complicated: it relies on a prior ethnographic investment in what the trust provides – that is, *access* to the stranger culture. To discuss friendship as strategically framed is not in any way to question Bell's intentions or the political importance of her work. To do so would individuate a complex set of textual as well as material relations. But we do need to rethink how the claim to intimacy may rework the ethnographic construction of 'the stranger'. For example, Sally McBeth also discusses her relationship to her informants as involving intimacy and an 'interpersonal and intracultural friendship', and then moves from that discussion to the discipline of anthropology ('the relation between text, audience and ethnographic field techniques') (1993: 146, 161). The move from one to the other, from friendship to the question of technique, constitutes that friendship *as a technique*, a technique of knowledge.[7] Bell's discussion of friendship – of the need to make friends with strangers – purely in terms of relationality and dialogue works to conceal the operation of an epistemic difference and division. In other words, the discussion of friendship conceals the ethnographic relation, which is based on the (re)production of stranger-ness, that already exists between Bell and Nelson.

What are the implications of Bell's concealment of the power relations involved in the ethnographic encounter through the use of a narrative of friendship? In her discussion of the letter sent to *WSIF* by the Indigenous women, Bell makes the following statement, 'It was authored by 12 well-educated urban Aboriginal women, none of whom, to the best of my knowledge has any in-depth fieldwork experience in the area in which we have written, but all of whom had claimed to speak *for* Aboriginal women' (1996: 108). Here, the effect of the concealment of the ethnographic investment makes itself evident. Bell implicitly claims a greater *ability* to speak on the rape of Aboriginal women as somebody who has had, 'in-depth fieldwork experience'. This is a claim to knowledge arrived at through the classical techniques of ethnography. The work of ethnography *in the field* provides the material context in which Bell's speaking for Nelson could take place.

We have a symptomatic shift in Bell's article that appears in the collection, *Gendered Fields*. In the first instance, Bell writes in a way which conveys a sense or intimacy as proximity: a closeness to each other, or togetherness in which no estrangement appears: 'It was only a glance, I was crying and so was she' (1993: 28). Although the 'I' and the 'she' work to indicate subjects who are differently positioned in the writing (there is no move from the 'I' and the 'she' to a 'we'), the two subject nevertheless remain bound together by the shared act of mourning, for 'her' father. So why not a 'we'? Bell writes, 'there were moments in the field when we move so finely tuned to the logic of the host culture that it feels as if we belong' (1993: 28). The 'we' that appears here, is not Bell and the Indigenous woman who is present only as a 'she', but the 'we' of those entering the host culture, those professional strangers called ethnographers. The 'she' is kept in place, through a shift from the 'I' who identifies with her, to the 'we' that only almost does. In between these two narratives is lodged yet another calling: 'how was I, as the anthropologist consultant to the judge on this case, going to give expert evidence on the local system of land tenure' (Bell 1993: 28). What we have then is the shift from the intimacy of mourning together (where the 'I' mourns *with* the stranger 'she'), to the structures of law that position the 'I' as expert, and then to the ethnographic 'we'. Such a narrative involves becoming closer to the stranger (being-with-her) as a means of representing her to the 'we' of the ethnographic (the production of knowledge of the 'host culture').

In the final article in *Gendered Fields* by Wasir Karim the implications of this shift become clear. Karim writes:

> Bell was subject to a double barrage of prejudices from both 'native' Aboriginal men and white Australians, but in the long term, was able to re-position herself against the 'other' – in particular, powerful white administrators of the law – by becoming an informant on 'Aboriginal' culture in courts of Australia. In a sense, her 'self' becomes the 'other', not so much by emulating native conduct *as by translating its meaning to others*.
>
> (1993: 249–250)

Here, Bell's constitution as expert by the Law operates *through* her designation as being close enough to the stranger to *stand in for her*, and stand against the Law's administrators. Her ability to occupy the position of an informant on Indigenous culture (rather than being an Indigenous informant) is not that she emulates strangers, but precisely that she can translate them. Translation here returns as a metaphor – even if it is for a different kind of ethnography. One gets closer to the host culture, one makes friends with strangers, in order to transform that friendship into an expert technique, *in order to represent strangers in Law precisely through translating them into the Law*.

Reading *Daughters of the Dreaming*

If Bell's ethnographic desire to know strangers (as a desire linked to a feminist concern to represent women's interests) leads to an ethnography of translation, whereby what is translated is strangerness into friendship and Law, then what kinds of knowledges are possible of those other women? I now want to look closely at Bell's earlier ethnography, *Daughters of the Dreaming*. This has rarely been mentioned in the Bell debate, but as my discussion suggests, *it is both presupposed and concealed by it*. At one level, *Daughters of the Dreaming* appears to challenge some of the traditional methods of writing ethnography, for example, by bringing the autobiographic into the ethnographic (Okely 1992). In this first chapter, there is little claim to objectivity or certainty: rather, the author is located in terms of a complex network of power relations (as a white, middle-class, divorced woman with two children), and as being ambivalent and confused. She writes of the difference of her account: 'to admit to one's inadequacies, to how fumbling one was in local language, to how socially inept, how angry and upset one became was not the done thing' (Bell 1983: 9).

This insertion of an 'I' into the narrative, an 'I' that is not centred and originary, but doubtful, does not depart significantly from the traditional ethnographic text in the way, say, Kamala Visweswaran's *Fictions of Feminist Ethnography* does. In Visweswaran's text, the 'I' keeps intruding into the writing in the form of a loss of a proper ethnographic subject. In *Daughters of the Dreaming*, the uncertain 'I' speaks only in the first chapter, and the narrativisation of the 'I' takes the form of an overcoming of doubt, uncertainty and ignorance through the acquisition of knowledge – the 'I' commands the narrative precisely by gaining access to the lives of strangers. As Mary Louise Pratt stresses, the personal account of fieldwork experience is 'a recognisable anthropological subgenre', that may accompany (as a first chapter) or precede a more 'formal' ethnography (1986: 31). Such personal accounts hence are the conditions of possibility for the ethnographic document rather than their radical undoing: they enable the document precisely by a writing of how it came to appear as such.

Pratt also discusses how it would be an 'ethnographic dream' to be invited into certain spaces (1986: 31). The ethnographic dream is narratable as the 'I' who gains access to the lives of strangers, who is allowed into their space, and whose documentable knowledge of the strangers hence expands. Noticeably, in the first chapter in *Daughters of the Dreaming*, Bell first writes, 'I was treated like a spy', by being asked questions such as, 'Will you write down secrets and publish them?' (1983: 9). Such 'treatment' becomes an obstacle to the ethnographic project. The narrative involves the overcoming of the obstacle: 'Later that day I sat chatting with the woman who had befriended me in the morning. She invited me to the women's business which was to be held that day. I couldn't believe my good fortune' (Bell 1983: 10). The last sentence is instructive. Gaining access to the spaces in which the indigenous women do their business is represented as 'my (her)' good fortune. The word, 'fortune', which suggests an economic gain, intrudes into the story as follows: what can *she* gain from another culture in terms of knowledge of that culture? In other words, the access to the intimate lives of strangers is the condition of possibility for the good fortune of the very document, *Daughters of the Dreaming* and the rendering proper of its name (authorship).

The first chapter emphasises the dialogues that took place between Bell as the ethnographer and 'the group of stranger women' (if I can reformulate Agar's phrase in gendered terms). Throughout, the dialogues are represented in terms of *learning*. In the first instance, Bell is learning *about* the Indigenous women: 'I wandered around, was swept up by an argument between two young mothers trailing toddlers and shielded by a talkative Warlpiri woman. She asked what I was doing. I said I had come to Warrabi to learn about women's lives' (1983: 10). While this project of 'learning about' involves speaking to Indigenous women, it also involves a prior reading of the ethnographic and anthropological literature: 'Before beginning my fieldwork at Warrabi I read all the available literature on Central Australia and discussed my project with other anthropologists' (1983: 9). The project becomes definable as follows: to what extent does traditional anthropology account for the reality of Indigenous women's lives and their place in their culture? Bell argues, through learning more about the women, that the traditional accounts don't recognise that Indigenous women are 'boss for themselves' (1983: 11).

In other words, Indigenous women are present in *Daughters of the Dreaming*, insofar as they establish a term in an argument that essentially has its terms of reference in anthropology. Although Bell learns about them, what she learns is already translated into the structure of an anthropological debate. I would not want to argue that such a translation is inherently wrong – such an argument would assume we could gain pure unmediated access to the lives of strangers. Rather, what is at stake is the concealment of the translation itself: a translation which both creates the strangers as a figure of speech (the 'they' in the narrative), then destroys the strangerness through designating the 'they' as that which returns us to the Law of argument. The role of translation in the appropriation of strangerness into the Law of argument is clear in the following passage:

> Through a study of Aboriginal women's ritual activity I hoped to answer questions which had nagged me since I began anthropology as an undergraduate in 1972. ... In some studies of Aboriginal religion I had read that women were deemed of less cultural importance than men, although their economic role and usefulness was acknowledged. Other studies assigned to women a separate and secret ritual life. How, I wondered, did Aboriginal women themselves perceive their role?
>
> (Bell 1983: 23)

The 'origin' of the document is clearly the relationship between the student and the master discourses of anthropology. The research question wonders about 'Aboriginal women themselves' through engagement with such master discourses. It assumes that you can gain access to 'Aboriginal women themselves' through the question which demands the establishment of an anthropological truth. The idea of 'themselves' is *created* through such an anthropological demand (what is it like for them?): a creation which *figures* the stranger insofar as the stranger poses a crisis for anthropological knowledge. The idea of 'themselves' is, at the same time, *destroyed* through the assumption that 'we' can know what they 'themselves' are: an assumption of access that abolishes the very possibility of an unknowable strangerness.

Given this double function of the category of 'Aboriginal women themselves', which creates 'Aboriginal women' as both strangers who must come to know (what do they think?), and then strangers who can be known (let

me document your thoughts), Bell is able to assert quite confidently, 'I
found this aspect of the document of women's ritual lives to be relatively
straightforward' (1983: 24). It is straightforward because the problem, 'was
essentially an ethnographic problem in that one must be accepted as a
person worthy of trust before attempting to participate and record' (Bell
1983: 23). In other words, the ability to know the strangers in the
ethnographic document becomes a sign of the ethnographer's *worth* and her
or his trust-worthy-ness. The strangers can be known in 'themselves',
because of the skills of the ethnographer. Those skills are here precisely the
skills of making friends with strangers, reinforcing my earlier suggestion
that friendship becomes a technique of knowledge insofar as it remains tied
to the desire to overcome barriers of strangerness and relations of power. The
intimate ethnographer here is assumed to overcome the distance implicated
in strangerness in the writing of the document. If ethnography structures
the origin of the research, then it also explains its proper destination.

However, the model of learning through dialogue is not just a question of
learning about 'Aboriginal women themselves' in order to displace
anthropological truths about the 'group of stranger women'. It is also about
learning *from* them. Hence, the new truths established in the ethnographic
document are supposed to *come from* the women themselves:

> At the slightest prompting women would lecture me on social struc-
> ture, drawing in the sand to show the way their society was divided into
> various cross-cutting categories, enumerating the classes of person, and
> where appropriate, the individuals, included in each division. ... As a
> student I had learnt of the division of Aboriginal society into two
> groups, that is, moieties, but I has been directed to the importance of
> patrimoieties in matters concerning land and Law. My female instructors
> were anxious to clarify and broaden my understanding of the intercon-
> nections of the divisions of their society. ... In some ways my anthropo-
> logical training was a hindrance and their attempts to clarify created
> confusion. In this respect I was fortunate to have Warlpiri women as
> teachers in the first months of fieldwork.
>
> (Bell 1983: 19–20)

The Warlpiri women are described as lecturers, teachers and instructors and
there is an apparent reversal of the power relation between the professional
stranger and the 'group of stranger women'. Indeed, earlier Bell draws an
analogy between herself and the Indigenous children: 'like me, they were
learning' (1983: 18). Her profession becomes 'a hindrance' and only serves to
create confusion. The ethnographer becomes repositioned as their student,
rather than as a student of anthropology. The dialogical element of the
documentation creates a conflict of discourses, whereby the different
'sources' of knowledge tell different stories. The Indigenous women are
positioned as better teachers of 'themselves'. What is learnt *from them* by the

ethnographer is, of course, still narrated to the reader through the ethnography: the ethnographer tells us what they teach her. The implications of the
retelling are important: as readers, we may be encouraged to feel that we too
are being taught by the Indigenous women, without the mediation of the
retelling. The learning from them, in that sense, creates the illusion that
they have authorised 'our' knowledge. Giving 'them' the status of 'authors'
authorises the document itself, by concealing both its origins and destination in the professional 'we' of ethnography. To some extent, we must
assume the ethnographer is a good student of them (that is, not just a good
writer) to assert our knowingness as readers.

The learning about and from 'them' also leads to a different model of
learning. Here what she is learning, is *how to be them*, where the ethnographer
'learn(s) by imitation' (Bell 1983: 28). So, towards the end of the first
chapter, the project to learn about and learn from 'the Aboriginal women
themselves', becomes reformulated as: 'The task of learning to be a woman
and a Nakamarra' (Bell 1983: 34). She later writes, 'In a very short time I
learnt with whom I might joke, with whom I might have affairs, whose
name I should not speak aloud and from whom I should seek favours. In all
of this I was learning to be a Nakamarra' (Bell 1983: 36). This narrative of
learning to be them entails that Bell positions herself as (like) an Indigenous
child: learning to be means learning to become an adult/Indigenous woman.
Her knowledge and learning enable her access to their being (learning-to-
be). She gets close enough: she gets inside their skin. But the position of
learning to be is very different from simply being. Her knowledge (learning)
sets herself apart from those that simply *are*. The difference can be set up as
the difference between knowing-being-them and being-them. The
professional stranger is reinstalled in this narrative of learning to be: she can
turn 'their' being into ethnographic knowledge by getting underneath their
skin and becoming like them (imitation). Learning to be is here a narrative
of becoming which gets closer to strangers, but at the same time reconfirms
the difference.[8] Knowing-being-strange (or becoming-a-stranger-through-
knowledge) functions as the model for this feminist ethnography: it enables
Bell to speak of 'the Aboriginal women themselves', for them, and as them
at the same time.

Furthermore, the knower is transformed into a hybrid subject, 'not
completely absorbed in the other world, but ... no longer the same'
(Hastrup 1995: 19). Is the hybridisation of such learning-to-be, one which
challenges the epistemic authority, or at least identity, of the knower? Or
does hybridisation itself become another technique of knowledge: *a way of
almost becoming the stranger in order to approximate the being of strangers through
knowledge?* For it is this narrative of knowledge-through-intimacy, premised
on a hybridity that belongs to the ethnographer (the 'natives' must stay the
same in the encounter, at least until they are represented in the Law),[9] that
explains how Bell comes to be close enough to speak for and with Topsy
Napurrula Nelson. The material relations of production embedded in the

ethnographic document hence provide a context for the battle over 'voice and representation' discussed by Anna Yeatman. Here, the skill of the ethnographer in learning-to-be-them (= knowledge through hybridisation), functions as the concealed labour in the battle over 'who speaks'.

But what to do with this knowledge? How to respond differently? If we cannot overcome the relations of force and authorisation implicated in 'knowing' itself, then is the answer *to come to know how not to know*? Interestingly, in one approach to ethnography offered by a female anthropologist, Hortense Powdermaker, there is a reflection on how the anthropologist both knows and fails to know. As defined by Malinowski, the anthropologist has a *double vision* as both participant and observer (see Hastrup 1995: 4). For Powdermaker, this double vision involves seeing the informants as both friends and strangers: 'To understand a strange society, the anthropologist has traditionally immersed himself in it, learning, as far as possible, to think, see, feel, and sometimes act as a member of its culture and at the same time as a trained anthropologist from another culture' (1966: 9). Here, getting to know the strangers involves both the intimacy of becoming-like-them, and the distanciation of knowledge. This double vision means presupposing the impossibility of becoming or going native: 'I never fooled myself that I had "gone native". I participated rather freely, but remained an anthropologist' (Powdermaker 1966: 115). Later she writes, 'I knew that no matter how intimate and friendly I was with the natives, I was never truly a part of their lives' (Powdermaker 1966: 116). Here, Powdermaker's knowledge of the natives renders her closer to them, but unable to be with them: her knowledge becomes, if you like, a knowledge *that admits the impossibility of being (with) them.* The proximity of ethnography leads to a recognition of distance: this is a knowledge which withdraws from that which one has laboured to know.

In this case, the impossibility of the 'we' that would place the ethnographer alongside the natives *is the knowledge of that which the ethnographer fails to know*. At the same time, the knowledge of failure *belong*s to the ethnographer. Such an ethnography of failure does not necessarily unlearn how to know, but rather learns how to know through failure (it learns what knowledge can be had from who one fails to know – 'I knew ... I was never truly part of their lives'). The natives are almost knowable as both strangers and friends: they still allow the knower to know precisely what she can and cannot know. Such an ethnography of failure still belongs to the ethnographer.

Does such a failed knowledge suggest alternative ways of understanding the relationship between the 'we' and the strangers? If we cannot overcome the barriers by making friends with strangers, and hence making the familiar an ever-expanding category, then do we simply keep in place the stranger as a figure, as a trace of that which must remain unknowable? These of course, are impossible questions insofar as they imply the possibility of some sort of resolution. What I am not arguing is that a different way of knowing or not knowing would lead to a better world. One model might be to make friends with all the strangers, to welcome them all into the room (to return to my opening comments in this chapter). While we might question the possibility of the abolition of strangerness, we could also problematise such a model as the ultimate violence of the 'we' of community living (all strangers become translated into the document). Another model might be to call ourselves strangers, insofar as we come to recognise that the 'we' needs the stranger if it is to appear. Does not such an approach, which we can read in Julia Kristeva's *Strangers to Ourselves* (1991), also perform the gesture of killing the strangers it simultaneously creates, by rendering them a universal: a new community of the 'we' is implicitly created. If we are all strangers (to ourselves), then nobody is. In contrast to either models of knowledge production where nobody is a stranger or everyone is, my concern with tracing the relations of knowledge that allow the stranger to enter the community as a figure has been precisely to situate figurable strangers within the relations of force and authorisation bound up with the 'who' that knows.

Do we need to distinguish between friendly or figurable strangers, and the absolute Stranger, the one who is beyond the singularity of such figures? Is the absolute Stranger the one who is destroyed by the figuring of strangers? Certainly, I think we need to consider the relation between knowledge and knowability: the desire, for example, to become friends with all strangers (to know them all) can be rearticulated as the violence of translation. However, to name the unknowable as the absolute Stranger is not appropriate precisely because strangers are forms of recognition embedded within community living (see Chapter 1). The unknowable is a relation to what is already assumed to be known: it is hence not an absolute. The unknowable is a limit that pushes us to the boundary of the historical and ontological: the ways of being in the world in which being-ness is constituted by the worldliness of the world. The naming of the knowable as the absolute stranger is to conceal the worldliness of being with others: it is to assume, that is, that the unknowable is unknowable *without* the particular and worldly beings who demand to know.

How I want to end is to consider the term, 'knowing strangers', more carefully. The term is more ambiguous than I have allowed it, so far, to appear. Within the ethnographic discourses of cultural translation, knowing strangers is the transforming of those who are recognised as strangers into knowledge. The ethnographer is situated as the professional stranger, the stranger who is all-knowing. But what of the possibility of the stranger, who is the object of his knowledge and recognition, coming to know? Does the knowledge always originate from and return to the one who knows? Bell writes that, 'In the field we meet with actual women who may well not agree with popular anthropological characterizations of their lives as impoverished and male-dominated. The women with whom I worked would not have endorsed Lloyd Warner's statement that women make little sacred progress through life but remain largely profane' (1983: 229). This is a fascinating claim. On the one hand, Bell assumes what 'the Aboriginal women themselves' would have endorsed or not. On the other hand, she names the possibility of the 'group of stranger women' knowing differently from how they are known in traditional ethnography. Bell hence opens out the possibility – though she does not explicitly deal with it – that if the Aboriginal women are knowing strangers, then they may know differently to the 'who' that knows in the ethnographic document, *Daughters of the Dreaming*. If the stranger is admitted as possibly knowing differently, then the document and the 'who' would lose the easy identification that allows the stranger to be figurable as the 'what'.

Our task, in opening out the possibility of strangers knowing differently to how they are known, is to draw attention to the forms of authorisation and labour that are concealed by stranger fetishism. Such stranger fetishism is implicit in the assumption that the stranger is any-body we do not know, or in the assumption that we can transform the 'being' of strangers into knowledge. It is only by contesting the discourses of stranger fetishism, that we can open out the possibility of a knowledge that does not belong to the (ethnographic) community, even in the event of its failure to 'know the stranger'.

Part II

Closer to home

4   Home and away

Narratives of migration and estrangement

> I strolled around in the Invalides for quite some time after my father's departure. There was always something comforting, familiar about airports and air terminals. They give me a sense of purpose and security. I was there with a definite destination – usually home, somewhere. In London, I came 'home' at the end of the day. During the holidays, I came 'home' to Paris and family. And once every two years, we went 'home' to India on 'Home leave'. India was 'real' home, and yet, paradoxically, it was the one place we didn't have a home of our own any more. We always stayed as guests. Of course we'd had a home once, but, when India was divided, it was all lost – the house, the city, everything. I couldn't remember anything.
>
> (Dhingra 1994: 99)

What does it mean to be at home? How does it affect home and being-at-home when one leaves home? In Dhingra's story, the familiar place, the place that is comfortable and comforting, is the inbetween space, the interval, of the airport. Such a space is comforting, not because one has arrived, but because one has the security of a destination, a destination which quite literally becomes the some-where of home. Home is here, not a particular place that one simply inhabits, but more than one place: there are too many homes to allow place to secure the roots or routes of one's destination. It is not simply that the subject does not belong anywhere. The journey between homes provides the subject with the contours of a space of belonging, but a space that expresses the very logic of an interval, the passing through of the subject between apparently fixed moments of departure and arrival.

It is the 'real' Home, the space from which one imagines oneself to have originated, and in which one projects the self as both homely and original, that is the most unfamiliar: it is here that one is a guest, relying on the hospitality of others. It is this home which, in the end, becomes Home through the very *failure* of memory: '*I couldn't remember anything*'. The very failure of individual memory is compensated for by collective memory, and the writing of the history of a nation, in which the subject can allow herself to fit in, by being assigned a place in a forgotten past: '*Of course we'd had a home once, but, when India was divided, it was all lost – the house, the city, everything'.* In the discussion of what 'was all lost' the subject moves from an 'I' to a 'we': when the subject returns to the real Home, the 'we' becomes writeable as a story of a shared past that is already lost. Through the very loss of a past (the sharing of the loss, rather than the past as sharing), the 'we' comes to be written as Home. It is the act of forgetting that allows the subject to identify with a history, to find out, to discover, what one has already lost: what is already lost is the fantastic 'we' of a nation, city and house.

The narrative of leaving home produces too many homes and hence no Home, too many places in which memories attach themselves through the carving out of inhabitable space, and hence no place that memory can allow the past to reach the present (in which the 'I' could declare itself as having come home). The movement between homes allows Home to become a fetish, to be separated from the particular worldly space of living *here*, through the possibility of some memories and the impossibility of others. In such a narrative journey, then, the space that is most like home, which is most comfortable and familiar, is not the space of inhabitance – I am here – but the very space in which one is almost, but not quite, at home. In such a space, the subject has a destination, an itinerary, indeed a future, but in having such a destination, has not yet arrived: *'There was always something comforting, familiar about airports and air terminals. They give me a sense of purpose and security. I was there with a definite destination – usually home, somewhere.'* Home is some-where; it is indeed else-where, but it is also where the subject is going. Home becomes the impossibility and necessity of the subject's future (one never gets there, but is always getting there), rather than the past that binds the subject to a given place.

Such transnational journeys of subjects and others invite us to consider what it means to be at home, to inhabit a particular place, and might call us to question the relationship between identity, belonging and home. You might think from such a narrative of homely subjects who have forgotten 'the Home', who are temporary guests in their place of origin, that this chapter takes the perspective of 'the stranger', that it examines 'home' from the point of view of those who, in leaving home, have become the strangers. Indeed, migrants are often constructed as strangers (Diken 1998: 123). In such a construction, the strangers are the ones who, in leaving the home of their nation, are the bodies out of place in the everyday world they inhabit, and in the communities in which they come to live. The editors of *Travellers' Tales* discuss how 'the migrant, journeying from "there" to "here" becomes a stranger in a strange land' (Robertson *et al.* 1994: 3). Here, the condition of being a stranger is determined by the event of leaving home.

Iain Chambers considers the 'drama' of the stranger as being 'cut off from the homelands of tradition' and the stranger becomes 'an emblem' and a 'figure' that, 'draws our attention to the urgencies of our time: a presence that questions our present' (1994: 6). The stranger is presented as figurable, as a presence in a contemporary landscape of dislocation and movement. It has been the argument of this book that to take the figure of the stranger as simply present is to overlook and forget the very relationships of social antagonism that produce the stranger as a figure in the first place. Such a fetishisation of the stranger, indeed, such an ontology of the stranger as given in and to the world, conceals how 'the stranger' comes into being through the marking out of inhabitable spaces, bodies and terrains of knowledge. To talk of the migrant as the stranger is not sufficient. It cannot deal with the complexities of the histories, not only of the displacement of peoples, but the demarcation of places and spaces of belonging (the dwellings which, in Chapter 1, I discussed in terms of neighbourhoods).

The problems of such a reduction of the stranger to a being (in which the figure is more than simply a figure of speech), are clear in the work of Madan Sarup when he suggests that, 'One may say the stranger is universal because of having no home' (1994: 102). According to Sarup, the stranger's lack of a home makes strangerness a universal condition, detached from the particularity of a given place. Quite clearly, assuming that one can inhabit the position of the stranger, by not inhabiting a given place (= being-at-home), creates a form of universality premised on the refusal of place itself, that is, the contingent and worldly relations that mark out habitable terrains. How can we read migrant narratives without taking for granted the stranger as a figure? Indeed, how else can we narrativise migrant subjectivities without reducing 'the stranger' to some-one that one can simply be, a being that is then premised on universality in the very loss of home?

In this chapter, I want to examine the affect of the transnational movement of peoples on the formation of identity without assuming an ontology of the stranger. While the argument will be developed through considering the perspective of the subject who has left home on the relationship between the subject and the place in which the subject inhabits, I will not assume that perspective *as* the stranger's perspective. Instead, the chapter will complicate our notion of what 'home' means, both for the narrative of 'being-at-home' and for the narrative of 'leaving home'. This chapter offers, not an ontology of the stranger, but a consideration of the historical determination of patterns of estrangement in which the living and yet mediated relation between being, home and world is partially reconfigured from the perspective of those who have left home. This reconfiguration does not take place through the heroic act of an individual (the stranger), but in the forming of communities that create multiple identifications through collective acts of remembering in the absence of a shared knowledge or a familiar terrain. The chapter will interweave a variety of different texts: short stories by Asian women in Britain, autobiographical reflection, theoretical constructions of migrancy, and literature from two very different nomadic or migrant communities, the Global Nomads International (GNI) and the Asian Women's Writing Collective.

Theorising migrancy

In order to interrogate the mediated and lived experiences of estrangement, their relationship to community formation, and the reconstruction of home, we need to challenge how migration and home have been theorised in the critical literature. This section will consider how migration is employed as a metaphor within contemporary critical theory for movement and dislocation, and the crossing of borders and boundaries. Such a generalisation of the meaning of migration allows it to be celebrated as a transgressive and liberating departure from living-as-usual in which identity (the subject as and at home) is rendered impossible. Certainly, in Iain Chambers's *Migrancy, Culture and Identity*, migration becomes a way of interrogating, not only the different social relations produced by the histories of the displacement of peoples, but the very nature of identity itself. Migration is one journey amongst a number of journeys that involve the crossing of borders: the migrant, *like* the exile and the nomad, crosses borders and breaks barriers of thought and experience (Chambers 1994: 2).

In Chambers's work, migration, exile and nomadism do not simply refer to the actual experience of being dislocated from home, but become ways of thinking *without* home: 'For the nomadic experience of language, wandering without a fixed home, dwelling at the crossroads of the world, bearing our sense of being and difference, is no longer the expression of a unique tradition or history, even if it pretends to carry a single name. Thought wanders. It migrates, requires translation' (1994: 4). Migration is generalised, such that it comes to represent the very nature of thinking itself, in which to think is to move, and to move away, from any fixed home or origin. While I will come back to how such a narrative itself constitutes home as a site or place of fixity in the next section, it is important to note here how migration becomes a mechanism for theorising how identity itself is predicated on movement or loss. What is at stake in such a narrative?

In the first instance, one can consider how different kinds of journeys become conflated through theorising identity as migrancy. The shift in Chambers's work between the figures of the migrant, the nomad and the exile serves to erase the real and substantive differences between the conditions in which particular movements across spatial borders take place. For example, what different effect does it have on identity when one is forced to move? Does one ever move freely? What movements are possible and, moreover, what movements are impossible? Who has a passport and can move *there*? Who does not have a passport, and yet moves? These provocative questions echo Avtar Brah's, when she asks: 'The question is not simply about who travels, but when, how, and under what circumstances?' (1996: 182).

However, what is problematic about Chambers's narrative is not simply that the differences between histories of movement are erased under the sign of migrancy, but also the slippage between literal migration and metaphoric migration. Literal migration suggests the physical movement of bodies within and across spaces. Indeed, there is no clear and obvious referent here: to talk about migration literally is to open oneself to the complex and contingent histories of the movements of people across borders. However, Chambers's narrative refuses to take migration literally. Instead, migration becomes a metaphor for the very process of dislocation. Migration becomes an impossible metaphor that no longer refers to the dislocation from place, but dislocation as such (thought already dislocates). The migrant becomes a figure: this act of granting the migrant the status as a figure (of speech) erases and conceals the historical determination of experiences of migration, even though those experiences cannot be reduced to a referent.[1] As Uma Narayan puts it, 'Postcolonial global reality is a history of multiple migrations, rooted in a number of different historical processes' (1997: 187). To talk literally about such migrations is to complicate rather than reduce the meaning of migration: it is to introduce questions of context (post-coloniality/globality), historicity, temporality and space.

In her discussion of the literature on exile, Anita Haya Goldman analyses the problems implicit in the metaphoric treatment of the term exile: 'there has been a rather misleading tendency to use the term metaphorically, so that the experience of exile has come to mean, more broadly, the experience of difference and estrangement in society, and most broadly, an aspect of what is human in all of us' (1995: 108). Goldman demonstrates how the gesture of taking exile as a metaphor works to generalise the meaning of exile, such that it becomes an element in the very staging of 'the human'. Indeed, such metaphoric readings of exile imply that what 'we' have in common is precisely the lack of being implicated in exile. In a similar way, the use of migrancy as a metaphor for the impossibility of the human – what we have in common is the absence of being or the absence of a home – ironically confirms the violence of humanism. It substantiates a 'we' based on what is common, even if what we have in common is the lack of being.

The metaphoric treatment of migrancy and exile is also clear in the introduction to *Travellers' Tales*, where the authors state that, 'Life is a journey, even for the stay-at-homes, and we are all exiles whose return is always deferred' (Robertson *et al.* 1994: 6). The creation of the 'we are all' demonstrates how the generalisation of the meaning of exile and migration can found a new form of humanism: what we share as 'humans' is the deferral of home. The humanistic 'we' in this migrant ontology is defined in terms of a particular set of experiences of what it means to depart from a given place. To say, 'we are all exiles', is to conceal the substantive difference it makes when one is forced to cross borders, or when one cannot return home.

In such metaphoric treatments of migration, migration is equated with a movement that already destabilises and transgresses forms of boundary making: 'Migrancy ... involves a movement in which neither the points of departure nor those of arrival are immutable or certain. It calls for a dwelling in language, in histories, in identities that are constantly subject to mutation. Always in transit, the process of home-coming – completing the story, domesticating the detour – becomes an impossibility' (Carter, cited in Chambers 1994: 5). Migration is defined against identity; it is that which already threatens the closures of identity thinking. However, the conflation of migration with the transgression of boundaries in the impossibility of arriving at an identity is problematic. It assumes that migration has an inherent meaning: it constructs an essence of migration in order to theorise that migration as a refusal of essence.

The implications of this gesture of essentialising migrancy as beyond essence are clear in a later passage. Chambers discusses how an *'authentically migrant perspective'* would be based on, 'an intuition that the opposition between here and there is itself a cultural construction, a consequence of thinking in terms of fixed entities and defining them oppositionally' (1994: 42). Such an assumption of an authentic migrant perspective immediately constructs an inauthentic migrant: the inauthentic migrant would be the one who believes in fixed entities and who refuses to transgress. The production of authentic and inauthentic migrant perspectives clearly relies on assumptions about what migration already is, as well as what it *should be*. Such an evaluative narrative, which creates a hierarchy of perspectives on migrancy assumes, not only that migrancy can be detached from the social relations in which it is lived, but also that there are better and worse ways of 'being a migrant'. The violence of this gesture is clear: the experiences of migration, which can involve trauma and violence, become exoticised and idealised as the basis of an ethics of transgression, an ethics which assumes that it is possible to be liberated from identity as such, at the same time as it 'belongs' to an authentically migrant subject.

The designation of an authentically migrant perspective also involves the privileging of a certain kind of theoretical work: Chambers's work, which at one level is on 'migrancy' (as its object of study), comes to name itself as an example of authentically migrant theorising, a theorising that refuses to think in terms of fixed entities. The claim to a migrant theory, or a theory which is multiple and transgressive given its dislocation from any secure origin or place, is also evident in Rosi Braidotti's work, although here the privileged figure is 'the nomad'.[2] Braidotti considers that, 'though the image of "nomadic subjects" is *inspired by* the experience of peoples or cultures that are literally nomadic, the nomadism in question here refers to the kind of critical consciousness that resists settling into socially coded modes of thought and behaviour. ... It is the subversion of conventions that define the nomadic state, not the literal act of travelling' (1994: 5; emphasis added). Again, the relation between the literal and metaphoric is important. By separating her understanding of nomadism from those that are literally nomadic, Braidotti translates the literal into the metaphoric, such that the nomads come to represent something other than themselves. The specificity and difference of particular nomadic peoples is alluded to (as an inspiration), and then erased (such that it is 'not the literal act of travelling'). The erasure of cultural difference through the figuring of the nomad as a general way of thinking, turns into a kind of *critical self-consciousness*: in the end, what the nomad comes to figure is the kind of subversion of conventions that the book constructs itself as doing.

The naming of theory as nomadic can be understood in terms of the violence of translation, a form of translation that allows the theory to name itself as a subversion of conventions – the erasure of others allows 'the self' as 'critical consciousness' to appropriate all that is threatening under the sign of the nomadic. Indeed, what is at stake here is a certain kind of Western subject, the subject of and in theory, as a subject who is free to move (see Ahmad 1992: 86). Braidotti later states that critical nomadism is about choice: 'Homelessness as a chosen condition, also expresses the *choice* of a situated form of heterogeneity' (1994: 17; emphasis mine). What is offered here is a liberal narrative of a subject who has autonomy and is free to choose, even if what is chosen is a refusal of the kind of subjectivity we might recognise as classically liberal. The subject who has chosen to be homeless, rather than is homeless due to the contingency of 'external' circumstances, is certainly a subject who is privileged, and for whom having or not having a home does not affect its ability to occupy a given space. Is the subject who chooses homelessness and a nomadic lifestyle, or a nomadic way of thinking, one that can do so, *because the world is already constituted as its home*? Is this an example of movement being a form of privilege rather than transgression, a movement that is itself predicated on the translation of the collective and forced movements of others into an act of individual and free choice?[3] We need to complicate the narrative whereby movement is read as necessarily transgressive, and examine the different kinds of movement available to subjects that are *already differentiated*.

We can offer a very cautious reading of Braidotti's later return to the 'real nomads'. She suggests that, 'just like real nomads – who are endangered species today, threatened with extinction – nomadic thinking is a minority position' (Braidotti 1994: 29). First, we might note the use of analogy: the narrative claims the real nomads and nomadic thought are *like* each other. They are presented as alike because both are on the margins, and by implication, both are endangered. What is at issue here is not only the loose nature of analogies that serve to flatten out real and substantive forms of difference into a form of indifference (we are alike), but also how those analogies serve to construct what is nomadic thinking. It is the abstraction of thinking that we need to problematise: the representation of nomadism in terms of thought, implies that it can be separated from the material social relations in which 'thought' itself is idealised as the rational capacity of well-educated subjects (see Pels 1999: 64). To make an analogy between nomadic peoples and nomadic thought hence does not simply flatten out differences, but serves to elevate such thought to the level of being (by thinking as nomad, I am endangered like the nomad). It is the privilege of some beings over others (in the very detachment of thought from being) that is concealed in the analogy.

For Braidotti, the nomad is 'a figuration for the kind of subject who has relinquished all idea, desire, or nostalgia for fixity', and a nomadic consciousness is 'an acute awareness of the nonfixity of boundaries' and 'the intense desire to go on trespassing, transgressing' (1994: 36). We might consider how the very theoretical approach which privileges 'transgression' and 'subversion' and a lack of fixity, does not necessarily define itself simply against the law, convention and boundaries, but may actually serve to reconstitute the law, conventions, and boundaries: we can ask, how does the desire to go beyond fixity serve to fix? How does the law require transgression in order to exist? How can migratory subjects (the subjects written by such theories of migrancy) reclaim space and identity in their refusal to inhabit a particular space, in their very transgression of the law of home? My own consideration of how migrant ontology works as a form of humanism – we are all migrants – might suggest a way in which migratory subjects can claim space in their refusal to inhabit it.

In order to consider how movements of migratory subjects can involve a form of privilege, and can allow the creation of new forms of identity thinking, rather than their necessary transgression, we can consider the narratives offered by Global Nomads International (GNI). This is a volunteer organisation that promotes the welfare of current and former 'internationally mobile' families and individuals through literature, conferences and education. Internationally mobile families is a term that refers largely to families who have spent significant time overseas as members of the diplomatic corps, the missionary movement, or the military. In order to examine GNI, I will discuss two contributions to the book, *Strangers at Home*, written by past presidents of the organisation.

Paul Asbury Seaman's contribution, 'Rediscovery of a Sense of Place', begins with the grief of feeling 'like a refugee in my own country' (1996: 37), of not being-at-home in one's home. The feeling of displacement becomes a question of memory: 'Instinctively, I understood that to connect more fully in the present – to *feel* at home – I had to reconnect with my past' (Seaman 1996: 38). The desire to make connections given the sense of alienation from home – or the 'feeling of being at home in several countries or cultures but not completely at home in any of them' (Seaman 1996: 53) – leads to the discovery of a new community: 'The community of strangers – our experience of family with other global nomads – is one of the large and often unrecognised paradoxes of this heritage' (Seaman 1996: 53). The sense of not being fully at home in a given place does not lead to a refusal of the very desire for home, and for a community and common heritage. The very experience of leaving home and 'becoming a stranger' involves the creation of a new 'community of strangers', a common bond with those others who have 'shared' the experience of living overseas. It is the constitutive link between the suspension of a sense of having a home to the formation of new communities that we need to recognise. The forming of a new community provides a sense of fixity through the language of heritage – a sense of inheriting a collective past *by sharing the lack of a home rather than sharing a home*. The movement of global nomads hence allows the fixing rather than unfixing of the boundaries implicated in community and identity formation. As Norma McCaig, the founding member of GNI argues, 'That global nomads share a common heritage is clear when they meet ... there is a sudden recognition of kinship' (1996: 115).

In McCaig's contribution, 'Understanding Global Nomads', she discusses the benefits of a global nomad upbringing: 'In an era when global vision is an imperative, when skills in intercultural communication, linguistic ability, mediation, diplomacy, and the management of diversity are critical, global nomads are better equipped' (1996: 100). McCaig discusses global nomads as a highly skilled workforce whose ability to move across places, and between languages and culture, makes them better equipped and hence more useful to a globalised economy of difference. The ability to travel clearly gives global nomads access to a set of privileges, a set of equipment, which makes them highly commodifiable as skilled workers on a global landscape of difference and cultural exchange.

The skills of the global nomads are also associated with their ability to move beyond the boundaries of a given culture, to question those boundaries, and perhaps even to recognise their cultural constructedness (to allude here to Chamber's notion of an authentically migrant perspective). McCaig suggests that, 'The ease with which global nomads cruise global corridors often gives rise to an expanded world view, the capacity to extend their vision beyond national boundaries' (1996: 101). The questioning of boundaries, and the movement across borders, leads to an expansion of vision, *an ability to see more*. The transgression of the border provides the subject who knows and can see with an *ease* of movement. Such a narrative clearly demonstrates how some movements across spaces become a mechanism for the reproduction of social privilege, the granting of particular subjects with the ability to see and to move beyond the confined spaces of a given locality.

McCaig quotes Margaret Push, who talks of the global nomad's ability, 'to view the world'. The expansion of the meaning of 'home' is clearly evident: by refusing to belong to a particular place, the world becomes the global nomad's home, giving this nomadic subject the ability to inhabit the world as a familiar and knowable terrain. The claiming of ownership of global space through the refusal to identify with a local space of inhabitance suggests that the GNI involves a new form of citizenship, which I would call *global-nomadic citizenship*. Here, citizenship is not predicated on the rights and duties of a subject who dwells within a nation-state, but is produced by a subject who *moves through space and across national borders* (see also Chapter 8).

We can consider how the expansion of the meaning of home involves the creation of a new imagined home and community, that of the globe itself. Globality becomes a fantastic space: for example, the notion of 'global corridors' imagines a space in which globalisation literally can take its shape, and through which global nomads can move. McCaig ends her article by quoting Lev, 'It's as if we [global nomads] have replaced the physical "home" [of] non-nomads ... with an internal home' (McCaig 1996: 120). The challenge to the very physical confinement of home leads to a home that travels with the subject that travels: a home that, in some sense, is internalised as part of the nomadic consciousness. As John Durham Peters puts it, 'For nomads, home is always mobile. Hence there is a subtle doubleness here: being-at-home everywhere, but lacking any fixed ground' (1999: 17). The internal home that moves with the subject who moves allows the world to become home. McCaig goes on to suggest that, 'I prefer to think of us looking out at the new world from a place inside ourselves that we share with other nomads' (McCaig 1996: 120). Not only does the 'home' become internalised as the world the nomad can take on the journey, but it is this interior space which is detached or unattached to place, that allows for the new identity and community of nomadism itself. The very detachment from a particular home grants the nomadic subject the ability to see the world, an ability that becomes the basis for a new global identity and community. In such a narrative, identity becomes fetishised: it becomes detached from the particularity of places which allow for its formation as such.

I am arguing, not that all nomadic subjects are implicated in such relations of privilege, and in the creation of a new globalised identity in which the world becomes home, but that there is no necessarily link between forms of travel, migration and movement and the transgression and destabilisation of identity. An investigation of migrant journeys has to examine, not only how migration challenges identity, but how migration can allow identity to become a fetish under the sign of globality. The assumption that to leave home, to migrate or to travel, is to suspend the boundaries in which identity comes to be liveable, conceals the complex and contingent social relationships of antagonism which grant some subjects the ability to move freely at the expense of others. As I argue in the next section, problematising such a narrative that equates migration with the transgression of identity thinking requires that we begin to ask the question of what it means to be at home in the first place.

Home

What does it mean to be-at-home? Certainly, definitions of home shift across a number of registers: home can mean where one usually lives, or it can mean where one's family lives, or it can mean one's native country. You might say I have multiple homes, each one a different kind of home: home is

England, where I was born and now live, home is Australia, where I grew up, and home is Pakistan, where the rest of my family lives. The different possibilities of 'home' are not necessarily either/or: where one usually lives can be where one's family lives, and this can be 'one's native country'. Does being-at-home involve the co-existence of these three registers? Can we understand 'leaving home' as the breaking apart of this co-existence, such that where one usually lives is no longer where one's family lives, or in one's native country? This rather obvious approach begs more questions than it can answer.

In the first instance, we can return to the narratives of migrancy examined in the previous section. To some extent, Chambers's and Braidotti's visions of migrancy and nomadism seem self-contradictory. On the one hand, migration and nomadism become *symptomatic* of what it means 'to be' in the world: migration and nomadism make clear that being cannot be secured by any fixed notion of home or origin. On the other hand, migration and nomadism are inscribed as *exceptional* and *extraordinary* in the very event of being defined against home: that is, an implicit opposition is set up between those who are authentically migrant (Chambers) or those who have a nomadic critical consciousness (Braidotti), and those who simply stay put. Both narratives, which seem in contradiction – migration as symptom and migration as exception – share a common foundation: they rely on the designation of home as that which must be overcome, either by recognising that being as such is not homely (migration as symptom) or by refusing to stay at home (migration as exception).

What is at stake in such a narrative of 'the home' as that which must be overcome? In both Chambers's and Braidotti's work, home is not given any positive definition: it is constructed only through reference to what it is not, that is, through reference to the homelessness of migration and exile. By being defined negatively in this way, home becomes associated with stasis, boundaries, identity and fixity. Home is implicitly constructed as a purified space of belonging in which the subject is too comfortable to question the limits or borders of her or his experience, indeed, where the subject is so at ease that she or he does not think. Such a construction of home as too familiar, safe and comfortable to allow for critical thought has clear resonance in some post-colonial literature. Nalina Persram, for example, defines 'home' as rest and respite, where there is 'being but no longing' (1996: 213). Home is associated with a being that rests, that is full and present to itself, and that does not over-reach itself through the desire for something other. To be at home is the absence of desire, and the absence of an engagement with others through which desire engenders movement across boundaries.

In such a narrative, home and away are divided, not only as different spaces, but as different ways of being in the world. Home is constructed as a way of being by the very reduction of home to being, as if being could be without desire for something other. Such a narrative of home assumes the possibility of a space that is pure, which is uncontaminated by movement, desire or difference, in order to call for a politics in which movement *is always and already a movement away from home as such*. I want to suggest that this narrative requires a definition of home that is itself impossible: it stabilises the home as a place with boundaries that are fixed, such that the home becomes pure, safe and comfortable. However, encounters with otherness which, in Persram's terms, would engender desire, cannot be designated in terms of the space beyond home: it is the very opposition between 'home' and 'away' that we must question.[4]

According to the model which assumes that the opposition between home and away is fully secure, home would be the familiar space, while 'away' would be 'a strange land' (Chambers 1994: 18). When one is at home, one would be a member of the family, a neighbour, a friend, and when one leaves home one would become the stranger. The problem with such a model of home as familiarity is that it projects strangerness beyond the walls of the home. Instead, we can ask: how does being-at-home already encounter strangerness? How does being-at-home already engender desire? For example, if we were to expand our definition of home to think of the nation as a home, then we could recognise that there are always encounters with others already recognised as strangers within, rather than just between, nations. To argue otherwise, would be to imagine the nation as a purified space, and to deny the differences within that space: it would be to assume that you only encounter strangers at the border (see Chapter 5). Within any home, it is not only the border line that brings our attention to the strangers that seem out of place. To return to an earlier argument, the stranger only comes to be recognised as such by coming too close to home (see Chapter 1).

Given this, there is always an encounter with strangerness at stake, even within the home: the home does not secure identity by expelling strangers, but requires those strangers to establish relations of proximity and distance within the home, and not just between home and away. The association of home with familiarity which allows strangeness to be associated with migration (that is, to be located as beyond the walls of the home) is problematic. There is already strangeness and movement within the home itself. It is not simply a question then of those who stay at home, and those who leave: *as if these two different trajectories simply lead people to different places.* Rather, 'homes' always involve encounters between those who stay, those who arrive, and those who leave. We can use Avtar Brah's notion of diasporic space here: there is an intimate encounter at stake between those who stay and those who leave, or between natives and strangers (1996: 181). Given the inevitability of such encounters, homes do not stay the same as the space which is simply the familiar. There is movement and dislocation within the very forming of homes as complex and contingent spaces of inhabitance.

However, to argue for the non-opposition between home and away is not to claim that it makes no difference if one leaves a place in which one has felt at home (this would turn migration into a symptom: we have all left home, as you can never simply 'be' at home). We need to think about ways of understanding this difference without identifying home with the stasis of being. We can begin by returning to my earlier attempt to define home across three registers: home is where one usually lives, home is where one's family lives, or home is one's 'native country'. Already this seems vastly inadequate – for example, it is possible that one's native country might not be *felt* as a home. Indeed, for me, while I was born in England, it never really felt like a home: England was what I read about in school text books; it was where it snowed at Christmas; or it was where I got birthday cards from, and the occasional funny five pound notes. The lack of a sense of England being my home was precisely because of a failure to remember what it was like to inhabit the place (I tried to remember – I was 4 when we left for Australia – but could never get past the blue window frames). So, England didn't really feel like home, despite the astonishing ability of my mother to keep her accent. The issue is that home is not simply about fantasies of belonging (where do I originate from?) but that it is *sentimentalised* as a space of belonging ('home is where the heart is'). The question of home and being-at-home can only be addressed by considering the question of affect: being-at-home is a matter of *how one feels or how one might fail to feel*.

Avtar Brah rethinks the difference between home as where one lives and home as where one 'comes from' in terms of affect: 'Where is home?' On the one hand, "home" is a mythic place of desire in the diasporic imagination. In this sense, it is a place of no return, even if it is possible to visit the geographical territory that is seen as the place of "origin". On the other hand, home is also the lived experience of locality, its sounds and smells' (1996: 192). Home as 'where one usually lives' becomes theorised as *the lived experience of locality*. The immersion of a self in a locality is not simply about inhabiting an already constituted space (from which one could depart and remain the same). Rather, the locality intrudes into the senses: it defines what one smells, hears, touches, feels, remembers. The lived experience of being-at-home hence involves the enveloping of subjects in a space which is not simply outside them: being-at-home suggests that the subject and space leak into each other, *inhabit each other*. We can think of the lived experience of being-at-home in terms of inhabiting a second skin, a skin which does not simply contain the homely subject, but which allows the subject to be touched and touch the world that is neither simply in the home or away from the home. The home as skin suggests the boundary between self and home is permeable, but also that the boundary between home and away is permeable as well. Movement away is also movement within the constitution of home as such. Movement away is always affective: it affects how 'homely' one might feel and fail to feel.

Migration and estrangement

We can now reconsider what is at stake if one leaves a space in which one has already been enveloped, inhabited by (rather than a space which one simply inhabits). The journeys of migration involve a splitting of home as place of origin and home as the sensory world of everyday experience. What migration narratives involve, then, is spatial reconfiguration of an embodied self: a transformation in the very skin through which the body is embodied (see Chapter 2). The experience of moving to a new home is often felt through the surprise of different skin sensations. When we came to Australia, what I first remember (or at least what I remember remembering) is all the dust, and how it made me sneeze and my eyes itch. When I returned to England, I felt the cold pinching my skin. The intrusion of an unexpected space into the body suggests that the experience of a new home involves an expansion and contraction of the skin, a process which is uncomfortable and well described as the irritation of an itch. So while Parminder Bhachu's question about migration is, 'how is cultural baggage re-located?' (1996: 284), mine would be, 'how do bodies re-inhabit space?' and even, 'how do spaces re-inhabit bodies?'

Migration is not only felt at the level of lived embodiment. Migration is also a matter of generational acts of story-telling about prior histories of movement and dislocation. I remember being told about my family's migration to the newly created Pakistan in 1947. A long hard train journey. My father just a child. Then the arrival at the house in Modeltown, Lahore where I lived when I was a baby (my grandmother and aunt looked after me when my mother was ill in England, or so I am told). My father used to have some old volumes of Shakespeare. He'd found them in the new house in Lahore. I used to finger those books, little brown objects, rem(a)inders of a lost inhabited space, of a space I might have inhabited. Now, it seems fitting that this is what we have left from that old house, volumes of Shakespeare, reminders of the impossibility of us inhabiting Pakistan without the discomfort of an English heritage (a heritage that is lived out through and in the 'constitution' of bodies). And then there was the story of my father coming to England. This was a more comfortable journey. It was a journey that was as much about colonialism (the young upper-middle-class Pakistani man coming to do his postgraduate medical training back at the centre), as it was about class privilege and gender. And then, having met my mother, we migrated as a family to Australia: again a story about class privilege (he was to take up a consultant position), as it was about racism (he couldn't get a consultancy in England), as it was about heterosexuality and gender (my mother followed him).

So many stories, so many journeys: each one, fantastic in its particularity (how did it feel, what happened here and there?) and yet mediated and touched by broader relationships of social antagonism (the history of the British empire, class relations and the politics of sexuality and gender). Migrations involve complex and contradictory relationships to social privilege and marginality (they are not necessarily about one or the other) and they involve complex acts of narration through which families imagine a mythic past. The telling of stories is bound up with – touched by – the forming of new communities. In this sense, memory can be understood as a collective act which produces its object (the 'we'), rather than reflects on it. As Keya Ganguly argues, 'The past requires a more marked salience with subjects for whom categories of the present have been made unusually unstable or unpredictable, as a consequence of the displacement enforced by post-colonial and migrant circumstances' (1992: 29–30). The stories of dislocation help to relocate: they give a shape, a contour, a skin to the past itself. The past becomes presentable through a history of lost homes (*unhousings*), as a history which hesitates between the particular and the general, and between the local and the transnational.

If we think of home as an outer skin, then we can also consider how migration involves, not only spatial dislocation, but also temporal disloca-tion: 'the past' becomes associated with a home that is impossible to inhabit, and be inhabited by, in the present. The question then of being-at-home or leaving home is always a question of memory, of the discontinuity between past and present: 'For an exile, habits of life, expression or activity in the new environment inevitably occurs against the memory of things in the other environment' (Said 1990: 366). Indeed, Poult suggests that the process of leaving home and coming home is *like* memory: 'it is the already lived that save the living. If the familiar places are sometimes able to come back to us, they are also able to come back to our notice, and to our great comfort to retake their original place. Thus one can see that places behave exactly like past memories, like memories. They go away, they return' (cited in Buijs 1993: 3).

The analogy between places and memories is suggestive, though we may want to make the analogy on different grounds: it is the impossibility of return that binds place and memory together. That is, it is impossible to return to a place that was lived as home, precisely because the home is not exterior but interior to embodied subjects. The movements of subjects between places that come to be inhabited as home involve the discontinui-ties of personal biographies and wrinkles in the skin. The experience of leaving home in migration is hence always about the *failure of memory to make sense of the place one comes to inhabit*, a failure that is experienced in the discomfort of inhabiting a migrant body, a body that feels out of place. The process of returning home is likewise about the failures of memory, of not being inhabited in the same way by that which appears as familiar.

The temporal and spatial dislocation implicit in migrant stories are linked: the question of memory – and its failings – is bound up with the reinhabiting of bodily space. The reinhabiting of bodily space is explored in Ameena Meer's story about migration, 'Rain'. Here, the memories of another place are felt through and on the skin:

Crossing the street on a steamy grey day in September, Zerina feels as if she's walked into a memory of last summer in Delhi, the last few days before the monsoon. When the air was thick and hot, tension building in the clouds and in her forehead, where the humidity made her sinuses swell and block, so that she could barely see a few feet ahead of her.

Still the grumbling clouds hold back, occasionally letting go a thunderclap or a flash of lightening like a stinging slap across someone's cheek, a sharp insult cuts through the skin. There is no release, just a regathering of explosive anger, like a mad woman screaming down a carpeted hallway.

The sweat gathers on the back of her neck, under her thick black hair, steaming her face, each wiry hair sticking to her fingers when she tries to brush it off.

(Meer 1994: 139)

The experiences of migration – of not being in a place one lived as home – are felt at the level of embodiment, the lived experience of inhabiting a particular space, a space that is neither within nor outside bodily space. Throughout the story, the trauma and pain of not being fully at home is narrated through skin sensations. The physical sense of moving through space is enough to trigger a memory of another place. Memory hence works through the swelling and sweating of the skin: the memory of another place which one lived as home involves the touching of the body, and the animating of the relation between the body and the space which it inhabits and is inhabited by. The story is one of suffocation, of smells and sounds that intrude into bodily space, of bodies 'overflowing', of bodies 'shuddering' and 'slipping'. As her skin becomes cut and sticky, the narrator remembers with and through her body. Migration stories are *skin memories*: memories of different sensations that are felt on the skin. Migrant bodies stretch and contract, as they move across the borders that mark out familiar and strange places.

Acts of remembering are felt by migrant bodies in the form of a discomfort, the failure to inhabit fully the present or present space. Migration can be understood as a process of estrangement, a process of becoming estranged from that which was inhabited as home. The word 'estrangement' has the same roots as the word 'strange'. And yet, it suggests something quite different. It indicates a process of transition, a movement from one register to another. To become estranged from each other, for example, is to move from being friends to strangers, from familiarity to strangeness. The term is suggestive precisely because it names the process of moving from one to the other, *rather than referring to different states of being.* The process of moving away or estrangement involves a reliving of the home itself: the process of moving is a movement in the very way in which the migrant subject inhabits the space of home.

In the work of Michael Dillon, 'estrangement' is what we have in common, rather than being that which divides us: 'the estrangement of human beings ... is integral to their condition of being here as the beings that they are' (1999: 136). In contrast, I would argue that we need to understand estrangement in a way which emphasises how the histories of movement of peoples across borders make a difference to the spatiality and temporality of estrangement. Estrangement is always an estrangement from a particular time and place. To universalise estrangement as that which brings us together is to conceal how estrangement marks out particular bodies and communities. Estrangement needs to be theorised as beyond that which we simply have in common.

For example, in Pnina Werbner's work on Asian migrants in Britain, she emphasises how migrants are strangers to each other, and how they make positive acts of identification in the very process of becoming friends: 'I start from the assumption of a void – from strangerhood, non-relationship. So when I find that these strangers ... create, generate, make multiple identifications with one another, then this is a process (not a pre-given static situation) which I find interesting' (1996: 69). Here, there is no shared terrain of knowledge which is presupposed by the gesture of identification. What is at stake is not, as in the case of the narratives of the global nomads, a 'sudden recognition of kinship' (McCaig 1996: 115), through which an automatic 'community of strangers' can be established (a common estrangement or commonality through estrangement). Rather, there is void or an absence: the other migrants are already known again as not known, they are already assigned a place as strangers before the identification can take place. In other words, it is through an *uncommon estrangement* that the possibility of such a migrant community comes to be lived. The gap between memory and place in the very dislocation of migration allows communities to be formed: that gap becomes reworked as a site of bodily transformation, the potential to remake one's relation to that which appears as unfamiliar, to reinhabit spaces and places. This reinhabiting of the migrant body is enabled through gestures of friendship with others who are already recognised as strangers. It is the role of community in the re-inhabiting of migrant bodies that is so important. The community comes to life through the collective act of remembering in the absence of a common terrain.

In order to examine the relationship between the reinhabiting of bodies community and estrangement in migration journeys and narratives we can consider the edited collection *Flaming Spirit*, which was produced by the Asian Women's Writing Collective in the United Kingdom in 1994. The book is itself a journey in migration: migration is not its object (not all the stories are *about* migration), but allows for the very gestures of identification through which the book becomes readable as a collection. The book is made possible through the forming of a migrant community of writers brought together under the problematic, if not impossible, signs of 'Asian', 'women' and 'writers'. Hence, the editors reflect on how the forming of the collective did not pre-suppose a shared identity (either as Asian, women or writers), but made apparent that the criteria for who should belong to the community can always be contested.

The forming of a community through the shared experience of not being fully at home – of having inhabited another space – presupposes an absence of a shared terrain: the forming of communities makes apparent the lack of a common identity *that would allow its form to take one form*. But this lack becomes reinscribed as the pre-condition of an act of *making*: how can we make a space that is supportive? How can we become friends? How can we write (as) a collective? The editors reflect on the differences of class, sexuality and religion between the women in the collective, as they also reflect more profoundly on the politics of the category 'Asian' and the uncertainty about which women are to be included within the category (Ahmad and Gupta 1994: xii). The forming of this community of migrant women writers makes clear that there is always a boundary line to be drawn. This lack of clarity makes a definition and redefinition of the community possible; it allows the group to emerge in the need to 'redefine our identity as a group' (Ahmad and Gupta 1994: xii).

The process of estrangement is the condition for the emergence of a contested community, a community which 'makes a place' in the act of reaching out to the 'out-of-place-ness' of other migrant bodies. The work of such community formation is hence always 'outreach work' (Ahmad and Gupta 1994: xiii): in this case, it is about reaching out to different women who might share, not a common background, but the very desire to make a community, a community of Asian women who write. The community is reached through reaching across different spaces, towards other bodies, who can also be recognised – and hence fail to be recognised – as out of place, as uncomfortable, or not quite comfortable, in this place. Migrant bodies, selves and communities cannot be understood as simply on one side of identity or the other, or on one side of the community or the other: rather, it is the uncommon estrangement of migration itself that allows migrants to remake what it is *they might yet have in common*.

5 Multiculturalism and the proximity of strangers

Multiculturalism is much more than the provision of special services to minority ethnic groups. It is a way of looking at Australian society, and involves living together with an awareness of cultural diversity. We accept our difference and appreciate a variety of lifestyles rather than expect everyone to fit a standardised pattern. Most of all it requires that we each can be 'a real Australian', without necessarily being 'a typical Australian'.

(Australian Council on Population and Ethnic Affairs 1982)

How does multiculturalism reinvent 'the nation' over the bodies of strangers? How does the act of 'welcoming the stranger' serve to constitute the nation? How is the 'we' of the nation affirmed through the difference of the 'stranger cultures', rather than against it?

In the above definition, the proximity of different ethnic groups becomes integral to the definition of the nation space. Multiculturalism is defined, not as providing services for 'specific ethnic groups', but as a way of imagining the nation itself, a way of 'living' in the nation, and a way of living *with* difference. Significantly, the role of difference in allowing or even establishing a national imaginary presupposes the proximity of those who are already recognisable as strangers as well as the permanence of their presence: living together is here simply a matter of being aware of cultural diversity. The strangers become incorporated into the 'we' of the nation, at the same time as that 'we' emerges as the one who has to live with it (cultural diversity) and by implication with 'them' (those 'specific ethnic groups'). By suggesting that multiculturalism is *not* about the provision of services to specific ethnic groups, and then defining multiculturalism in terms of cultural diversity, this statement powerfully evokes and then erases particular histories of racial differentiation: racial difference, already construed as ethnic difference, is redefined in terms of cultural diversity, that is, in terms that erase any distinctions between groups. The 'acceptance' of difference actually serves to conceal those differences which cannot be reduced to 'cultural diversity'. In such a story of 'multicultural Australia', the differences and antagonism between white settler groups, Asian immigrants and Indigenous peoples are hidden from sight.

The tension between the incorporation and refusal of that which is different is clear in the final two sentences. Difference is immediately 'our difference': it is a difference that belongs to the inclusive 'we' of the nation. The claiming of difference as that which 'we' have involves the erasure of differences that cannot be absorbed into this 'we'. Furthermore, differences become immediately defined in terms of 'lifestyles', ways of being in the world that find easy commodification in terms of an aesthetics of appearance (appearing as different might make no difference to the difference that is ours: in such a fantasy, we might seek to glimpse almost white skin or an almost human heart beating underneath the stranger's dress).

The acceptance of a variety of lifestyles is defined against the expectation that everyone fits into a 'standardised pattern'. Is such an acceptance, an acceptance of those who don't fit? Or does the welcoming of the strange culture's difference itself require that culture *fit into this model of cultural diversity as a normative model of who 'we' already are?* To accept that which is different from the 'standard' is already, in some sense, to accept difference *into* the standard. Those who do not fit into a standardised pattern must still fit into the nation: they fit, not by being the standard, but by being defined in terms of their difference. The nation still constructs itself as a 'we', not by requiring that 'they' fit into a 'standardised pattern', but by the very requirement that they 'be' culturally different (that they 'not be' typical Australians). The strangers who do not fit such a pattern are still fitting into such a nation space: they fit into the nation precisely because they allow the nation to imagine *itself* as heterogeneous (to claim their differences as 'our difference').

The final sentence in this statement maintains this critical tension around the question of difference: 'we each can be "a real Australian", without necessarily being "a typical Australian" '. In the first instance, the use of the inclusive pronoun – '*we* each can be' – works to conceal further the differences that the first sentence of this statement had set up (however precariously through reference to 'specific ethnic minorities'). This 'we' is both the 'we' of each individual Australian as it alludes to the 'we' of Australia. The double possibility of the 'we' relates to the distinction set up between real and typical Australians. The implication is that any-body in Australia can *be* a real Australian even if they are not typically Australian, even if, that is, they appear to be different. The notion that any-body can be a real Australian is extremely powerful: it imagines a neutral national space in which authenticity itself is inclusive: it is open to all; it *sees no difference*. The failure to see any difference involves a form of individuation: there is a slip from the 'we' of the authentic nation to the 'we' of the abstract individual, the any-body who can be a real Australian (the *any-body* who might conceal *some-bodies* who are already recognised as 'typical Australians'). Such a narrative in which anyone can be a real Australian hence fails to take account of social differences at the level of group formation, at the same time as it claims to do justice to (individual) differences by not allowing such differences to define who has the right to be an Australian (a model of justice which erases its own object). It is the collapse between the individual and nation that allows the narrative to imagine the multicultural nation as singular and inclusive in its very difference.

In this chapter, I want to examine how nations become imagined and contested through the recognition of strangers. Much work has been done on how nations define themselves against strange cultures by finding means of keeping strangers out (see Cohen 1994). It has been assumed that strangers are found at the borderlines or 'frontiers' of nation spaces. Certainly, we can consider how nations are invented as familiar spaces, as spaces of belonging, through being defined against others who are recognised, or known again, as strange and hence strangers. In some sense, the stranger appears as a figure, as a way of containing that which the nation is not, and hence as a way of allowing the nation to be. As Michael Dillon argues, 'with the delimitation of any place of dwelling, the constitution of a people, a nation, a state, or a democracy necessarily specifies who is *estranged from* that identity, place or regime' (1999: 119, emphasis added). The stranger appears as a figure through the marking out of the nation as dwelling, as a space of belonging in which some bodies are recognised as out of place.

I want to consider what happens to the construction of nationhood in the context of multiculturalism: what happens to the nation when 'strange cultures' are not only let in, but are redefined as integral to the nation itself? The strangers would not simply be those who, as I argued in Chapter 1, are already recognised as out of place, and as the origin and cause of danger. Rather, in the multicultural nation, the strangers would come to have a place in the nation: this in-place-ness would be made possible given that the strangers, as in the case of immigrants, have already arrived from-another-place (being out-of-place would become, in this framework, its own place). My analysis will examine how multiculturalism involves stranger fetishism: the act of welcoming 'the stranger' as the origin of difference produces the very figure of 'the stranger' as the one who can be taken in. I hence support Ien Ang's argument that othering can take place by acts of *inclusion* within multicultural discourse (1996: 37). I will also suggest that multiculturalism can involve a double and contradictory process of incorporation and expulsion: it may seek to differentiate between those strangers whose appearance of difference can be claimed by the nation, and those stranger strangers who may yet be expelled, whose difference may be dangerous to the well-being of even the most heterogenous of nations.

Nations and strangers

How are nations invented and imagined? The work of Benedict Anderson is crucial for an understanding of how 'the nation' is imaginary or fantastic. According to Anderson, both nationalism and nationhood are 'cultural artefacts' (1983: 13), with their own particular 'style in which they are imagined' (1983: 15). Such an approach allows us to recognise that the boundaries of nations are not simply geographical or geopolitical (though they take both these forms), but also discursive. The nation does not refer to something that simply exists: nations are produced and constructed as places and communities in which 'a people' might belong. Of course, to say that nations are imagined is not to say that they are not real. The question of nationhood cannot be properly addressed without a recognition of the political economy of modern nation-states. An entity can be imagined and real at the same time: in some sense, the opposition between imaginary and real must be suspended if we are to understand how the nation comes to be *lived* as an 'organic community'. The imagining of the nation as a space in which 'we' belong is not independent of the material deployment of force, and the forms of governmentality which control, not only the boundaries between nation states, and the movements of citizens and aliens within the state, but also the repertoire of images which allows the concept of the nation to come into being in the first place.

To think of the nation as simultaneously imaginary and real (the nation as both fantasy and material effect) is also to think of the processes of identification which allow the nation to be secured as one of the organising assumptions of 'public life' (Goffman 1972: ix). What forms of identification are produced with the nation? How does 'the nation' come to be produced as a form of identification? In other words, we need to examine how the invention of the nation as a bounded space requires the production of a *national identity* which can be *claimed* by the individual ('I am ... ') through reference to the apparent transparency and coherence of the nation itself. The *investment* of the individual in being or having a nation suggests that the discourse of nationhood operates at both a psychic and social level. The individual, who encounters others in daily life, comes to identify as not only *having* but *being* a nationality, through referring to public symbols and expressions which themselves tell stories of what it means to be that nationality (the fleshing out of the 'national character'), and also through identifying with other individuals with whom such stories can be shared. The production of the nation involves not only image and myth-making – the telling of 'official' stories of origin – but also the everyday negotiations of what it means 'to be' that nation(ality). The production of the nation involves processes of self-identification in which the nation comes to be realised as belonging to the individual (the construction of the 'we' as utterable by the individual).

Crucially, then, the production of nations constitutes individuals as belonging to the nation: the work of 'the nation' is done as much through the everyday encounters in public life, as it is done through the political machinery of the nation-state. But the production of the nation also involves imagining the nation *space*: it involves the projection of boundaries (nationhood as cartography), and the telling of stories about the authentic landscape (for example, in travel writing and tourism), and the production of interiority (imagining 'the heart of the nation'). The construction of the nation space takes place alongside the production of national character as instances in which 'the nation' itself is fleshed out *as place and person*. The nation becomes imagined as a body in which personhood and place are precariously collapsed. Through a metonymic elision, the individual can claim to embody a nation, or the nation can take the shape of the body of an individual ('bodyscape').

But how do the complex and multiple sites of the production of nation-hood involve the reification of the figure of the stranger? As I pointed out in my introduction, the formation of a dwelling or place of residence involves a definition of who or what does not belong (estrangement). At one level, such distinctions between the familiar and the strange take place in everyday encounters. The self-identification with the nation also involves the recognition of others as belonging to the 'same' community. If we return to my discussion of recognition in Chapter 1, we can consider how the act of hailing or recognising some-body as a shared member of a community serves to produce or flesh out that community through or against the bodies of strangers. For example, the recognition of another as belonging to the same nation when travelling abroad relies on techniques for reading and telling the difference between that which is familiar and strange. The recognition of the other as from a shared nation requires a rehearsal of a public discourse of nationhood (shared memories of the nation space, the use of jokes, reference to sporting events or national achievements). The recognition of others as being from the same nation, or as sharing a nationality, hence involves an everyday and much rehearsed distinction between who does and does not belong within the nation space.

The production of the nation, in such a model, requires some-body or some-where to not-be in order for it to be. This demarcation of spaces of belonging through estrangement is central to Said's now classical theory of Orientalism: the Occident comes into being as a material place through the creation of an ontological distinction between it and the Orient. The Orient comes to embody that which the Occident is not. That is, the Orient creates Europe (or the Occident) as a bounded space in the very event of being positioned as its Other. The fascination with the Orient within Western imperial culture is a fascination which, in Said's terms, creates an idea of Europe, 'a notion collectively identifying "us against the non-Europeans" ' (1978: 7). Orientalism creates *an imaginary geographical divide* based on the binarism of Occident/Orient. In this sense, the creation of a space of belonging (the 'we' that remains unspoken, or is spoken only through the claiming of the right to speak) requires that which is strange in order to be.

The nation is one such space of belonging. Robin Cohen's reflection on the discourse of nationhood emphasises how national identity is produced through the differentiation between familiar and strange: 'a complex national and social identity is continuously constructed and reshaped in its (often antipathetic) interaction with outsiders, strangers, foreigners and aliens – the "others". You know who you are, only by knowing who you are not' (1994: 1). In Cohen's model, strangers are not external to the formation of national identity: the nation requires strangers in order to exist. Despite this, the formation of identity is defined in terms of *frontiers:* strangers are the ones who are encountered at the border, and whose proximity threatens the coherence of national identity. Féher and Heller's consideration of nations poses an analogy between 'the nation' and the 'house': 'a country has a certain number of inhabitants who are supposed to close the doors behind them, not to let in any casual stranger without a preliminary agreement; however it can also open its doors' (1994: 143). Here, the question of the stranger in the nation is a question of opening or closing the doors: the stranger can either *be let in or kept out.* What I want to suggest in contrast is that the definition of the nation as a space, body, or house *requires the proximity of 'strangers' within that space,* whether or not that proximity is deemed threatening (monoculturalism) or is welcomed (multiculturalism).

A key problem in this literature on nationhood is the use of the model of 'generalisable other', in which national identity is simply defined through and against an other, as such (Cohen 1994: 1). What is demanded is a much more contextual and nuanced understanding of the role of differentiated others in the demarcation of national identity. In Chapter 2, I examined how bodily integrity is produced, not simply through or against a generalisable other, but by differentiating between others, who have a different function in establishing the permeability of bodily space. The very habits and gestures of marking out bodily space involve differentiating 'others' into familiar (assimilable, touchable) and strange (unassimilable, untouchable). While I would not want to imply that we can make a simple analogy between bodies and nations, I think we can understand how bodily and social spaces leak into each other, or inhabit each other (see also Chapter 4). The nation becomes imagined and embodied as a space, not simply by being defined against other spaces, but by being defined as close to some others (friends), and further away from other others (strangers). In this sense, only some others are read as strangers within the nation space. The proximity of strangers within the nation space – that is, *the proximity of that which cannot be assimilated into a national body* – is a mechanism for the demarcation of the national body, a way of defining borders within it, rather than just between it and an imagined and exterior other.

As Christine Inglis demonstrates, the encountering of cultural difference within the fantastic nation space allows the work of nation formation to be sustained: strangers, those who are not recognised as 'typical' of a nation, might allow the question of what it means to be a nation to be posed (again and again). Inglis argues that, 'Many nations are having to confront the issue of how they respond to these "strangers" in their midst and how they incorporate them within their existing society and institutions. In so doing, the issue of national identity as a symbolic and legal issue inevitably comes to the fore' (1997: 204). The proximity of strangers requires the nation to respond: there is a constant process of adjustment and transformation. The nation is not secured in the process of keeping strangers out: the stranger's proximity is required if the stranger is to be known as the limit of 'the nation'. National identity emerges as a site of social conflict: there is a constant redefinition of who 'we' are through the very necessity of encountering strangers within the nation space. As Zygmunt Bauman puts it, the question is not, 'how to get rid of strangers and the strange, but how to live with them – daily and permanently' (1997: 55). National identity is unstable, and emerges through multiple encounters between those who assume themselves to be natives and those recognised as strangers, as out of place, in this place. The response to strangerness in the discourse of nationhood is hence built around the question of what it means to be 'in place'.

The assumption that strangers only populate the borders of the nation is in danger of reifying those borders: rather we need to understand the process of negotiation between identity and strangerness as ongoing, and as moving across different spatial formations (the body, home, the neighbourhood, the city, the country, the region, the nation, the globe). Immigration policy and border controls are not the only places in which the question of 'the stranger' is posed for and by the nation. National identity is metonymically related to other sites of identity formation: through marking out spaces of dwelling, spaces which are familiar and inhabitable, subjects are interpellated into multiple regimes. Like other forms of identity, nationhood is constantly renegotiated, and that negotiation is crucially dependent on encountering those who are recognisable as strangers, and who demand a response from the citizen: who are they? do they belong here? who am I? who are we? The distinction between native and stranger within a nation is not simply enforced at the border: rather, that distinction determines different ways in which subjects inhabit – which involves both dwelling and movement (see Chapter 1) – the space of the nation. The figure of the stranger is also constructed at the level of governmentality as the 'origin' of the very question of national identity: how do we live together, as one or many (= the strategic question of monocultural or multicultural government policy)? Or even, who is the 'we' of the nation if 'they' are here to stay?

Inventing the multicultural nation

Thinking about multiculturalism must begin, therefore, with an understanding that the coherence of the 'we' of the nation is always imaginary and that, given this, such a 'we' does not abolish cultural difference, but emerges through it. Multiculturalism is always contested, whether at the level of government policy, or whether in critical scholarship and resistant political activity. Multiculturalism is one of many historically specific negotiations of 'the nation'. There are key national and regional differences in how a discourse of multiculturalism emerges and is contested (see Rystad 1997). As

Theo Goldberg argues, 'Multiculturalism and commitments to cultural diversity emerged out of the conflictual history of resistance, accommodation, integration and transformation' (1994: 7). Multiculturalism can name a range of activities in education, as well as in grass roots political campaigns, which are based on the revaluing of minority cultures, and hence on the promotion of differences that are not accommodated within the official discourses of nationhood (Gunew 1994: 5). But, in other instances, multiculturalism works as an 'official' discourse: that is, it involves the setting of governmental agendas on what it should mean to be 'a nation'.

In this section, I will avoid speculating about what multiculturalism *is*, as it can clearly refer to contradictory forms of political mobilisation. As I am interested in *how* nations get constructed, I will analyse an example of 'official multiculturalism'. I will examine how multiculturalism works as a set of official 'responses' to cultural diversity in Australia. I will concentrate on Australia as an example, partly as this is where I first came to think about the implications of identifying a nation *as* multicultural, but also because Australia is an interesting example of how nationhood can be redefined through rather than against difference. In order to do this, I will read the *National Agenda for Multicultural Australia*, a policy framework document produced by the office of Multicultural Affairs when Paul Keating's Labor Government was still in office in 1989 (Department of Immigration and Multicultural Affairs 1989). This document is very much about setting an agenda, rather than making specific commitments to policy. It was widely circulated within the public domain and is still available on the Internet. I will also consider the more recent *Multicultural Australia: The Way Forward* (Department of Immigration and Multicultural Affairs 1997), which is an issues paper prepared by the National Multicultural Advisory Council since the election of John Howard's Liberal government, and is also available on the Internet. Although the former has received a lot of critical responses from academics in Australia, there has not been much close attention given to how the document is written. I want to read this document closely *as a text*, that is, *as a construction of multiculturalism, rather than as a response to it*. Such political documents are important instances in the forming of the national imaginary: as they describe the nation, they actively produce it. Rather than discuss the politics of multiculturalism at a general level, we need to look at the very 'grammar' of multiculturalism, in specific instances, in order to consider how it constructs the nation through mobilising a rhetoric of difference.

The *National Agenda* begins by assuming the descriptive power of the term, multiculturalism. It opens with the question, 'what is multicultural-ism?', to which it answers, 'multicultural is simply a term which describes the cultural and ethnic diversity of contemporary Australia. We are, and will remain, a multicultural society.' As a descriptive term, multiculturalism refers to that fact that there are many cultures in the nation space. As such, multiculturalism is defined as an accurate description of what Australia *already is*. Australia is defined *as* a multicultural nation: 'we' are and will be so. Immediately, the use of the term, 'multiculturalism', to describe the nation allows cultural diversity to reinforce, rather than undo, the fantastic inclusiveness of the nation: what 'we' are is not 'one', but 'many'. What binds Australia together as a 'we' is the fact of our differences: differences that belong to us, and that allow Australia 'to be' as a nation.

The second response to the opening question, 'what is multicultural Australia?', is as follows: 'As a public policy, multiculturalism encompasses government measures designed to respond to that diversity. It is a policy for managing the consequences of cultural diversity in the interests of the individual and society as a whole.' Multiculturalism comes to stand for a set of official responses to cultural diversity. Multiculturalism is both a name for cultural diversity and a name for government responses to cultural diversity. In the second sense, multiculturalism refers to a response to itself; it responds to itself. By using the same term to describe diversity and particular government approaches to diversity, the *National Agenda* closes a gap between description and prescription. The effect of this closure is to give the prescription – the response to difference – the status of description: the response to difference hence comes to refer to the 'real' of Australia.

The response to difference is defined in terms of the management of the consequences of difference. The term 'management' implies that differences themselves need to be contained and given a shape or coherence by government policy, and that without such policy, differences would be unmanageable (they would have problematic and unpredictable conse-quences for 'the individual and society as a whole'). The emphasis on the *consequences* of differences posits differences as originary: they simply and already exist. Such a positing of originary difference works to fetishise difference: what is concealed is precisely the histories of determination in which differences come to mark out terrains, subjects and bodies. Rather than 'differences' themselves being the 'consequences' of social processes, the document posits 'differences' as only *having* consequences. The detachment of differences from the social relations in which they are embedded allows the *National Agenda* to define itself as an agenda for dealing with differences, as such. Such an agenda then immediately becomes a question of 'interests'. Differences will be dealt with 'in the interests of' the individual and the undifferentiated nation. As a result, dealing with differences becomes a matter of concealing any differences that cannot be contained within the discourses of individualism and nationhood. That is, dealing with differences is a matter of refusing any differences that cannot be recognised as in the interests of the disembodied individual or the unified nation.

The *National Agenda* then defines three dimensions of multicultural policy. They are: cultural identity, social justice and economic efficiency. Cultural identity is defined in terms of 'the right of all Australians, within carefully defined limits, to express and share their individual cultural heritage, including their language and history'. Noticeably, cultural identity is defined as an *individual right* available to 'all Australians'. Later in the document, the term 'all Australians' is repeated, and the policies of multiculturalism are defined as applying 'equally to all Australians'. What is noticeable, then, is that the right to cultural identity is both individuated (it is something an individual owns, possesses or has) at the same time as it is universalised, such that it does not recognise any differences between social groups within Australia, but instead establishes what is 'common' to 'all Australians'. The *National Agenda* concludes, 'Fundamentally, multiculturalism is about the rights of the individual – the right to equality of treatment; *to be able to express one's identity*' to be accepted as an Australian without having to assimilate to some stereotypical model of behaviour' (emphasis added). The right to express 'one's cultural heritage' becomes a mechanism for re-establishing the 'we' of the nation as commonality, made up of individual Australians, whose differences are neutralised under the banner of 'equality' and under the assumption that being (accepted as) an Australian is the proper telos of different forms of cultural expression.

What is at stake here is a certain definition of culture as something that one simply has, and something one seeks to express. Not only is culture defined as possessive and expressive, but it is immediately associated with 'heritage', that is, with a fixed notion of 'the past'. The mixing of different cultures is here given an awkward temporality: the here and now of the nation space does not clash with the individual expressions of cultural difference. Such expressions of difference can be contained within the temporality of the nation insofar as they can only return 'us' into a static and uncontestable past which belongs elsewhere (not only to another time, but to another place). In this sense, 'cultural differences' are assumed to be static and fixed, something that can be displayed in the present, but that do not present difficulties for the cultural imaginary of 'all Australians'.

These 'stranger cultures' are not only to be fixed in the past *as heritage*, but they are also presented as objects that are self-contained, free from contradiction and difference. Those cultures that are different are hence assumed to be self-identical, as lacking any differences within. As Jon Stratton and Ien Ang argue, 'the very validation of cultural diversity tends to hypostatise and even fetishise "culture", which suppresses the heterogeneities existing within each "culture" ' (1994: 153). To some extent, the coherence of multicultural Australia is made possible by defining difference purely in terms of the difference between self-identical cultures that inhabit the national landscape and the culture of Australia itself: these stranger cultures are a 'gift' to all Australians, something to be 'expressed' and 'shared', and I would add, consumed (see Chapter 6).

The way in which official versions of multiculturalism define culture has been one of the most contentious issues in the critical literature on multiculturalism, in Australia and elsewhere. For example, Laksiri Jayasuriya (1997) discusses how the expressive definition of culture implicit in this version of multiculturalism restricts culture to the private domain.

The emphasis on culture over and above issues of political economy – or at least the refusal to understand culture as a site of a struggle that is also political and economic – means that multiculturalism neutralises the differences that it apparently celebrates: 'the social accommodation afforded through cultural pluralism avoided the potential of social disharmony by channelling the social and economic strivings of migrants into the private domains of their cultural needs' (Jayasuriya 1997: 23). This restriction imposed by such a definition of culture can be related to my earlier point about how national identity can be claimed through turning 'their' differences into 'our' difference: those who are 'culturally different' from the 'typical Australians' can display their difference, but only in such a way that it supplements *what is already assumed to be the coherence of culture itself*. As John Frow and Meaghin Morris conclude in their introduction to *Australian Cultural Studies*:

> it is always possible for the category of culture with which it operates to remain at the decorative level of folklore ethnic markers detached from substructures of real and agonistic difference; conversely it tends to reproduce imaginary identities at the level of the ethnic 'community' and thereby to screen differentiations and contradictions within the community.
>
> (1993: x)

The *National Agenda* later comments:

> Multiculturalism is concerned to encourage all Australians, including those from non Anglo-Celtic backgrounds, to share their diversity of culture, rather than excluding one another or being forced into separate enclaves. It seeks to make it clear that colour or language, style of dress or mode of worship, are no indication of the degree of personal commitment to the future of our nation. Being an Australian has nothing to do with outward appearance.

In this extraordinary statement, the right to cultural identity is again about sharing diversity amongst all Australians: it is a difference that not only belongs to, but must *return to*, 'the nation'. Cultural identity is defined in terms of 'outward appearance': one can appear culturally different, but still 'be' an Australian. The narrative works through the displacement of a binary opposition: cultural difference is set up against being 'Australian' through an opposition between appearance and being. Such a narrative reduces 'culture', understood in terms of 'cultural difference', to an outward appearance that actually conceals an Australian being. Here, multiculturalism is about accepting differences at the level of appearance in the assumption that they conceal a unified core or 'Australian being'. Being an Australian – and being committed to Australia – is hence 'nothing to do with outward appearance', nothing to do, that is, with the expression of one's cultural identity. As long as one is truly Australian underneath one's dress one can appear as different. Culture is reduced to a matter of style or dress and any cultural differences that question what it means 'to be' Australian are excluded from the concept of cultural identity altogether.

As Gillian Bottomley puts it, 'Australia's official policy of multiculturalism advances a kind of repressive tolerance towards cultural practices of the large immigrant population. But some cultural forms are more acceptable than others' (1992: 49). Those cultural forms that are 'more acceptable' are precisely those that may look different, *but are in fact the same underneath*. As a result, this multicultural nation accepts those differences that do not threaten the 'we' of an Australian being: the differences that cannot be reduced to mere appearance become *the unassimilable*. Those others who are (like) natives underneath their dress are assimilated into the 'we' of the nation (they do not have to be *culturally assimilated*, but must assimilate at the level of being), while those others who are strange beings define the limits to what or who can be assimilated (the unassimilable would be evoked by a figure of a stranger who refuses to be 'a real Australian' underneath).

The implicit differentiation between others who are more and less familiar and strange functions as a way of defining the potential and limits of the multicultural nation. The 'we' of the nation can expand by incorporating some others, thus providing the appearance of difference, while at the same time, defining other others, who are not natives underneath, as a betrayal of the multicultural nation itself (such other others may yet be expelled from the national body). Alternatively, what we have in operation in this multicultural discourse is two figures of 'the stranger' who are constructed through their different degrees of proximity to the white Australian 'native'. In one figure, the stranger appears different, but is the same underneath; this stranger can be assimilated, and even welcomed, insofar as it enables *the nation itself to appear as different*. In the other figure, the stranger's dress can reveal only a strange being; this *stranger stranger* cannot be assimilated. The stranger stranger, however, cannot simply be understood as the unassimilable other: rather, such strangers are assimilated precisely *as* the unassimilable and hence they allow us to *face* the 'limit' of the multicultural nation ('we' are open to some strangers, but not stranger strangers, who refuse to be 'native' underneath).

Multiculturalism as an official discourse hence involves narratives of partial assimilation or incorporation (through which the 'we' of the nation can appear different) as well as narratives of partial expulsion (through which the 'we' of the nation defines the limits of what it 'can be'). Both the narratives of incorporation and expulsion involve differentiating *between* others, which produces simultaneously, two figures of 'the stranger', including the one who can be taken in (the other who *appears* as a stranger), and the one who might yet be expelled (the other who *is* a stranger). This double construction of the 'we' of the nation in relation to the figures of the stranger reminds me of Ghassan Hage's consideration of the difference between 'being' and 'having' difference within multiculturalism (1998: 140). Hage suggests that Australian multiculturalism tends to define 'difference' as something that the 'we' of the nation 'has' rather than 'is': such a narrative still keeps in place the difference between that 'we' and those different others whom the nation 'has'. I am suggesting that the 'we' of the nation has a more complex and ambivalent relationship to difference, precisely because the multicultural nation remains predicated on a prior act of *differentiating between differences*. The multicultural nation claims 'to be' different, insofar as it incorporates those others whose difference is a matter of appearance. It hence takes on their difference (*becomes* different) by requiring that they *appear* different. At the same time, the multicultural nation claims to 'have' difference, insofar as the 'we' that becomes 'different' is still differentiated from those that simply *are* different. Hence, in the very same moment, the multicultural nation can claim *to be* and *to have* difference. The figure of the familiar stranger *appears* as that which allows us to be(come) different and to have difference, while the figure of the stranger stranger (who is nevertheless still familiar in its very strangerness), *disappears* as that which the 'we' cannot 'be' or 'have'.

The second key aspect of multiculturalism in the *National Agenda* is social justice, defined as, 'the right of all Australians to equality of treatment and opportunity, and the removal of barriers of race, ethnicity, culture, religion, language, gender or place of birth'. Here, we have a clear statement of multicultural justice within the liberal framework of equality of opportunity (with its negative model of freedom) and individualism. The markers of difference are defined as *barriers* that restrict the movements and capacities of essentially disembodied individuals. The commitment to social justice is defined through a neo-liberal discourse: multiculturalism can be just in this framework, *only insofar as it refuses to recognise the differences that it supposedly not only describes but also manages*. Again, such differences are not only managed, but erased under the signifier of individual freedom, the individual who embodies the justice of Australian 'multiculturalism for all'.

The final key aspect of multiculturalism is economic efficiency, 'the need to maintain, develop and utilize effectively the skills and talents of all Australians *regardless of their background*' (emphasis added). Later, in the section on human resources, the following statement is offered:

> People, as much as machines, are a crucial input to economic perform-
> ance and growth. Effective and efficient development and utilisation of
> our human resources is essential if Australia's economic potential is to be
> realised fully. ... Multicultural policies seek to maximise the contribu-
> tion – the experience, job skills and entrepreneurial talents of all Aus-
> tralians to the economic life of the community.

The term 'all Australians' is qualified by the phrase, 'regardless of their background'. This suggests that the goal of economic efficiency in multicultural Australia is partly about making the most of the resources and skills offered by those 'real' but not 'typical' Australians (despite the sustained emphasis on the blanket term, 'all Australians').

We can refer back to my discussion of global nomads in Chapter 4, where I argued that they become highly commodifiable as skilled workers in a global or transnational economy of difference. Likewise, within the modern late capitalist nation-state, multiculturalism can also be about the production of a better workforce who can deal with the multiple networks and forms of exchange in global capitalism. This is what makes most sense of Paul Keating's declaration, 'I am Asian', and his description of Australia as a 'multicultural nation in Asia'. Here, multiculturalism is about achieving a workforce that is better equipped to trade with nearby Asian countries: it is about the maximisation of profit in the interest of 'the Australian economy'. Such a discourse of economic efficiency, at the very same time, conceals the class and racial stratification of the Australian workforce: it conceals, for example, how migrant workers tend to occupy lower paid and unskilled positions. This narrative defines multiculturalism as a better form of management and use of 'the resources' of those from a non-English speaking background,[1] at the very same time as it conceals *the historical determination of difference as profit* (by explicitly defining multiculturalism in terms of *human* resources). Lisa Lowe's comments on multiculturalism in the United States have a clear resonance here: 'the production of multiculturalism at once "forgets" history, and in this forgetting, exacerbates a contradiction between the concentration of capital within a dominant class group and the unattended conditions of a working class increasingly made up of heterogeneous immigrant, racial, and ethnic groups' (1996: 86)

The *National Agenda* also attempts to define 'the limits to Australian multiculturalism'. In the first instance, the limits are that all Australians should have an 'overriding and unifying commitment to Australia, to its interests first and foremost'. Here, there is a clear assumption of the importance of a 'common culture' to a 'multicultural nation': while other Australians do not have to assimilate fully (to become 'typical Australians'), their difference cannot be a justification for not 'being Australian', that is, for not being committed to 'Australia' as such. The nation is clearly imagined as a singular and unified space: those untypical Australians must 'fit in' by expressing their difference only given a prior attachment and loyalty to the 'future of the nation'.

The second defined limit is even more important: 'multicultural policies require all Australians to accept the basic structures and principles of Australian society – the Constitution and the rule of law, tolerance and equality, Parliamentary democracy, freedom of speech and religion, English as the national language and equality of the sexes'. Here, the institutions, language and discourse of Australia, as a Western nation state, provide the framework in which all differences must be negotiated. As Jayasuriya argues, 'all statements of Australian multiculturalism from the Whitlam to the Keating era ... sought to accommodate difference and plurality strictly within a uniform and monistic political and social framework' (1997: 5). What is not acknowledged in the *National Agenda* is how these institutions themselves require an assimilation to a set of values that have historically been linked to colonialism and other forms of domination. There is an organising assumption that these institutions are themselves neutral and can not only accommodate differences, *but can become a mechanism for their advancement*.

The inclusion of 'the equality of the sexes' as a 'limit of multiculturalism' is hence extremely important. In this first instance, one can consider how a version of liberal feminism is easily accommodated into the universalist premises of 'the common culture'. Such a feminism can be accommodated precisely insofar as it is set up as *beyond difference*. However, the relationship between the limits of multiculturalism and feminism is more complex than this precisely because of the failure of gender to appear elsewhere (as an explicit category). The abstract individual who is privileged as the true subject of multicultural Australia (the *body* which is *any-body*) is clearly gendered: its lack of a gender is a mark of its masculinity. The incorporation of a version of liberal feminism functions to conceal the privileged relationship between the masculine subject and the multicultural nation. Such a nation is imagined as gender neutral, and then supplemented through reference to the discourse of liberal feminism as that which 'transcends' the limits of cultural difference. In this sense, feminism can be incorporated into the multicultural nation only through *a double concealment*: first, the already gendered nature of the multicultural subject is concealed, and second, by *reducing* feminism to a liberal discourse of equality that is our 'common culture', the cultural differences which cannot be reconciled into liberalism are concealed (which then allows feminism to be constructed *simultaneously* as a limit of multiculturalism and as advanced by multiculturalism).

The way in which multiculturalism assumes the inherent neutrality of that which is marked by differences is clear in the case of the law. The discussion paper from the Australian Law Commission on multiculturalism and the criminal law suggests that: 'The fact that Australia is a multicultural society does not mean that different standards of criminal behaviour should be applied to different groups. Communities within Australia have distinctive religious or cultural values which may influence what is right or wrong and what should be punished. However, while people are free to follow their own beliefs and have their own values, the imposition of standards by the power of the state should apply equally to all' (ALRC 1991: 4). What is noticeable here is that law can accommodate only some differences given the assumption that its standards must apply equally to all. Any element of another culture which contradicts the assumed neutrality of the legal standard, despite the recognition of points of difference, is hence *outlawed* within multicultural Australia.[2] The reliance on the uniformity of standards and institutions that have historically been linked to forms of domination, suggests that multiculturalism can only allow those differences that can be neutralised and accommodated within 'one' culture: *it sets up unassimilable differences as a failure or betrayal, not just of the Australian nation, but of the discourse of multiculturalism itself.*

Any real conflicts of value are mediated by a framework that presents its values as neutral. John Horton suggests that, 'multiculturalism becomes a problem when conflicts between groups about values or their interpretation cannot be comfortably accommodated within a particular social structure' (Horton 1993: 3). In contrast, I would suggest that multiculturalism is the solution to conflicts that cannot be accommodated: by presupposing that differences must be reconciled within a common culture, multiculturalism *excludes any differences that challenge the supposedly universal values upon which that culture is predicated.* Or, to put it more strongly, the official discourse of multiculturalism implies that differences *can be* reconciled through the very legislative framework which has historically defined Western values as neutral and universal. This use of difference as a form of reconciliation is possible because 'differences' have already been set up as simply expressive, private or a matter of appearance; they are not defined in terms of difference in values or ways of being. What we have then is a *disavowal of differences that are incommensurable*: a fantasy that, through the very legislative mechanisms of law, language and the polity, differences can be reconciled into a unified being-with-strangers-for-the-nation.

Multiculturalism and common culture

The *National Agenda* has been followed by other official documents defining Australia's commitment to multiculturalism. The National Multicultural Advisory Council produced an issues paper, *Multicultural Australia: The Way Forward* in 1997. This document endorses the principles of the *National Agenda*, but provides a different history of the coming-into-being of 'multicultural Australia' and a different – or perhaps more explicit – narrative of the proper goals of multiculturalism (there is also a list of more specific policy shifts which I do not have the space to discuss here). In the first instance, the narrative is prefaced with a message from the Minister for Immigration and Multicultural Affairs, Philip Ruddock, who begins the story of multiculturalism with a display of patriotism (sustained throughout the document). He suggests, 'We have been able to build upon the richness and strengths of many cultures to create a nation of which we can justifiably be proud.' Here, multiculturalism is an achievement of the 'nation': 'we' were able to combine the best of 'many cultures' to create a superior *multiculture* that remains ours. The 'we' is asserted as heroic, as being able to combine and build on others to create a better culture. Noticeably, such a 'we' is located outside culture, defined in terms of cultural difference. The 'we' is the subject of history that authorises itself as a subject precisely by telling the story of how it came to be through the appropriation or 'mixing' of those who are culturally different. In this sense, the 'we' *claims hybridity*, by assigning others to the category of pure difference, which 'it' alone can mix into something that is not one or the other.[3]

The story of multiculturalism as 'our' national achievement is sustained throughout the report. Indeed, the ability to build upon 'many cultures' is linked to a peculiarly 'Australian' set of values: 'As a community we have and support core values, principles and institutions which, while shared with many countries, have a special Australian quality. These include a "fair go".' The emphasis on 'fair go' as a core value throughout the report is extremely important: 'fair go' has historically been the utterance of the *typical Aussie battler*, the ordinary bloke, upon which the myth of an egalitarian society rests. Importantly, then multiculturalism is defined as the outcome of a core value which confirms the place of the typical (white, male) Australian in the origin of 'the nation'. According to such a narrative, multiculturalism exists, not as a way of breaking the relationship between Australian national identity and the typical Australian, *but as an outcome of that very relationship*: it is the ordinary values of typical Australians that have allowed 'us' to become a 'multicultural nation'. In this sense, the document makes explicit that the *any-body* who can be a real Australian in multicultural Australia still takes the shape of the body of the ordinary bloke, the white masculine hero of Australian settler history.

By evoking the figure of the ordinary Australian, *Multicultural Australia* actually prefigures the monocultural narratives offered by the extreme right-wing party One Nation, led by Pauline Hanson.[4] In *Multicultural Australia* the ordinary or typical Australian is represented as a hero for his ability to welcome and incorporate others. In One Nation rhetoric, the figure of the 'ordinary Australian' who embodies the values of 'mainstream Australia' is also central (see Stratton 1998: 76–84; Hanson 1997). However, in the narratives offered by One Nation, '*the ordinary Australian' is transformed from hero to victim* (or rather his heroism made him a victim of those incoming others he once welcomed). One Nation represents the figure of the ordinary Australian as the victim of multiculturalism itself, which they represent as privileging those who are marginal at the expense of the mainstream (Hanson 1997). Both One Nation and *Multicultural Australia* hence evoke the figure of the ordinary Australian in order to call for a politics in which difference should not threaten the common culture and 'ordinary values' of the nation.

The identification of core values with the figure of the typical Australian does an enormous amount of historical work in the report, *Multicultural Australia*. Throughout, the emphasis is on taking pride in 'our' history of tolerance and openness to newcomers: 'we should build upon our proud record of compassion and concern which has made ours a welcoming and caring society'. This writing of the history of the Australian nation as predicated on openness, tolerance and a 'fair go' could be considered a direct attempt to overcome the national discourse of shame about the historical dispossession of Indigenous peoples.[5] Ironically, the diversity of Indigenous peoples is mentioned, or indeed claimed, as part of 'our' history of cultural diversity, alongside the diversity of migrant cultures: 'Our Aboriginal and Torres Strait Islander peoples have many cultures and languages and our migrants have come from all parts of the globe'.[6] The use of the term 'our' is quite astonishing in its violence. As 'our' possessions, these natives and strangers have allowed 'us' to be 'culturally diverse'. Such a narrative not only overlooks histories of violence, but it also performs its own violence: it signals an-other appropriation of 'strangers' into the achievement of multiculturalism itself ('they' have allowed us 'to be').

Not surprisingly, then, in the account of the goals of multiculturalism more emphasis is placed on unity: throughout the document, the aim of multiculturalism is defined as 'ensuring that cultural diversity *is a unifying force*'. The document asks us to question any impression 'that multicultural policy has been primarily concerned with migrants': 'We believe that multicultural policy must become more inclusive by embracing and being relevant to all Australians.' The term 'all Australians' erases any differences between white settler groups, migrants and Indigenous groups: the celebration of difference must bring us together. Such a story of multiculturalism is a story of an *inclusive multiplicity*: a multiculturalism that includes all of us, that unites us together as 'fellow' natives. In this story, multiculturalism is not even about unity-in-diversity – which is how we could read the narrative offered in the *National Agenda* (see Stratton and Ang 1994). Rather, it is about unity-from-diversity. The definition of a multicultural nation takes place through the use of a monocultural framework: multiculturalism can be described as a cultural diversity that, at least to some extent, must be overcome or, to put it better, must be transformed into a unifying force. In this framework, differences that cannot be assimilated into the white, masculine core of the Australian being (the typical Australian who calls for a 'fair go') are defined as a betrayal of the multicultural nation. At the same time, cultural differences that have historically been sites of struggle and antagonism are appropriated and neutralised as a sign of 'our' history.

In such multicultural constructions of the nation space, strangers become a means of defining 'who' we are, not by being represented as 'outside' that we (although some strangers are known in this way), but by being incorporated as elements in the 'making' of the 'we' that can be uttered by the national subject. I hence broadly support Ghassan Hage's argument that multicultural tolerance and monocultural intolerance are structured around a similar fantasy of the national subject who alone is afforded the will to define who should and should not inhabit the nation space (1998: 17). However, unlike Hage, my argument is not simply that both multicultural-

ism and monoculturalism involve white supremacy (1998: 232). My
argument has attended to the grammatical specificity of the construction of
the multicultural nation by considering how the 'we' of the nation is
established by an act of differentiating *between* those stranger others who
have already entered the nation space.

Multiculturalism, by defining difference purely in terms of appearance,
can only value the differences that, beyond the level of culture, can be
incorporated into the 'ordinary values' of 'fair go', or the institutional and
political frameworks of neo-liberalism itself. Indeed, in some multicultural
constructions of the nation, the 'we' itself emerges through the very *gesture of
claiming difference*. Those who appear as different are incorporated *as*
difference – a process that allows the nation to imagine *itself* as heterogeneous (to claim their differences as 'our difference'). This process of incorporation also involves acts of differentiation. While some strangers can be
assimilated, as their strangeness is 'seen' as only a matter of appearance,
other strangers can only be assimilated *as* the unassimilable. Their
strangeness is represented as a matter of being, and hence betrays the very
appearance of difference within the discourse of multiculturalism itself. These
strangers hence disappear and reappear as embodying the danger of the one
who does not want to become 'a real native' underneath the appearance of difference.
The strangers who refuse to receive the gift of multiculturalism by being
natives, in the very act of appearing as different, hence function to define the
limits of multicultural hospitality.[7] We can only welcome those others who
allow us to be ourselves and be different, at one and the same time.

At one level, it might be assumed that the emergence of new (or not-so-
new) forms of right-wing populism that organise their narratives through
constructing strangers as phobic objects, might lead us to endorse multiculturalism as a way of opening ourselves to strangers, or as a way of imagining
a more heterogeneous sociality. But for me, the emergence of extreme
monocultural agendas, in Australia as well as elsewhere (most notably, in the
United States and France), calls for a different response. It calls me to ask
how we can turn an opposition to monoculturalism into a mobilisation of a
different politics of multiculturalism, and a better form of hospitality
towards others (see Chapter 7). Such a politics would refuse to celebrate the
figure of the stranger as the origin of difference: it would also be concerned
with how the 'we' of the nation can violently reproduce itself in the name of
liberal inclusion. Such a politics would attend to how incorporation and
expulsion can both work *simultaneously* to fetishise the stranger as the origin
of difference. Such an oppositional politics may hence find 'a place' for *that
which refuses to be assimilated into the heterogeneous 'we' of the nation*.

6   Going strange, going native

Even if you don't have a magic carpet to transport you to the exotic East, you can enjoy a Turkish bath of your own with this rich, luxurious cream bath. Enhanced with rose extract to soothe and silk protein to help moisturise, Turkish Bath will leave your skin feeling soft and smooth.

The people of Oshima are famed for having luxurious hair. Oshima, Japan, is the traditional source of material camellia extract renowned for its softening and cleansing benefits. The wonders of the world are now yours to enjoy.

(Boots, *Global Collection*)[1]

In consumer culture, the commodity object which is, at once, an image and a material thing, enables subjects to have a close encounter with a distant other (the one already recognised as 'the stranger'). Through consuming objects that are associated with other places and strange cultures, either in how those objects are represented and framed (as in Boots's *Global Collection*), or how they are produced and travel, subjects can almost become the stranger, or can become or smell *like* the stranger. The strange encounters that produce the figure of the stranger do not necessarily involve the immediacy of the face to face. The subject does not have to travel to meet the one who is apparently from another place: 'Even if you don't have a magic carpet to transport you to the exotic East, you can enjoy a Turkish bath of your own.' Objects and images mediate such encounters between bodies-at-home (or bodies-in-the-bath) and those recognisable as from a strange or 'exotic' place.

Returning to my discussion of fetishism in the introduction to this book, we can see an immediate relationship between commodity fetishism and stranger fetishism. First, the object comes to be valued (is 'enigmatic') only through a prior act of detachment from the social relationships of labour and production that produced it. Second, the object is invested with meaning by being associated with the figure of the stranger: indeed, the object becomes the stranger; it is consumed as that which contains the 'truth' of the strange or exotic. The fetishism of the commodity becomes displaced onto the fetishism of cultural difference: we value the lost object by assuming *it contains difference in its own form* (a containment which is enabled by a double concealment of the history of its production and the history of determination that allows the stranger to appear).

The objects and images used and expelled in postmodern consumption come to stand for, or stand in for, the impossible figure of the stranger itself: by using the cream bath, you can enjoy Turkey, or by using the camellia extract, you can have hair like the people of Oshima. The assumption that you can be (almost) like the stranger through consuming a product works through a series of metonymic associations: the softness and silkiness of the product is *like* the softness and silkiness of exotic Turkish baths which is *like* what your skin will be if you use the product. The narrative which sells the commodity object incorporates the consumer into the 'world' of strangers (a discourse of globality), an incorporation which is also an imperative: *you will enjoy* the 'wonders of the world' through the act of consuming the object. The object that sells itself as 'difference' also transcends differences; through the double displacement of commodity and stranger fetishism, it comes to stand for globality, *but a globality that touches the skin of the body-at-home in the very moment of consumption.*

In this chapter, I consider some key modalities in which the contemporary Western subject encounters the stranger. Rather than examining the encounters with the stranger as the one who is already recognised as out of place (see Chapter 1), I examine encounters in which the 'stranger' is the object of desire, or comes to embody 'the place' that the subject seeks to inhabit. What happens in such encounters? How do contemporary Western subjects enter relations of proximity with strangers and become transformed? I will examine three key modalities of *going strange, going native*:[2] consuming, becoming and passing. What are the effects of these different ways of entering the stranger's space, or even getting inside the stranger's body? How do they reproduce the fetishism which allows the stranger to appear as a figure, a figure that may no longer be see-able as stalking the streets, because it comes to be inhabited by the subject?

Consuming strangers

How are 'strangers' consumed? How does the consumption of strangers involve a transformation in the subject who consumes? Such questions cannot be addressed without a consideration of the impact of globalisation on consumer culture. Mike Featherstone argues in his introduction to *Global Culture: Nationalism, Globalisation and Modernity* that globalisation involves not just global cultural inter-relatedness, but 'persistent cultural interaction and exchange' (1990: 6). This series of global cultural flows involves a repertoire of images and information, that is, a *mediascape* (Featherstone 1990: 7). The mediascape undermines the boundaries of the nation-state (Featherstone 1990: 2). I think this model of cultural inter-relatedness needs some qualification. We could argue, in light of my discussion in Chapter 5, that the boundaries of nation-states (or geographic entities such as the 'West') have always been imaginary. While the contemporary mediascape may involve a global flow of images and objects this is not to say that those images and objects do not create and reinforce such imaginative boundaries (and hence the deployment of power) between, for example, the 'West' and 'East'. The flow of cultural images and objects across national boundaries means that 'difference' as the basis of *imaginary divides* ('us' and 'them') is increasingly available to Western consumers. William M. O'Barr's work, *Culture and the Ad: Exploring Otherness in the World of Advertising*, suggests that images of 'otherness' and 'difference' function to *sustain* rather than *problematise* the imaginary boundaries between different nations, or groups of people. He argues that the fascination with otherness within advertisements helps define the boundaries of a product's market: that is, to define who is and is not the consumer audience (O'Barr 1994: 2, 12). The flow of cultural images and objects which play with 'otherness' and 'difference' may serve to reproduce *as well as* threaten the imaginary boundaries between social or racial groups.

The flow of images and objects across border lines invites us to consider how identity is reconstituted in an intimate relationship to 'the strange' and the exotic. The Western consumer is invited to 'go ethnic' through what she or he might eat, drink, or wear. However, what is at stake is not only the actual flow or movement of commodity objects across national borders, but the imaginary construction of 'other places' in the selling of commodities. In the case of Boots's *Global Collection*, it is important that we do not assume that the commodities themselves have 'come from' the places they cite as the origin of the commodity: rather, what is at stake is how the commodity is sold through the fixing of difference in a discourse of origins.[3] The process of consuming the strange does not mean that the strange is the 'real' origin of the commodity object: the 'stranger' is precisely that which is produced, marketed and sold in order to define the value of the commodity object. In other words, through the commodity, the stranger becomes a fetish: it becomes consumed as something the object simply *has*. This perception of objects as *having* difference is itself an effect of the very processes of production and exchange embedded in consumer culture.

Consumer culture involves the production of the stranger as a commodity fetish through representations of difference. Differences are defined in terms of culture, and culture, as in the official discourses of multiculturalism (see Chapter 5), is restricted to the privatised and the expressive domain of 'style'. Increasingly differences have become a matter of style in consumer culture. As Henry Giroux put it, 'difference is stripped of all social and political antagonisms and becomes a commercial symbol for what is youthfully chic, hip, and fashionable' (1994: 15). The definition of difference in terms of style involves the detachment of difference from relationships of antagonism. Difference is used to *bind together in the present moment of consumption* that which, historically, has been in conflict.

The reduction of difference to a matter of style can be linked to the shift from biological racism to cultural racism (Balibar 1991: 22). Rather than racial difference being fixed through reference to the biological body, racial difference is increasingly fixed through culture itself. For example, Boots's *Global Collection* represents difference in terms of style: the commodity object *carries difference* in that it can allow you to alter the surface of the body (your hair, your skin) in order to become *like them*. In other words, *its difference* (that is, the difference of and in the commodity) is immediately *their difference* which can become *your difference*: 'The people of Oshima are famed for having luxurious hair. Oshima, Japan, is the traditional source of material camellia extract renowned for its softening and cleansing benefits. The wonders of the world are now yours to enjoy.' It is through (rather than despite) the assumption that difference is a style that can be consumed (insofar as the commodity object is assumed *to have it*), that difference is fixed onto the bodies of others. They appear as strangers (with 'a life of their own') in order to enable the consumer to take on their difference, that is, to take on their style.

One of the most powerful critiques of the exoticisation of difference as style is offered by bell hooks in her article, 'Eating the Other'. Eating involves the bodily processes of consumption: one swallows, digests, farts and shits. One takes in, and lets out. The food which is eaten is partly incorporated into the body. hooks suggests that, 'Within commodity culture, ethnicity becomes spice, seasoning that can liven up the dull dish that is mainstream white culture' (1992: 21). In other words, ethnicity becomes constructed as 'the exotic' through an analogy with food: black people are spicy and different. The white consuming subject is invited to eat the other: to take it in, digest it, and shit out the waste. The exotic and strange foods are incorporated into the bodies of Western consumers as that which is different, but assimilable. This incorporation allows 'difference' to be associated with something that simply livens up the ordinary or mainstream diet. Of course, some differences cannot be assimilated. Horror stories of what 'they' eat elsewhere abound to define the limits of what can be incorporated into the (multicultural) diet, or assimilated into the (multicultural) body (at least, in ethnic restaurants at home, we can subject them to our standards of hygiene).

A key aspect of multiculturalism as a policy for managing difference is food and eating. One of the benefits of multiculturalism is often cited as the range of restaurants that the consumer can visit: the range of flavours and spices that can be tasted. Ethnicity becomes a spice or taste that can be consumed, that can be incorporated in the life world of the one who moves between (eating) places. Differences that can be consumed are the ones that are valued: difference is valued insofar as it can be incorporated into, not only the nation space, but also the individual body, the body-at-home (this body does not have to leave home to 'eat' difference). By implication, *differences that cannot be assimilated into the nation or body through the process of consumption have no value.*

If we consider multiculturalism and food in more detail, we can examine how the consumption of strangers allows the redefinition of the consuming subject and an expansion of her or his agency. In Australia, multicultural food is defined as 'fusion cooking' (or 'Mod Oz'). Here, it is multicultural Australia that brings together all the differences that make up the separate 'dishes' of the world, by fusing or combining spices and ingredients that are normally the authentic mark of each particular national dish. Some dishes are fixed as a mark of authentic strangeness, and then reconstituted through the act of mixing and bringing them together.[4] The multicultural dish confirms the agency of the consuming self who alone can combine differences, to create something that is not one or the other (see Hage 1998: 118–123). The stranger foods simply are what they are: it is only by being fused by the multicultural cook, that they can become something other. Consumer culture fixes difference onto strange cultures and foods, those that are 'elsewhere', in order to unfix them through the act of 'bringing them home', and transforming them into a commodity (defined as a movement from nature to culture, from one to many). It is the *fixing* of difference onto the strangers (this is what 'they' eat, wear or smell like) that allows the *unfixing* of the consumer self. It is the consuming self who has the agency *to become different*, rather than simply *be different* (the authentic stranger, or the authentic spice).

The identity of the consuming subject is established through the proximity of the strange culture, a proximity that is mediated by the commodity object. As the multicultural nation incorporates cultural differences as *its difference* (Chapter 5), so too the consuming subject establishes its agency through an act of incorporating differences as *its difference*. That is, the act of consuming strangers through objects and images allows the subject to establish its difference from itself, which is, at once, its difference from those recognised as simply 'being' strangers. Although the subject might become (like) the stranger through consuming objects and images which 'come from' strange places, or which are narrated as coming from strange places, that becoming is clearly separated from simply being strange. The consuming subject in approximating the smell or look of strangers is clearly not the stranger: this proximity allows rather than disallows the (ontological) distinction between the one who becomes (the consumer), and the one who merely is (the stranger). The agentic nature of the consuming self is established through, rather than against, the proximity of strangers; it is a proximity that requires that the stranger be fixed in the 'beyond' of the commodity form, and hence it does not assume the stranger's co-presence in bodily and social space. The fascination with difference within such spaces allows the appropriation of difference into the permeable 'constitution' of the consumer self.

Becoming strangers

Consumer culture provides consumers with the fantasy that they can become the stranger, however temporarily, or that they can be like the stranger, by using certain products or by eating their food. In this section, I analyse 'becoming' as itself a particular form of proximity to strangers. In my discussion of ethnographic knowledge in Chapter 3, I already gestured towards how becoming can work as a means of getting closer to the other in order to sustain a difference. Here, I want to consider how contemporary Western culture is imbued with fantasies of becoming, in which the Western self ceases to define it-self *against* the bodies of strangers. What are the implications of such narratives? How do they rework the classical nineteenth-century narrative of 'going native'?

Becoming has also been privileged within recent Western critical theory as a way of understanding the subject that does not assume the stasis of being. Theories of becoming are read as theories of transgression, movement, fluidity, difference and desire (see Probyn 1996). One of the most influential approaches to becoming is offered in Deleuze and Guattari's *A Thousand Plateaus*, a text which has had a significant impact on critical theory and cultural studies.[5] While I do not have the time to offer an account of their complex theory of becoming here, it is important to note that their model of becoming has been used within cultural studies to elaborate a different relationship between self and other. This is clear in Marcus Doel's paper, 'Bodies without Organs' where he affirms that, 'the subject swarms with these modalities of disappearance which Open onto the motionless voyaging of Becoming other' (1995: 240). Here, becoming is immediately becoming other: such a journey of subjects towards the other is premised on the *disappearance* of the subject. By getting closer to that which was cast as other to the self, the self ceases to be. I want to challenge this narrative, by discussing becoming other as a fantasy that is increasingly offered to the Western subject. To what extent do such narratives of becoming other reconstitute rather than transgress the integrity of the Western subject who becomes?[6] How does the narrative of the disappearance of the subject through proximity to strangers *allow 'the subject' to reappear as 'the stranger'*?

The narrative of becoming as 'getting closer' to that which was defined as other is problematic in that it implies the 'other' is, in the first instance, far away. As I have already argued in this book, through a reflection on the figuring of the stranger, that which is recognisable as the stranger *must be close enough*. The other becomes imaginable as familiar (assimilable) or strange (unassimilable) as a mechanism for establishing the permeability of the boundary lines of the body-at-home or the home-land. Given this, becoming the stranger is not simply about a move from distance to proximity: rather, we need to consider the way in which 'being' and 'becoming' might involve different *modes* of proximity or closeness. What are the different narratives in circulation that describe and constitute the relationship between natives and strangers in terms of becoming?

In order to investigate ways in which becoming is offered as a narrative of proximity to strangers, I want to look closely at the film, *Dances with Wolves* (1990). This is an important film: it is a Hollywood blockbuster that offers the cinemagoer a reworking of the classical colonial story of 'going native'. Its importance is precisely that it has put a story of becoming other/going native into circulation that *has appeal*. It provides an attempt to rewrite the history of the American West by describing and visualising the becoming native of a white man through his friendship with an Indian tribe. The natives cease to be the strangers: rather the white man becomes the native.

Dances with Wolves does, at least to some extent, transform the narrative of conquest, confrontation and development implicit in classic Westerns. The Sioux are not just there as an obstacle to be removed. They speak in their own language which is translated for the reader by the use of subtitles. They have names and faces. The narrative seems to offer a movement from distance to proximity: we, as spectators, get closer to the Indians, as does Dunbar, the white male hero of the film.

The film begins by positioning the white, male subject as an anti-hero; he becomes heroic through an act of cowardice, a suicidal ride into gun fire, a desire for death. The narrative reworks that act as the site of agency; for a desire to meet life at its limits. Dunbar's desire for life is reframed as a desire to see the borders of life – he says, 'I've always wanted to see the frontier'. Insofar as the narrative begins with Dunbar's desire to see the frontier – the desire to see where civilisation and wilderness meet, where civilisation reaches beyond itself – then the narrative begins with the *distancing* perspective of the masculine, colonising gaze. In other words, the hero of the film must keep his distance *in order to see*. When Dunbar reaches his post he is alone; the emphasis on his alone-ness, not only positions him as a solitary hero (confronted by the multiplicity of the other), but also suggests a lack, a lack that is inscribed on his face (his search for connection), as well as on the face of a culture (the lonely outpost on the border). Already, there is a sense that there is something lacking, that there is a need for something beyond the structure of the self who stands alone on the border between life and death. Although the Indians are at a distance, they come into the seen: it is the proximity of the Indians that already allows Dunbar to see the limits of the space that he inhabits.

However, the narrative does not maintain this distancing and lonely perspective. The spectator first see traces of the Indian subjects through violence littered in the landscape; a skeleton and a bow announce their presence as a danger and a threat. The story of becoming begins as a story of confrontation between the solitary white male and 'the multiplicity' of the Sioux tribe. They are the 'many figures' of the strangers: the ones already recognised as the origin and cause of the danger, as the out of place in this place as it ceases to be the frontier. The early encounters do involve the language of confrontation, as a confrontation that engenders the desire to know: 'I have made first contact with the wild Indian', he says. The desire for contact emerges through a sense of the multiple: 'I assume where there is one, there will always be another.'

The shift from confrontation to becoming emerges through his desire for company; his desire for access to the multiplicity that he lacks: 'It's good to finally have some company.' Dunbar becomes fascinated by the Indians. His fascination with them involves unlearning the violence of the stereotypes of the native as 'strangers' to civilisation, or even civil society: 'Nothing I've been told about these people is correct. They are not beggars and thieves. They are not the boogey man they've been made out to be. They are polite guests and have a sense of humour that I enjoy.'

The shift from positive to negative images of the Indians does not keep the subject/object relation in place. For Dunbar gets too close. His proximity to the Indians, to those who were defined as strangers to civilisation and civility, breaks down his identity as a soldier policing the borders of empire (he gets too close to 'see' the frontier). He is becoming Indian. This becoming is related to becoming animal. The Sioux rename him as Dances with Wolves, when they see him chasing the wolf he has befriended, attempting to prevent the wolf from coming to the Sioux's village with him. The chase presents itself as a playful dance – the wolf became his company in the lonely outpost. The friendship between man and animal shifts into becoming through authorisation from the Sioux tribe. This renaming of Dunbar, this merging of the wolf and the man through the structure of the name, opens the narrative to another way of 'coding' the friendship between man and wolf. Dunbar ceases to define himself against the animal, but enters into a relation of physical proximity to the animal, and moves through him. Likewise, Dunbar ceases to define himself against the Indians (a definition that already required them to be close enough), but enters a relation of physical proximity to them, and moves through them.

Both becomings are visually coded through dance. Through dancing with the wolf, through the meeting and touch of two bodies, Dunbar's transformation is made possible, he is no longer distinguishable as a lonely subject. This dance is echoed by other dances. First, Dunbar dances *like* an Indian by his fire. This dance suggest a desire to be the other which works through imitation rather than becoming. In the second dance, Dunbar, or Dances with Wolves, dances with the Indians by their fire. Here, *he ceases to stand out as a white man dancing like an Indian*. The multiplicity of the dance reshapes his body. In the physicality of merger, of lines of flight made possible through proximity, Dances with Wolves becomes something other. He is not white man or Indian: the dance produces a hybridity that does not belong to one or the other. We can no longer see his face. There appears to be no distinction between natives and strangers: all we have left is the physical merger of dancing bodies: 'the subject swarms with these modalities of disappearance which Open onto the motionless voyaging of Becoming other' (Doel 1995: 240).

However, this narrative of becoming other does not simply leave us with the proximity of dancing bodies. Or, to make a slightly different point, such a proximity needs to be read in terms of a fantasy which still serves to substantiate the 'body' of the stranger, but through the very proximity of the dance. The tale of becoming involves fantasy at a number of levels. It involves fantasy at the level of the fascination with the 'strangers' that the subject enters a relationship with through becoming. It also involves fantasy at a more structural level in terms of the organisation of the narrative itself by a particular self–other dynamic. In other words, the story of becoming involves not just a destructuring of white masculinity, but its restructuring in relation to the other, who ceases to be a stranger, but instead becomes one's 'native self'.

The fantasies of Indian-ness and wolf-ness crucially rest on fantasies of woman. It is the act of returning the woman to the Sioux tribe that produces new possibilities for the relationship between Dunbar and the Sioux. Dunbar finds a woman mutilating herself as he carries his flag over a hill on his first visit to the Indians. He uses his flag to cover her wounds. This highly charged gesture – in which the symbol of conquest is rendered a symbol of rescue and redemption – gives the woman a pivotal status in his story of self-transformation. Significantly, the woman is a white woman who had been 'stolen' by the Indians. Although, she has been brought up as Indian, the film obsessively focuses on her difference to the Indians; her 'look' is differentiated mainly through the visual coding of her hair as being out of place (it is too 'big' to be confined to plaits). Dunbar's movement to proximity with the Indians is mediated then by his desire for the white woman. The woman's memories (of her language and her family) mean that she acts as translator between Dunbar and the male Sioux. The woman is returned to Dunbar by the Sioux tribe as the sign of his inclusion. The woman is positioned within the narrative as the first mediating term; as the primary means by which his becoming is engendered. It also frames the narrative of becoming as a narrative based on the 'difference' of the white heterosexual couple. They stand out as different from the 'many' of the Indian tribe, even if they are marked as 'not quite white' in the process of becoming.

The narrative of becoming Indian involves fantasies of who the Sioux tribe already are. However much the narrative of becoming unleashes a transformation in Indian-ness as it has been contained by empire, the fascination with the Indian reconstructs the Indian as other-than-(him)self. Dunbar's transformation relies on a very precise imaging of the Indian as more in tune with nature, as more in tune with each other, and as 'prior' to the alienations of the outpost: 'I've never known a people so eager to laugh, so devoted to family, so dedicated to each other'. Indeed, the contrast of the outpost to the Sioux's village works primarily by images of fire (suggesting heat and passion) and colour (suggesting affectivity and love). The Sioux are visually constructed as more emotive, more passionate, more loving. The fascination with the Indians and the fascination with the wolf inhabit a similar terrain; the wolf and the Indian come to 'stand for' what is lacking in the white man's face, the desire, movement and closeness of nature itself.

The narrative of becoming does not just involve particular fantasies about the other, in the movement from strangeness to familiarity. It also functions more structurally as a fantasy of strangerness in relation to the self. Firstly, one must consider how the narrative is framed. The blurb on the cover of the video reads: 'one man went in search of the frontier and found himself'. This description of the film cannot be read as fully grasping the play of the film; we should not take on board this text as a proper reading or as authorising our reading. However, the construction of the narrative as a story of his self-discovery is significant. Although Dunbar does not discover what he is expected to as a soldier (the frontier), the narrative remains about his discoveries. What he discovers is his lack. His (self)-discovery is mediated as a discovery of the truth about the Indians. In other words, although the narrative involves him becoming other, it does so by positioning the Indians as a means to his discovery. The Indians remain other – they remain at the service of a white, masculine story of (self)-discovery. Rather than being annihilated as a threat, they become reincorporated to provide what is lacking in his self. One must consider that throughout Dunbar is positioned as a scribe – he writes down 'his story' in his journal, a story that becomes authorised for the spectator in the form of a voiceover. Becoming could be read as the de-forming and re-forming of the white masculine face through the absorption of the other. This is a transformation, but one that expands the force of mastery as beyond the limitations of the singular face.

The organisation of becoming around his self-discovery (*his* becoming) returns us to the question of agency. I argued that the narrative began with a definition of his agency as the desire to see the border; the border between death and life, wilderness and civilisation. Becoming, in this sense, does not reassert but erodes agency. However, I would argue that becoming reinscribes agency elsewhere, not necessarily at the level of the individual (or individuated) subject. The story of transformation could be read differently – as the story of the ability to transform oneself. The link between becoming and agency within the narrative is clear. Dunbar still stands out as a 'hybrid hero'; he discovers the buffalo (after which he becomes 'a celebrity') and he gives the Sioux his guns so they can fight the Pawnee. The materiality of this becoming suggests that the hero and agent is not the white male subject per se. It is the very force of hybridisation (the undoing of pure whiteness) that enables the white male subject who is becoming to offer something other to those through which he becomes. Although both the white subject and the Indian subjects are transformed through becoming, that transformation is framed as the Indian's *debt* to the white man's overcoming of himself.

Hybridisation becomes, not a means of transgression, but a technique for getting closer to strangers which allows the reassertion of the agency of the dominant subject. The story remains organised around his ability to move and to overcome differences (his 'difference' from them). The ending names this ability as a danger (he has to leave the tribe to prevent them from being discovered in the military's search for the white man who is a traitor to the race). However, it is also the energising force behind the plot itself. The way in which this narrative of becoming Indian most clearly involves fantasy is in the very assumption that the structural relations of *antagonism* between Indians and white men can be simply overcome through the act of getting closer. His agency is central to this fantasy of overcoming; *not only can he make but he can unmake the border between self and other, between natives and strangers.*

Within the narrative, the process of 'going native' as 'going strange' still differentiates between more and less assimilable others. While Dunbar gets closer to the Sioux tribe, such that he is renamed as *one of them* (Dances with Wolves), that proximity aligns him with them and against some 'stranger strangers', the Pawnee. The Pawnee are represented as brutal, violent and threatening. The narrative of the good versus bad Indians is classic to Western films (see Shohat and Stam 1994: 67): here, the process of becoming the stranger still requires other strangers to define the limits of the act of becoming. Beyond the Pawnee, the white soldiers are also represented in the ending of the film as brutal and violent: they are the ones that kill, in a literal as well as symbolic act of annihilation, the horse and dog whose friendship with John Dunbar enabled him to become Dances with Wolves. Dunbar's 'natives' become Dances With Wolves's 'strangers'. However, Dances with Wolves then becomes John Dunbar (with a difference): he re-enters the white community in an attempt to save his fellow Indians/natives/strangers. While there is a differentiation between good and bad Indians, there is also a differentiation between good and bad whites. As a result 'going strange, going native' involves crossing the border between *some selves* and *some others*, and not *other selves* and *other others*, or between *some natives* and *some strangers*, and not *stranger natives* and *stranger strangers*.

Within this film, the narrative of becoming allows the agency of the white masculine subject to be re-established through the proximity of the bodies of some strangers. Through becoming (like) them, he is able to undo the history of violence which fixes the Indians into the bodily life of strangerhood. Such a narrative of becoming the stranger or 'going native' offers itself as a rewriting of a history: it deals with the shame of the colonial past by the very fantasy that getting closer to strangers can allow the 'white man' to live for and as the native. Just as the multicultural narrative of the past reimagines violence as cooperation and the mutuality of difference (see Chapter 5), so too the narrative of becoming reimagines violence as the opening out of the possibility of friendship and love. The possibility of love is tied to a liberal vision of the white self as always open to others ('if only we'd got closer, there would have been love, we would have lived as one'). Not only do such multicultural fantasies of becoming involve releasing the

Western subject from responsibility for the past, but they also confirm his agency, his ability to be transformed by the proximity of strangers, *and to render his transformation a gift to those strangers through which he alone can become.*

Passing for strangers

How do such fantasies of becoming work to reproduce knowledge of 'strangers' or, more accurately, to produce the figure of the stranger through the accumulation of knowledge? As I have already suggested, consumer culture is one site in which becoming other is offered to Western subjects through the commodity form ('stranger fetishism'). Such commodities are assumed *to contain* the difference of the strange culture. Implicit in the narrative of 'eating the other' (hooks 1992) is the assumption that the Western subject can *have* the difference and hence *knows* the difference. In this section, I consider how narratives which enable the one to get closer to the many – 'the group of strangers' (Agar 1980: 41) – are premised on epistemic authority. In other words, I will examine how narratives of proximity are *authorised as knowledge*, and so extend the analysis of ethnographic knowledge offered in Chapter 3. In order to do so, I analyse passing as a particular form of proximity to strangers.[7]

Passing has been theorised, like migrancy, nomadism and becoming, as a form of transgression. Such approaches assume that 'passing' destabilises and traverses the system of knowledge and vision upon which subjectivity and identity precariously rest. The subject who passes for that which they are not has increasingly become a point of entry for an approach to identification that emphasises the fantasies, ruptures and breakages which prevent identity from being assured as the ontological given of the subject. For example, in Lola Young's, *Fear of the Dark: 'Race', Gender and Sexuality in the Cinema*, passing is read 'as a sign of racial duplicity which threatens to undermine the stability of racial categorisation' (1996: 85), and as 'transgressing racial boundaries' (1996: 91).

Within such work there is a failure to theorise, not the potential for any system to become destabilised, but the means by which relations of power are secured, paradoxically, *through this very process of destabilisation* (we all know, I think, how the language of crisis is managed by a conservative politics). Rather than assuming a link between passing and transgression, we can ask: How are differences that threaten the system recuperated? How do 'strange bodies' get read in a way which further supports the enunciative power of those *who are telling the difference* (see Garber 1992: 130)? In what ways is 'passing' implicated in the very discourse around tellable differences? That is, we need to investigate how the disorganising of social identities can become a mechanism for the reorganising of social life through an expansion of the terms of surveillance (how are we to know 'the stranger' if we cannot see her?). The economy of desire 'to tell the difference' is itself an apparatus of knowledge which already fixes others into a certain place. Such an economy of desire to tell the difference assumes that the difference can be found somewhere on (or in) the bodies of strangers (on or underneath their skin). Strange bodies that do not fit existing criteria for identification keep in place, or are even the condition of possibility for, the desire to tell bodies apart from each other through the accumulation of knowledge.

So why consider passing as a mode of proximity to strangers in which 'the subject' is transformed? This question assumes there is a general logic to passing, and a general logic of 'the subject'. However, passing is not identifiable as a discrete practice that has discernible political effects. On the contrary, passing is intelligible only in relation to a complex set of social antagonisms; passing for white as a black subject has a very different relation to power than passing for black as a white subject. Equally, passing may function at the level of the intentional subject (the subject who seeks to pass in order to secure something otherwise unavailable to them), or it may function as a misrecognition on the part of others (one may pass for something other than one's self-identification but not seek to, or know it). Passing may be successful – in which case the difference between the subject and the image assumed becomes unrecognisable – or it may fail – the subject may be detected as 'not being' the identity assumed. Passing may not be a special case that we can speak of as throwing up a crisis of identity in and of itself.

And yet, we must resist the temptation of generalising passing as simply a condition of identity formation. I would problematise the shift in Carole Ann Tyler's work from her consideration of passing as 'a politically viable response to oppression', to the argument that, 'all subjects therefore are passing through the signifier which represents them for another' (1994: 212, 220). I would not deny that identity – any identity – involves passing in some form. It involves assuming an image that has no proper 'fit' with the structure of the subject; it is the act of assuming an image that constitutes the subject (passing demonstrates that the subject is the effect rather than the origin of a fantasy of being). However, the problem that resides with using this model of identification is that we can no longer differentiate between kinds of identifications and particular forms of 'crisis' over identity. If we take Lacan's definition of identification – 'the transformation that takes place in the subject when he assumes an image' (1977: 2) – we can consider how the misrecognition which founds or finds the subject involves an economy of difference. Rather than simply understanding identification as something that has already taken place in the formation of subjectivity, we can consider how identifications perpetually fail to grasp 'others' in social encounters. Subjects assume images that they cannot be or fully inhabit, but the images they assume are *already differentiated*: subjects and others become differentiated in the very moment that they are constituted as such (see Chapter 1).

So while the process of identification involves a form of passing – the transformation that takes place in the assumption of an image – we can still theorise how passing itself involves a form of social differentiation. Not only do we have the difference between images already assumed in social encounters with others (such as 'being assumed' as white or black), but in the temporal lag of passing for an-other, we have the potential of a difference between an image that is already assumed in and by a subject (however much the assumption does not hold or contain the subject), and an image that is *always yet to be assumed*. So, for example, I would argue that we can differentiate between a black subject who passes for white, and a white subject who passes for white. While whiteness is an assumed image which is often invisible, one's relation to whiteness as something which is passed through depends on a prior history of self-identification and identification by others. Would one fear being caught out, if one did not *already* perceive oneself to be passing for white? In other words, passing for something that one is not already assumed to be makes a difference to the politics of passing.

The difference between the black subject who passes as white and the white subject who passes as white is not then an *essential* difference that implies that blackness or whiteness simply exist before passing. Rather, it is a *structural* difference that demonstrates that passing involves the reopening or restaging of a fractured history of identifications that constitutes the limits to a given subject's mobility. To refuse that difference by arguing that passing constitutes a general logic of assuming an identity (since all identities belong, so to speak, to the Other), is to refuse to recognise the constraints that temporarily fix subjects in relations of social antagonism. The white subject who passes as white (that is, the subject already constituted as white by structures of identification that precede the encounter) has a degree of comfort and security about identity as the crisis of not-being is, so to speak, hidden from memory (it is not representable or liveable as such).

In much Black feminist literature, there is a reflection on how passing as white takes place given the invisibility of the mark of whiteness as a mark precisely of its privilege. As Jayne O. Ifekwunigwe, argues there is a 'prevailing and inconsistent social and political stance that anyone who does not look white is seen as black' (1997: 210). We can turn this around and emphasise that one is assumed to be white unless one looks black. Here, 'looking black' becomes a deviation from the normalised state of 'being white'. Passing as white hence guarantees a form of social assimilation in which the gaze of others hesitates only upon those that are already marked as different (such a hesitation on strange bodies allows the 'community' to imagine itself as unmarked and hence white). Harryette Mullen's reflection on passing for white emphasises how the individual and familial acts of passing become mechanisms for the re-creation of the nation space (1994: 72). Passing as white supports a national desire to assimilate difference into a generalised white 'face of the nation'. The spatial configuration of communities of belonging involves the legitimation of passing for white as an individual and national story of progress.

Passing as white allows both the redefinition of (nation) space – the white community assimilates the difference – and a renarrativisation of the history of the nation/subject (a forgetting of the forms of racial antagonism that are concealed by the white nation face). Passing becomes narratable as an individual act only through being *joined* to forms of social and national belonging in which being passed as white, by others, allows one to pass into an invisible and privileged community. The difference between the white subject who passes as white and the black subject who passes as white is determined by a different relation to this imaginary space: the crisis of 'not belonging' for the black subject who passes becomes then a crisis of knowledge, of knowing there is always a danger of *being seen*.

A consideration of passing as constitutive of such contradictory social identifications involves an understanding of the processes whereby subjects come to be seen as 'having' a prior and fixed identity. The erasure of that process from regimes of knowledge involves the erasure of the social conflicts which structure inter-subjectivity. If passing can be seen as threatening, it is in the making visible of the fractured history (the time, the labour and the crisis) that is concealed by identity. Through fetishism, identity hides passing, and by hiding passing, identity hides the conflict and antagonism that determines the 'work' needed to be done to reproduce a given sociality.

Passing then cannot be simply theorised as a logic of the subject (= the transformation that takes place in the subject when she or he assumes an image). Rather, we can consider how passing takes place through strange encounters with embodied others in which there is a crisis of reading, a crisis that hesitates over the gap between an image that is already assumed and an image that is yet to be assumed. Given this, passing is not best understood as an event that is clearly definable in time and space. Passing, by definition, is a movement through and across. Passing as the literal act of moving through space (in which there is no moment of departure or arrival), can be linked with passing as a set of cultural and embodied practices (passing for others). In the act of passing through a given place one does not come to a halt and inhabit that place. Likewise, in the act of passing for an-other, or passing through the image of an-other, one does not come to inhabit the image in which 'one' moves (away from one-self). Acts of passing cannot be thought of as events: they involve encounters between others whose boundaries are not fixed. Passing involves strange encounters: encounters where 'what is encountered' is under dispute. Such encounters represent precisely the impossibility of fixing the meaning of passing; it is the undecidable moment that repeats itself as others are addressed, as we address each other.

Take the following event.[8] I was stopped by two policemen in a car when walking near my home in Adelaide when I was 14. The first policeman asked, 'are you Aboriginal?' I replied no, rather indignantly. The second policemen winked and said, 'it's just a sun-tan, isn't it?' I smiled and did not reply. One must note that the first policeman's assumption of his right to stop and interrogate me operated through the politically sanctioned conflation between Aboriginality and criminality. My denial of being Aboriginal and my failure to name or declare my 'race' (which of course was unnoticed or invisible to them) implicated me in their structure of address, by rendering Aboriginality something to be disavowed. The gesture of smiling can here be figured as a collusion, a desire in some sense to be figured as white, as respectable, as somebody who has a legitimate right to walk in these leafy suburbs (to be read not as a stranger, but as a neighbour). Or it could be read as motivated by fear; fear of being positioned as a suspect who must be excluded.

The exchange of glances and the hailing of the policemen did not simply interpellate me as a subject. It also opened out a space in which the subject becomes 'unfixed' by almost, but not quite, 'fitting' the visual prompt that triggers identity thinking. The difference in passing, as Carole Ann Tyler has suggested, is an uncanny one (1994: 212). Or, to put it differently, it is a disturbance that lacks a sign. I have taken up elsewhere how the reference to sun-tanning in this address positions me as a white woman, as a woman whose colour is not natural or real, but is a sign of her proper attention to the cultivation of her body (Ahmed 1998b). Tanned colour is understood as an adornment and not a stain, as 'a paying attention to the body'. The colour of my body is read as a detachable signifier, a 'mask' that can be put on and taken off, inessential to the subject, and hence acceptable. By reading colour as a mask rather than as essential (as something on the skin rather than of the skin), the exchange rendered my body something to be valued, adorned, protected. Colour became inscribed as a detachable signifier, positioning me as essentially white, as truly and properly white underneath the luxury of a brown veil. Inscribed as a white woman, I became the legitimate object of the policeman's protective gaze.

The reference to sun-tanning enabled me then to pass as a white woman, and to pass into the white neighbourhood (see Chapter 1). Now, between these two addresses – to the Aboriginal woman and the (sun-tanned) white woman – something slipped beyond, something passed through. No, not some-thing. There is no nameable object that was not spoken. The language could not name what was beyond the two identifications. Passing here allows mobility precisely through not being locatable as an object that meets the gaze of the subject; passing here passes through the limits of representation and intentionality. That mobility has its limits precisely in *the reopening of histories of encounter which violate and fix subjects*. The policemen necessarily return to interrogate those they see as not white, or as not quite, not white (see Bhabha 1994). So while passing unfixes by the impossibility of naming the difference, it also fixes. In this example, fixation occurs by the policeman resolving the crisis of an uncertain identity by re-reading the ambiguous body according to a pre-existing regime of identity cards: if not Aboriginal, then sun-tanned, then white. Passing here involves both fixation and the impossibility of fixation determined through strange encounters between embodied others within the context of law.

As Ellen Brinks points out, the passing subject desires to become (like) the other (1995: 4). In this process of miming and approximating the identity of an-other, 'identity' itself becomes decontextualised. The traversing of distinct identities materialises itself in *the discontinuities of the subject's biography*. In miming the identity of an other, identity itself becomes an object of exchange that resists the realms of the proper and property. How to approximate her look? How to look white? Here, in desiring to capture an identity, the subject has to work and labour. It takes time and knowledge to see the difference that one may desire (or need) to assume. The labour that is hidden in the assumption of identity as self-presence is re-created on the surface of the subject who passes. But passing does not just reveal the labour and antagonism that is concealed by identity. It also reproduces identity as a fetish, by rendering it an object that can be known, seen and approximated. If I desired to pass for a particular other, I can imagine myself saying: 'Look, this is what you are, so I will become you. I will move, talk, eat, smell and be like you. By adopting your dress and manner, I will pass for you.' The subject who seeks to pass may assume *the knowability of strangers* (see Chapter 3). The contradictions embedded in passing suggest the impossibility of placing passing on one side or the other of identity politics. While identity may be dislodged through the act of theft, and hence become subject to reiteration, it also determines the economics of passing, that which it takes for granted as the measure of desire.

How does passing constitute rather than simply transgress identity? Passing for the one who is already recognised as the stranger (who is estranged from the dominant narrative of the self, home and nation) has a particular set of effects. Passing for black as a white subject can certainly assume a knowable stranger and can fetishise the stranger's body (by approximating its image). Such an assumption of a stranger's image in which there is a perpetual reconfirmation of the knowability of strangers is clearly evident in John Griffin's *Black Like Me*. This text is an autobiographical account of a white man who receives medical help to alter the colour of his skin so that he can 'discover' the truth of being black. It is quite clear that the story about the truth of the Negro involves a fetishising of skin colour. By altering his skin, the narrator becomes a Negro: 'How else except by becoming a Negro could a white man hope to learn the truth?' (Griffin 1970: 9). Here, the becoming-black of the skin is reducible to the assumption of a true and proper Negro identity. He asks himself, will they realise I am the same man, 'or will they treat me as some nameless Negro?' The reply is, 'As soon as they see you, you'll be a Negro' (Griffin 1970: 12). One becomes a Negro in the event of being seen as black, in being found and fixed in the horrified gaze (or 'hate stare') of others. The relation between identity and looking is demonstrated when the narrator catches his image in the mirror:

> In the flood of light against white tile, the face and shoulders of a stranger – a fierce, bald, very dark Negro – glared at me from the glass. He in no way resembled me.
>
> The transformation was total and shocking. I had expected to see myself disguised, but this was something else. I was imprisoned in the flesh of an utter stranger, an unsympathetic one with whom I felt no kinship. All traces of the John Griffin I had been were wiped from existence. Even the senses underwent a change so profound it filled me with distress. I looked into the mirror and saw reflected nothing of the white John Griffin's past. No, the reflections led back to Africa, back to the shanty and the ghetto, back to the fruitless struggles against the mark of blackness. Suddenly, almost with no mental preparation, no advance hint, it became clear and it permeated my whole being. My inclination was to fight against it. I had gone too far. I knew now that there is no such thing as a disguised white man, when the black won't rub off. The black man is wholly a Negro, regardless of what he once may have been. I was a newly created Negro who must go out that door and live in a world unfamiliar to me.
>
> (Griffin 1970: 18–19)

Here, the transformation of skin colour from white to black becomes causally linked to a total personal and collective transformation. Skin in this way is seen to hold the 'truth' of the subject's identity (like a 'kernel') as well as functioning as the scene of the subject's memory and history (with a black skin there is no *trace* of his previous identity).[9] The essentialising image of his black skin leading (back) to Africa creates an absolute link between skin colour and racial origin. His transformation into a stranger, where he passes as black in the mirror, produces the naked face of a black man, a face that immediately gets coded as fierce and glaring, as monstrous and bestial. In passing as black in his own mirror image, the vision of the black face is hence over-determined by the 'knowledges' available of blackness central to the violence of colonialism. In other words, what one sees as the stranger (or in oneself, as one passes for the stranger) is already structured by the knowledges that keep the stranger in a certain place.

Passing involves an apparatus of knowledge that masters the stranger by taking its place. Within such a narrative, it is 'the stranger's body' which is assumed or inhabited: 'I was imprisoned in the flesh of an utter stranger, an unsympathetic one with whom I felt no kinship.' Griffin sees himself both *as* a stranger, and as imprisoned *by* the stranger. He sees himself as inhabiting the figure and the body of the stranger insofar as he sees himself as black (*Black Like Me*). The black skin is both seen and inhabited *as* the stranger's skin. In this way, the taking of the place of 'the stranger' involves the fixing of the association between the strange and those embodied others who appear to hesitate at the boundary lines of nations and homes: being estranged from one-self by passing for a stranger is hence narratable only as a story of 'being imprisoned' by flesh. Passing for the stranger turns the stranger's flesh into a prison – it reduces the stranger to flesh that can only be inhabited as a temporary loss of freedom. The stranger becomes known as the prison of flesh through the fantasy that one can pass, that is, that *one can pass through the stranger's body*.

Passing as black as a form of appropriation/knowledge is central to Gail Ching-Liang Low's concerns in *White Skins/Black Masks: Representation and Colonialism* (1996). In successfully passing, the white subject inhabits the place of the other; the possibility of surveillance is expanded, exceeding the divisions imposed by time and space. The act of passing is informed by a hegemonic white masculinity, the ability to be anywhere, at any time. Such a fantasy of 'going native', while threatening to some anthropological models of the other as always already the stranger, becomes a mechanism for the reconstitution of the other *through* the hegemonic self. Indeed, Low shows how the fantasy of 'going native' works as a theatrical display which, like fetishism, both affirms and disavows the difference (1996: 203). The difference is disavowed in the assumption that the subject has assumed the place of the other; and yet in assuming the place of the other rather than simply being the other, the difference is perpetually reaffirmed. The fantasy, for example, seeks to uncover a glimpse of white skin beneath the native costume (Low 1996: 203).[10] Passing is here the fantasy of an ability (or a technique) *to become without becoming*.

Passing for black as a white man can demonstrate the labour involved in the assumption of a white, masculine identity. It puts on display the other within the face of the same in order to manage and contain that other (= the domestication of the other). Through adopting or taking on signifiers of the subordinated other, passing becomes a mechanism for reconstituting or reproducing the other as the 'not-I' *within* rather than *beyond* the structure of the 'I'. Hence, when Griffin looks in the mirror he can say with conviction, 'he in no way resembles me'. The split between the 'he' and 'I' is seeable within the mirror image of the face. Passing for black as a white man can be understood as an 'ability' insofar as it is a technique; it is a set of practices through which knowledge of strangers functions to affirm a white, masculine identity (to affirm the structure of the white face).

Significantly, with the shifts in form of racism towards a fetishising of cultural rather than biological difference (Balibar 1991: 22), passing for black has become an increasingly powerful individual and national fantasy. Passing for black is enabled by 'adopting' elements of black culture, a process of adoption which then fixes and freezes those elements as indicators of what it means to be black. In Sunderland's sympathetic account of white women who pass as black, she emphasises how these women imagine and project what it means to 'be black'. To quote from one of her interviewees:

'And I find that very much about black people. You know I think, um. I just find the warmth there' (Sunderland 1997: 40). While Sunderland clearly supports this representation of the white self through claiming affiliation with black culture – for her this indicates a shift towards a recognition of mixed identities (1997: 53) – we can be more cautious. Not only is there a fetishising and exoticising of blackness at stake. We also have the re-creation of the white subject as the one *who knows the difference*, even if that difference is no longer seen as external to the self and community. The white feminine subject becomes re-created through her *sympathy* for strangers (the stranger's warmth). They become a means through which she can *know herself* (as black), by providing what is lacking in her self. Passing for black is a technique of knowledge insofar as it remains tied to the narrativisation of the white female subject's knowledge of herself through her sympathetic incorporation of others (by assuming an image of blackness, it becomes known as that which is lacking in the white self).[11] The narrativisation of hybrid and mixed identities expands the force of mastery as beyond the limitations of the singular face. The face of the dominant self and nation expands through hybridity; it expands by passing for what it is not (hence allowing 'the stranger' to exist within 'the native face'). One can consider how such individuated acts of passing legitimate the national fantasy of multiculturalism, in which one passes for strangers by adopting or assuming *their style*.

Multicultural national spaces and multicultural bodies come to be inhabited precisely through the construction of assimilable difference: difference becomes a style that the white nation and body can put on and take off. Consuming, becoming and passing are hence techniques that confirm the subject's ability to 'be itself' by getting closer to, and incorporating some strangers (a form of proximity that produces the figure of the stranger as *that which can be taken in*). Although, as my reading of *Dances with Wolves* suggested, the figure of the stranger may be produced as that which can be taken in only by the simultaneous production of the figure of the stranger stranger, *who may yet be expelled by this very act of taking in*. What is clear in the narratives offered of consuming, passing and becoming is the reduction of the stranger to the level of being, and the association of being with the body: hence to consume, become or pass as the stranger is always to pass through, or move through, the stranger's body. The very techniques of consuming, becoming and passing are informed by access to cultural capital and knowledges embedded in colonial and class privilege which give the dominant subject the ability to move and in which 'the stranger' is assumed to be *knowable, seeable and hence be-able*. In the end, 'the stranger' becomes 'the truth' insofar as it exists to confirm the ability of the Western self to find the truth: 'How else except by becoming a Negro could a white man hope to learn the truth?' (Griffin 1970: 9).

Part III

Beyond stranger fetishism

7 Ethical encounters

The other, others and strangers

> If the other is not my enemy (as he sometimes is in Hegel – albeit a be-
> nevolent one – and especially in the early writings of Sartre), then how can
> he become the one who wrests me from my identity and whose proximity
> (for he is my neighbour) wounds, exhausts, and hounds me, tormenting me
> so that I am bereft of my selfhood and so that this torment, this lassitude
> which leaves me destitute becomes my responsibility?
>
> (Blanchot 1986: 22)

I am mesmerised by the poetics of Blanchot's writing about 'the writing of
the disaster'. It is a writing that poses the question of 'the other' as a
question to itself and of itself. It hesitates and pauses as it writes of 'the
other' and as it turns the other into a question that troubles the very concept
of selfhood, at the same time as it fleshes out the self, allowing it to appear
in writing as tormented, vulnerable and tired, faced as it is, right from the
very beginning, with the face of the other. The question of 'the other' as
posed by Maurice Blanchot, in the horizon in which one cannot not glimpse
the ghostly presence of Emmanuel Levinas, is essentially a philosophical one,
not in the sense that his writing contributes to an ethical philosophy
(although it may do so), but in the sense that he demonstrates, with Levinas,
that the whole philosophical enterprise can only be written as about 'being'
and the adjacent questions of identity, essence and truth, with a prior
forgetting of the intimate responsibility for the other who is, in a very
precise sense, 'before' being, as that which makes being possible. Philosophy
is ethics, and can only betray itself as ethics, if it forgets its intimate
responsibility for the other.

Blanchot's writing of the disaster, as a writing of and for the other, begins
with the refusal to identify the other as enemy. We can recall Plato's analogy
between philosophers and guard dogs that suggests that the ability to
smell/tell the difference between friend and enemy is essential to philosophy
itself. In such an analogy, a link is forged between knowledge and community: philosophy is about the love of knowledge insofar as it can establish a
boundary line between friends (other 'nosey' philosophers) and enemies or
strangers (those who do not know, the savage, or the non-philosopher).

Rather than define the other as the enemy, Blanchot admits to the proximity of the other, the other's nearness, and the impossibility of fully excluding the other from the (philosophical) body. The other, then, the one whom I may not know, is always my neighbour, living by my side, living 'with' me. The other is the 'stranger neighbour': she is distant in the sense that I cannot assume community or commonality with her, and yet she is close by, so that she will haunt me, stay with me, as a reminder of the unassimilable in my life, or that which cannot be assimilated into the 'my' of 'my life'. The pain of the other's nearness suggests that encountering the other opens the self to the world, an opening that touches the self, makes it feel: the self becomes an opening, a boundless space of torment, the tiredness of being by the other, and of being with and for that which is *not yet*.

The turn to ethics in the poetic and philosophical writings of Blanchot and Levinas is hence bound up with the figure of 'the other'. To this extent, ethics is about encountering that which is 'beyond' and 'before' being: ethical philosophy involves the critique of ontology, which starts out with the question of 'what is', or what it is 'to be'. In such writing, ethics is quite distinct from morality, if understood as a set of rules or codes for conduct. Ethics is instead a question of how one encounters others *as* other (than being) and, in this specific sense, how one can live with what cannot be measured by the regulative force of morality. Importantly, then, a concern with ethics involves a rethinking of the relationship between philosophy – and by implication, community – and the/its other.

So, for example, Levinas's ethics also involves a critique of Heidegger's fundamental ontology, despite the fact that Heidegger's concern with the question of 'being' – and the ontological difference between Being and beings – emphasises 'withness' (*Mitsein*) and dwelling. Levinas suggests that ontology privileges 'home' and the world only insofar as it is here or mine. He contrasts the homeliness of ontology with ethics and metaphysics, which start from here, but go elsewhere: 'It is turned toward the "elsewhere" and the "otherwise" and the "other". For in the most general form it has assumed in the history of thought it appears as a movement going forth from a world that is familiar to us ... from an "at home" [*chez soi*] which we inhabit, towards an alien outside-of-oneself [*hors-de-soi*] towards a yonder' (Levinas 1979: 33). Levinas's ethics of the infinite is bound up, not just with 'the other' as such, but with the strange and the stranger: such a thinking thinks itself as moving from the familiar to the strange, from proximity to distance, and from here to there.

We need to hesitate on this question of the relationship between ontology and ethics, and the familiar and strange. Levinas suggests that the ontological enterprise involves a form of violence against the otherness of 'the other' to the extent that the posing of the question of being must first incorporate others into the same (being it-self). But, as Derrida points out in his critique of Levinas's critique of Heidegger, the posing of an opposition between ontology and ethics is itself problematic for its ontological implications: it implies that the question of being can be posed without a detour through the other, in the first place (Derrida 1978). We can consider how the question of being, of what it means to be in the world, can only be thought through, and in relation to others, as that which exceeds being, and makes it possible. As I have already argued, if we think of 'home' purely as proximity and familiarity, then we fail to recognise the relationships of estrangement and distance within the home (see Chapter 4). The opposition between being and the other, as with home and away, needs to be called into question.

What we need is an analysis of how philosophy already encounters others in its very turn to ontology. If we think of philosophy as a body of knowledge (and like all bodies, it is with other bodies, and with them in a certain way), then we can consider the encounter between philosophy and its others in terms of bodily processes (see Chapter 2). In my analysis of strangers and knowledge, for example, I discussed Plato's understanding of philosophy as a sneeze: the guard dogs and philosophers 'smell' the strangers (again, they have to be close enough) and by sneezing (a practice so habitual that it has become an autonomic reflex), expel the strangers from the philosophical body, or the body of the good philosopher (see Chapter 3). Other forms of bodily expulsion might be shitting and vomiting, both of which imply a process of partial incorporation as well as expulsion: the other/stranger must be taken in, and digested, before what is undesirable is both trans-formed and expelled. In light of Levinas's own critique of ontology, including Heidegger's fundamental ontology, we might consider the ontological encounter as a form of *eating* and digestion: the other is valued as that which one is *with*, but only insofar as it can be taken in by, and incorporated into, the philosophical body (or into the thinking of being). Levinas's distinction between need and desire in *Totality and Infinity* corresponds to his distinction between ontology and ethics: 'in need I can sink my teeth into the real and satisfy myself in assimilating the other; in Desire there is no sinking one's teeth into being, no satiety, but an uncharted future before me' (1979: 117). By defining desire as beyond need and the assimilation of the other, Levinas calls for an ethical encounter that does not satisfy the ego – that does not fill it up – but which is beyond its grasp. In this sense, his ethics is about finding a better way of encountering the other which allows the other to live, as that which is beyond 'my' grasp, and as that which cannot be assimilated or digested into the ego or into the body of a community.

Levinasian ethics slides between the descriptive and the prescriptive: using the best aspects of the phenomenological tradition he cannot fail to inherit, Levinas provides thick and poetic descriptions of how the other is encountered in the forming of the self (such encounters are primordial and hence before being), at the same time as he suggests ways of encountering the other, that are *better* than others, in the sense that they may allow the other to exist beyond the grasp of the present. These better ways of encountering the other are, in part, described through bodily processes: in *Totality and Infinity*, Levinas describes the caress, the erotics of touch, as a form of encounter that does not grasp, but which 'consists in seizing upon nothing, in soliciting what ceasingly escapes its form towards a future never future enough, in soliciting what slips away as though it *were not yet*' (1979: 258). Later, in *Otherwise than Being*, Levinas describes breathing as a way of encountering the other that does not grasp the other, or turn the other into a theme or thing, 'breathing is a transcendence in the form of an opening up' (1991: 181). Breathing is contrasted to other forms of encounter such as building, insofar as it simply opens the self to the other, a proximity or exposure that is traced in and through the air that is breathed and that, in the cold, can be seen, but only as an indeterminate mist coming from the body. Breathing does not establish territory or fix the relation between self and other, and yet breathing is that which allows one and the other to live in a co-inhabitance that is not premised on the commonality of a bond, but on the intangibility of air. Quite clearly, then, although Levinasian ethics does not prescribe a strict set of codes, norms or rules of conduct, it still has a normative basis; it differentiates better from worse ways of being with (or, more precisely, for) others. The criteria which allow Levinas to prefer some bodily processes over others as ways of encountering the other (breathing and caressing over eating and grasping) are clearly that some processes are more able to protect or preserve the otherness of the other.

What are the problems of defining ethical encounters in terms of protecting the otherness of the other? One could construct an argument that questions the very normative basis of the Levinasian discourse on otherness – that is, that questions why it is the case that some forms of encounter are assumed to be better than others or, to put it more strongly, why preserving the otherness of the other is *necessarily* a good thing. However, there is a more generous reading of Levinas that would ask us to question the role of the 'encounter' in the determination of the relationship between philosophy and its other. If we return to sneezing and eating as two forms of encounter that violate the otherness of the other, we can begin to question whether it is 'the other' at stake in this violence at all. For as my reading of Plato's analogy between guard dogs and philosophers suggested (see Chapter 3), the philosopher does not simply differentiate friends from strangers in order to expel the strangers. Rather, the processes of recognition and expulsion produce the very figure of the stranger in the first place. We can see a parallel between the processes of sneezing and eating in philosophy and the construction of other bodies and spaces: for example, my reading of multicultural national imaginaries emphasised how processes of incorporation and expulsion involve the figuring of 'the stranger' as the 'outsider within' (see Chapter 5). The figure of 'the stranger neighbour' is not the one whom we might welcome in an ethical encounter (by not grasping). Rather, the figure of the stranger is an *effect of the processes that imagine 'it' can either be taken in, welcomed or expelled in the first place.*

As I have already suggested, the recognition of strangers is a way of assimilating the unassimilable into the body (including the body of imagined communities such as philosophy). At the same time, there is always a left-over, there is always something that exceeds the recognition of an other as either friend or stranger (precisely because both terms lack a secure referent – there are no friends or strangers, but only those who are recognised as such, and who are 'missed' in this moment of recognition). In this chapter, I suggest that an ethical mode of encountering others is a way of working with that which fails to be contained within ontology (being), but also the figures of 'the stranger' or 'the other'. An ethics based on 'Yes-saying to the stranger' (Critchley 1992: 219) is hence inadequate. My task here is to think about the role of the particular and finite, as well as economy and difference, in decoupling the relationship between philosophy and itself, and philosophy and the other. Not only do we need to examine how encounters produce the figures of 'the other' and 'the stranger' in the first place, but we also need to consider how others and strangers are differentiated, such that there is never simply an encounter between self and self, or between self and other. There is always more than one *and* more than two in any encounter. In this chapter, I deal with multiple encounters: I encounter Levinasian ethics and Derrida's ethics of hospitality alongside the work of Gayatri Spivak and Mahasweta Devi. This chapter provides an attempt, necessarily inadequate, to consider the ethical implications of my investigation of the relationship between 'strangers' and identity formations. Such an investigation requires a more proper and rigorous thinking of what it means to 'encounter' an other in the first place.

The other and others

Levinasian ethics begins with 'the other' and, in so doing, defines itself against ontology. This much may seem clear. But Levinas's texts cannot themselves be grasped through this simple formula. Others have attempted to do so. For example, Colin Davis in his introduction to Levinas's thought, describes Levinasian philosophy as entailing, 'a reorientation of the whole philosophical project. Rather than just talking *about* the other, the philosophical texts become engaged in the project of giving the other voice, or trying to find an idiom in which the other may be heard' (1996: 144). He then describes Levinas's texts as, 'the philosophical counterpart of those seeking in numerous theoretical and practical ways to empower traditionally muted or disenfranchised groups' (Davis 1996: 144). In such a representation, Levinas is read as *on the side of* the others, those who are marginalised, or who are disempowered.

Certainly, in Levinas's work, the other is the weak, the poor and the marginal: the relationship to the other is always asymmetrical (1987: 83).

However, what is at stake in reading Levinas as being on the side of the other? First, it assumes that it is possible to take the other's side through philosophical language: in terms of Levinas's thought, the act of taking sides would certainly already thematise the other as *some-thing* or *some-body* that one can be for. As I have argued elsewhere, while Levinas's revisiting of philosophies that have prioritised the ontological may involve a critique of how otherness has been domesticated, his texts also assume the impossibility of rescuing the other from this entrapment in the obligation to thought or thinking (Ahmed 1998a: 59). On the one hand, to be on the other's side would be to grasp the other. On the other, the other is already grasped through the very languages in which thought can be said. As a result, the relationship between Levinasian ethics and 'the other' is neither one of siding nor of not siding. The difficulty of the relationship between the texts and 'the other' is part of the project – to reduce that difficulty is to make it appear as possible to rescue the other from philosophy through philosophy, an appearance which would also be a disappearance, insofar as it would preserve the fantasy that one can find and present the other, in philosophy, as such.

How then can the other be written otherwise in philosophical writing? How does the other *appear* in Levinas's texts? In *Differences that Matter*, I attempted to examine how Levinas writes the other *as* the other, by employing various figures of the other, including the widow, the poor and the orphan (all of which appear in the Bible, as figures for the needy whom one should welcome and help), whose specificity he then erases (1998a: 60–61). Here, I want to examine how 'the other' itself is figured, or already recognised, *in the very event of being named as 'the other'*. One way of beginning this critique is to think through how asymmetry may function both as a way of describing the mode of encounter, and then as a *character* of the other. To talk about the other as having the character of asymmetry is surely to fill the other in, to know the other as being in a certain way, and thus to ontologise the other as a being, albeit an alien one. This might seem, then, an un-Levinasian move – it defines the other as other only insofar as it is an-other being. Yet in *Time and the Other*, 'the other' is always the weak one, and this weakness is constitutive of what the other, in some sense, is. To name others as 'the other' and as being characterised by otherness is, in a contradictory or paradoxical way, to contain the other within ontology. That is, the nature of being becomes alien being: 'The other's *entire being* is constituted by its exteriority, or rather its alterity' (Levinas 1987: 76; emphasis added).

Derrida's critique of Levinas is on the opposite grounds. Derrida suggests, in his defence of Husserl, that the other must be understood as an *alter ego*, if its otherness is to be ethically preserved: 'The other, then, would not be what he is (my fellow man as foreigner) if he were not alter ego. A necessity due to the finitude of meaning: the other is absolutely other only if he is an ego, that is, in a certain way, if he is the same as I' (1978: 127). In contradis-tinction to Derrida, I would argue that by describing the other as having the character of otherness, Levinas does imply that the other is other because he is an-other being, despite his explicit refusal to define or flesh out the other within the language of ontology. In this sense, like Derrida and Drucilla Cornell (1992: 52), Levinasian ethics is premised on both ethical asymmetry and on phenomenological symmetry: the other is radically other than me, but as his being is characterised by such otherness, he is, like me, a being. Why is this problematic?

To describe 'the other' as having the character of 'otherness' is to recognise the other in a certain way: the other is abstracted from particular others (the 'the' turning the other into an article of speech). Through that abstraction, the other becomes a fetish: it is assumed to contain otherness within the singularity of its form ('entire being'). Such a cutting off of 'the other' from the modes of encounter in which one meets an-other allows 'the other' to appear in Levinas's texts as an alien being, whom one might then encounter, in the *entirety* of that very form. This model – which may rest on a concealed phenomenological distinction between beings and alien beings – hence both thematises the other in a particular way (as 'the other'), as it conceals that thematisation by defining 'the other' as beyond thematisation. The question of ethics, then, cannot be asked given the prior act of separation of 'the other' as 'alien being' from the particular and worldly encounters in which beings are constituted in and through their relationship to one another. The signifier, 'the other', which is assumed to contain otherness as a character of its 'entire being', hence operates to conceal the particularity of others, who may be other than this alien being.

In much of the criticism on Levinasian ethics, it is presumed that to describe or name or even to imagine the other as a particular other is to psychologise that other as a being with characteristics I am willing to respect. Zygmunt Bauman, for example, suggests that the response to Levinas which queries, 'Surely the other is not merely a face, but somebody's face' is misguided (1993: 74). Such a response fails to read Levinas insofar as it assumes the other can be presented as a particular being, and hence moves from the primordial domain of ethics – which is before being – to sociality (being with others) and ontology (being). Bauman does not mention the contradictions in Levinas's work on the question of being and otherness – as I have suggested, Levinas does describe the other as an alien being, even though, in other places, he defines the other as before and beyond being. Bauman also implies that the particular other – the some-body whose face might arrest our gaze – can only be a force in the ethical relation given the presumption that this other is already constituted as another being. He hence collapses sociality (being with) into ontology (being).[1] If we think of the encounter as sociality – that 'being' only emerges through and with others – then we can think about how meetings between particular others do not necessarily presuppose a meeting between two already constituted beings (in the introduction to this book, I argued quite the opposite – encounters are prior to ontology, the concept of separate beings is produced through the encounter, rather than preceding it). By attending to the encounters that take place between others, within particular or finite circumstances, we may open up the possibility of an ethics that is not only 'beyond being', but which would also resist thematising others as 'the other'.

Cynthia Willett provides a critique of Levinas's effacement of difference and particularity in her book, *Maternal Ethics and Other Slave Moralities*. She argues that, 'Without the possibility of individual self-expression, the Other is denuded of its speaking. Denuded of her accents, cries [and] lamentations, the Other is, precisely in her concrete difference, that is, in her embodied specificity, effaced' (Willett 1995: 81). However, there is a need for caution here. According to Willett's position, what is missing in Levinas is precisely an account of individual self-expression, concrete difference and embodied specificity. She presumes that by moving beyond the infinite nature of the Levinasian other, we can *gain access to* the concrete difference and embodied specificity of this other at the level of her individual self-expression. Such an argument does involve a certain psychologism: it assumes the possibility that we can make an other present at the level of her individual expression – that we can simply hear what she has to say. This assumption that we can access her difference does precisely imagine that 'the other' can be grasped in the 'this-ness' of an other.²

To introduce particularity is not necessarily to assume the other is grasp-able in 'this other'. One possibility is to avoid using particularity as a description of an other, which turns 'this-ness' into a property of her body or her speech. Instead, we can begin to think of particularity as a question of *modes of encounter* through which others are faced. That is, we can move our attention from the particularity of an other, to the particularity of modes of encountering others. Such an approach would avoid assuming that we can gain access to the individual expression or the 'real' of her body. Particularity does not belong to an-other, but names the meetings and encounters that produce or flesh out others, and hence *differentiates others from other others*. In this sense, introducing particularity at the level of encounters (the sociality of the 'with') helps us to move beyond the dialectic of self-other and towards a recognition of the differentiation between others, and their different function in constituting identity, and the permeability of bodily space (see Chapter 2).

Quite clearly, then, I am calling for an approach to the particular that does not assume it is simply present on the body or face of this other. We might begin by rethinking the very notion of what it might mean to face an other, to face her face, to be faced by her. To name her as particular in the face-to-face encounter is in danger of reifying the very moment of the face to face: it locates the particular in a present moment (or present body), and hence associates the particular with the here and the now (with what I am faced with). In contrast, I would suggest that we need to complicate the very notion of the face to face by discussing the temporal and spatial dislocations that are implicated in the very possibility of being faced by this other. Certainly, this is partly about locating the encounter in time and space: *what*

are the conditions of possibility for us meeting here and now? The particularity of
the meeting is hence bound up with a notion of generality, with a movement
outwards, and towards other others, who are already implicated in the face to
face. If we begin to think of the relationship between ethics and difference,
then we can examine differentiation as something that happens at the level
of the encounter, rather than 'in' the body of an other with whom I am
presented. So, for example, rather than thinking of gender and race as
something that this other *has* (which would thematise this other as always
gendered and racialised *in a certain way*), we can consider how such
differences are determined at the level of the encounter, insofar as the
immediacy of the face to face is affected by broader social processes, that also
operate elsewhere, and in other times, rather than simply in the present
(though this is where they may be presented or faced).

Given this, to discuss the particular modes of encounter (rather than
particular others), is also to open the encounter up, *to fail to grasp it*. We have
a *temporal* movement from the now to the not yet. We could ask, not only
what made this encounter possible (its historicity), but also what does it
make possible, what futures might it open up? At the same time, we have a
spatial movement from here to there. We need to ask, not only how did we
arrive here, at this particular place, but how is this arrival linked to other
places, to an elsewhere that is not simply absent or present? We also need to
consider how the *here-ness* of this encounter might affect *where we might yet be
going*. To describe, not the other, but the mode of encounter in which I am
faced with an other, is hence not to hold the other in place, or to turn her
into a theme, concept or thing. Rather, it is to account for the conditions of
possibility of being faced by her in such a way that she ceases to be fully
present in this very moment of the face to face, a non-present-ness which, at
one and the same time, opens out the possibility of facing something other
than this other, of something that may surprise the one who faces, and the
one who is faced (the not yet and the elsewhere).

Such an emphasis on particular modes of encounter involves a radical
rethinking of what it might mean to face (up to) others. Levinas is quite
clear that his notion of the face is not a phenomenology of the face: 'You
turn yourself towards the Other as toward an object when you see a nose,
eyes and a forehead, a chin and you can describe them. The best way of
encountering the other is not even to notice the colour of his eyes. When one
observes the colour of his eyes one is not in a social relationship with the
Other' (1985: 85–86). The best way of encountering an other is hence not to
notice the face's appearance, but to be in a direct relation to the face: the face
is presented to you.

I would suggest that the face is mediated, rather than simply presented to
the subject. However, that mediation does not take place at the level of
perception (like Levinas, I would not call for a phenomenology of the face),
but at the level of the encounter (sociality). The face-to-face encounter is
mediated precisely by that which allows the face to appear in the present as

such. It is through such a notion of the mediation of the face-to-face encounter that we can begin to encounter that which cannot be grasped in the face, and that which cannot be made present by the face. This is not a question of describing the face's appearance, but describing what is already at stake in allowing some faces to appear, to be encountered or faced, in the first place (the face is hence always an encounter, a matter of facing, or being faced). She is not found in her face: what is faced, as we face her face, is precisely that which cannot be contained and grasped in her face (in this sense, facialisation involves textuality: the face, as signifier, requires other signifiers, in order to be faced).

How does this emphasis on the particular modes of encounter, or of modes of facing (up to) an other, relate to an ethics of responsibility in the Levinasian sense? Does this emphasis on particular and finite encounters fail to do justice to the infinite nature of my responsibility, by naming who I might be responsible for? We can examine how a notion of infinite responsibility must respond to the finite and particular modes of encounter between others. Certainly, in Levinasian ethics, the responsibility for the other is infinite and before being:

> Responsibility for another is not an accident that happens to a subject, but precedes essence in it, has not awaited freedom, in which a com- mitment to another can be made. ... The word *I* means *here I am*, an- swering for everything and for everyone. Responsibility for the others has not been a return to oneself, but an exasperating contracting, which the limits of identity cannot retain.
>
> (1979: 114)

Here, powerfully, the responsibility for others is not only absolute and unconditional, but it also is the very condition of possibility for subjectivity and identity: prior to being, one is hostage to the other. What is prior to being, is also that which makes being as separation – as ego – impossible. Responsibility for others is what makes it impossible for one to be one-self – it is that which both constitutes identity and renders it impossible. Why is this important? Why is it that responsibility for others is prior to being and hence absolute and unconditional – as a responsibility for 'everything and everyone'? Clearly, if we make our responsibility conditional then we are occupying the regulative order of morality – we are relying upon distinc- tions of worth (or worthiness) and need, by saying, I am responsible more for you (for example, the needy or the poor), than I am for the others. Such an approach, by imposing conditions and hence limits on my responsibility, forecloses it: and, even more so, it imagines the possibility in which one *has been* responsible, in which one has measured out responsibility and fulfilled one's debt. To say that responsibility is infinite, is to imply that it is a debt that cannot be paid back, and hence that there is always a call, a demand, for a future response to an other *whom I may yet approach*. To assume that I have been responsible – to this or to that – is to measure out responsibility, to contain it, and hence to violate its condition of possibility altogether. To say that 'I am responsible' here and now is a form of irresponsibility: it refuses to accept the possibility of an approach of an-other other or, more simply, of an-other approach.

How then does my emphasis on the finite and particular modes of encountering others relate to this call for an infinite responsibility, for everything and for everyone? I want to suggest here, that the intimacy of response and responsibility needs to be rethought. To be responsible *for the other* is also, at the same time, to respond to the other, to speak to her, and to have an encounter in which something takes place. While responsibility is infinite – and cannot be satisfied in the present encounter – to respond is to be in the order of the finite and the particular. We need to recognise the infinite nature of responsibility, *but the finite and particular circumstances in which I am called on to respond to others*. A responsibility that does not respond to the particularity of the call for a response would be one that fails (or fails to fail in the right way). To respond to each other as if they were other *in the same way* would be a violence. One's infinite responsibility begins with the particular demands that an other might make, but the particularity of my response, cannot fulfil my responsibility: I cannot satisfy such demands, and fulfil my debt. How to respond to the particular at the same time as one takes responsibility for that which exceeds the particular would be the quest and the question of such an ethics.

How would such an ethics work? I can only begin with the particularity, then, of how I might encounter an other, an encounter that is always mediated, which is never simply here and now. I want to think through how I might encounter an other as text. Thinking of the other in terms of textuality is a way of recognising the mediation of the encounter without reducing that mediation to the order of the perceptive or intentional. Which text? What has touched me? There is a text I want to face. So I ask myself, I ask you: how did I encounter the text of Mahasweta Devi, a woman writer from India (and yet so much more than this)? My encounter with this text is mediated; it could only take place given the staging of other encounters, impossible to grasp in the present. I came to this text through the translation of Mahasweta Devi's writing, by the 'post-colonial' critic, Gayatri Spivak. This translation is itself a particular mode of encountering the other. Spivak writes of her act of translation, as a form of love and proximity that always fails to grasp the text, yet brings it to life in that failure, in the very act of transforming it into a different language, for a different audience. My encounter with this text must remember the particularity of that mode of translation, which allows the words on the page to be readable, legible in English to me, for me.

Spivak writes of translation in terms of an experience of the impossibility of ethics – the impossibility that pure presenting, pure communication can take place (an impossibility which is also what makes ethics possible). Through her encounter with Devi, through the singularity and the irreducibility of their meeting, this story can be presented to the reader of English. And yet, there is something that does not get across; there is something that remains a secret. The proximity of this translation as encounter hence leads, not to knowledge, communication or sympathy, but to a sense of the limits of what can be got across, to a sense of that which cannot be grasped in the present. That which cannot be grasped is mediated by this encounter; the response to the particularity of this text is also a response to the historical and colonial legacy of translation, in which English becomes the authorised language, and the subaltern woman is spoken for (see Chapter 3).

And so I face this text. I must respond to it. But in responding to this text, already mediated by the failed proximity of translation, I cannot fully face this text, I cannot transform the text into a face. I miss it. But, my missing of it, my failure to face up to it, is also an encounter with it, and engagement with it, and a responsibility for it. *Here I am*, working in Britain, reading English, unable to read the text in anything other than English. *Here I am*, arriving at this text due to the authorisation of the translator, whose name I know, given its value in the property system of Western Knowledge. I read the translator's preface and afterword. In fact, I have written on the translator's preface and afterword before, without reference to the translated text, and have even noted the irony without transforming that irony into labour. Now, I turn to this text, I work with it and for it, having already failed it. I face up to my complicity in not having read it before. I think of the histories and spaces that divide us, of the international and gendered division of labour that enables me to consume it, and the antagonism that cannot be overcome in the proximity of my reading, and yet which allows me to get close enough to face (up to) it. How to do justice to these differences, how to let them animate my reading, how to respond to the particularity of these modes of response without assuming I can live up to my responsibility, without assuming I can present myself to the text, or have it present itself to me? How to get closer, to take responsibility, and yet to take up the impossibility of that very gesture, at one and the same time?

I must come back, again, to this text, to this encounter with this text, as that which demands and exceeds my response. Before I can do this, I need to ask: how is it possible for me to respond to this text in a way which is generous, in a way which gives?

Welcoming the stranger?

In this section, I want to think about ways in which one can respond generously to others in particular encounters, and how such generosity might work with and against the impossible figure of 'the stranger'. In Levinas's writings, 'the stranger' appears as a figure everywhere, cropping up here and there with other figures (such as the poor, the widow, and the orphan) that can be found in the Bible, and that symbolise that the other is always the weak one, asking something of the subject, asking for a generous response. In *Totality and Infinity*, the stranger is distant, and yet close by: 'Neither possession nor the unity of number nor the unity of concepts link me to the Stranger [l'Étranger], the Stranger who disturbs the being at home with oneself [le chez soi]. ... But I, who have no concept in common with the Stranger, am, like him, without genus. We are the Same and the Other' (Levinas 1991: 39). The Stranger is the one who causes a disturbance in the very order of being as homeliness, as rest and respite. The Stranger is the other with whom one does not have anything in common – but who, in not being in common, one is, paradoxically, alike. The Stranger is the one to be loved: one must give to the stranger, as the one who is close by (the neighbour), as a giving without the assumption of commonality or return. As Derrida puts it, 'the neighbour [is] a distant stranger, according to the original ambiguity of the word translated as the "neighbour" to be loved' (1978: 105).

In *Totality and Infinity*, Levinas moves from the 'infinite distance of the Stranger' to, 'my orientation toward the Other' as a 'generosity' that is 'incapable of approaching the other with empty hands' (1979: 50). The powerful image of the full hands, the hands that give to the Other who has come close enough, despite the distance, does evoke a liberal notion of charity as benevolence, of the rich giving to the poor (without recognising what they have taken from the poor). And yet, it does more than this. As with Derrida's notion of the gift, there is no expectation of return, no exchange, or circulation of objects between hands (and yet, unlike Derrida's, Levinas's gift is defined as economic (1979: 50)). Derrida says, 'For there to be a gift, there must be no reciprocity, return, exchange, counter-gift or debt. If the other *gives* me *back* or owes me or has to give me back what I give him or her, then there will not be a gift, whether this restitution is immediate or whether it is programmed by a complex calculation of a long-term deferral or difference' (1992: 12). In Levinas's image of the approach as full hands, all there is is the gesture, the fullness of the gesture, which is not necessarily full of *something* (we must not know what the hands are carrying), but just full. The fullness is not that which one gives, but the very act of giving, without which one could not approach the stranger, without which one could not get close enough to have an ethical encounter with the one who is distant or remote. There is no exchange, no communication, no reciprocal gesture. The stranger becomes present in this ethical encounter as the one to whom one must give, endlessly, and without return. This endless obligation to give defines the form of hospitality as an opening to the other, an open home: 'Recollection in a home open to the Other – hospitality' (Levinas 1979: 172).

This notion of generosity and hospitality as an opening to that which is infinite and distant (partly figured as the stranger, partly as the other) finds a strong parallel with Maurice Blanchot's work. He suggests that the supplicant and stranger are one – and that the stranger is the one who might arrive at one's doorstep and whom one must therefore receive, as a host: 'Hospitality consists less in nourishing the guest than in restoring in him a taste for food by recalling him to the level of need, to a life where one can say and stand hearing said, "*And now, let us not forget to eat*" ' (Blanchot 1993: 95). Here, eating with those whom one has welcomed into one's home, those who are, in that moment, homeless, and yet who speak, is the condition of hospitality, *a way of being together with strangers*, without assimilating them fully into the home (eating with them, rather than, perhaps as in ontology and multiculturalism, eating them).

The critical literature on Levinasian ethics has placed considerable emphasis on his model of hospitality towards strangers (Vasseleu 1998: 103). Indeed, Jacques Derrida suggests, in his most recent and loving encounter with Levinas, that hospitality or 'welcoming' is the 'immense treatise' of *Totality and Infinity* (1999: 21). In his reading of Levinas, 'the stranger' is the one who is loved, if love is understood as an opening which does not reveal the presence or absence of the one who is loved: 'Who loves the stranger. Who loves the *stranger*? Whom else is there *to love?*' (Derrida 1999: 105). Hospitality is also bound up with the figure of the stranger in Edith Wyschogrod's ethics of remembering. She suggests that hospitality is *the act of welcoming in the absence of commonality;* it establishes 'a community of strangers' (Wyschogrod 1998: xvi).

However, as I have argued throughout this book, the 'stranger' cannot be simply used as a word to describe the one who is distant, the one whom I do not yet know. To name some-body as a stranger is already to recognise them, to know them again: the stranger becomes a commodity fetish that is circulated and exchanged in order to define the borders and boundaries of given communities. To welcome an other as a Stranger is to assimilate that which cannot be assimilated: it is to establish a community based on a principle of uncommonality in which their difference becomes 'our own' (see Chapter 5). The model of hospitality based on 'welcoming the stranger' assumes that to welcome the stranger *is* to welcome the unassimilable: it hence conceals how that very act of welcoming already assimilates others into an economy of difference. In order to problematise such a model of hospitality we need a double approach: first, *we need an analysis of the economies of differentiation that already assimilate others as the strangers* (which is economic in the precise sense of involving circuits of production, exchange and consumption); second, we need an analysis of how encounters with others who are already differentiated in this way *can move beyond the economic by welcoming, or being open or hospitable to, that which is yet to be assimilated.*

Derrida's approach to hospitality in *Aporias* suggests that hospitality might be an openness to that which is yet to be assimilated. Derrida introduces another term, 'the arrivant' as an attempt to signify the neutrality of *that* which arrives but also the singularity of *who* arrives (1993: 33). For Derrida, hospitality is premised on the very failure to recognise the one who arrives; it assumes that the event of an arrival is unexpected. The arrivant, 'does not cross a threshold separating the identifiable places, the proper and the foreign, the proper of the one and the proper of the other, as one would say that the citizen of a given identifiable border of another country as a traveller, an émigré or a political exile, a refugee or somebody who has been deported, an immigrant worker, a student or a researcher, a diplomat or tourist' (1993: 34). If the arrivant is to disrupt the identity of place and property, then she or he must not be identifiable as coming from a particular place, and as having simply crossed a border, arriving here from there. That is, if there is to be hospitality, there must be surprise: the host must be surprised by that which is encountered as other within the home. As a result, 'one does not yet know or one no longer knows which is the country, the place, the nation, the family, the language and the home in general that welcomes the absolute arrivant' (Derrida 1993: 34).[3]

However, while Derrida is providing us with a model of hospitality which is an opening to that which is yet to be assimilated (as either a friend or stranger), there is still a failure to acknowledge the relationship between this opening and *the forms of assimilation that already function to differentiate others.* Such a hospitality is based on the *forgetting* of the names that are used, however inadequately, to locate subjects in a topography of time and place. In contrast, what is required is a hospitality that *remembers* the encounters that are already implicated in such names (including the name of 'the stranger'), and how they affect the movement and 'arrival' of others, in a way which opens out the possibility of these names being moved *from*. This hospitality, premised on the surprise of an opening or gift, would begin by admitting to how the assimilation of others, and the differentiation between others, might already affect who or what may arrive, then or now, here or there.

In his analysis of the politics of friendship, Derrida explicitly defines the importance of the particularity of an other whom I might encounter. He writes that the desire for friendship, 'engages me with a particular him or her rather than with *anybody*. ... This desire of the call to bridge the distance (necessarily unbridgeable) is (perhaps) no longer of the order of the common

or community, the share taken up or given, participation or sharing'
(Derrida 1995: 298). Friendship is both a friendship with a particular him
or her, as it is a form of sharing that is not premised on community or
commonality. One is hence surprised by, and open to, that which is
particular, in some sense, *one is surprised by who is already assimilated into 'my
life'*. Perhaps it is here that we can begin to think of hospitality differently.
Being hospitable, or generous, is being open to the particularity of the 'who'
I might encounter, but in such a way, that this particularity does not hold
this 'you' in place. However, as I argued in the previous section, we must be
careful not to locate the particular in the present of a given 'who' we might
encounter: rather, what is at stake, is the different modes of encounter that
allow us to face (up to) others. A generous encounter may be one which
would recognise how the encounter itself is implicated in broader relations
and circuits of production and exchange (how did we get here? how did you
arrive?), but in such a way that *the one who is already assimilated can still
surprise*, can still move beyond the encounter which names her, and holds her
in place. Is it here that an ethics of welcoming that which is other than the
stranger might begin?

So, again, I turn to you, I face you. I order the book from the
Routledge catalogue. I admire and value the translator's work. I hardly
notice what or who is being translated. A slight anxiety passes through
me. I think of the word 'post-colonial' and how it works, and who it
works for. I think of how it sells. Suddenly, I cannot think of the
gendered and international division of labour, the relations of third
world production and first world consumption, without thinking of the
intimacy of this moment, in which I buy this book, as a reader of post-
colonial theory. I grimace. I am in it. The encounter is in it. This book,
this commodity object, that moves across the world, is that which
makes us face each other, but a facing in which I consume you. Am I
eating you up?

Of, course, this is how I arrive at you. But still I want to be generous.
And yet when I think of full hands, I am sickened. I feel nauseous. This
idea of me approaching you with full hands is nauseating. I approach
you with hands that have taken, taken from you: my little acts of reading
already involve relationships of debt. The reproduction of the economic
legacies of colonialism, here and now. I cannot simply give. To give in
the face of such debts is to forget what has already been taken,
including the very names that allow me to pick up this book, to desire to
read it, to shelve it, to make it part of 'my collection'. It is not me that
gives to you. A gift cannot be given without responding to the violence
of that which has been appropriated and transformed into a collection.

Read on. Read more. It is the story, 'Douloti the Bountiful' that moves me. It is a story of a peasant woman sold into prostitution, as a repaying of her father's debt. The story moves me. Douloti moves me. I encounter her story through you, and you through the translator, and the translator through the others acts of reading that have allowed me to define a terrain where I think I am at ('the post-colonial'). There she is, Douloti, presented to me, and yet absent, a little sketch, hard to read behind, beneath, beyond these other encounters, these prior and mediating relationships of debt that are already accrued, even as I say her name. In the story, Douloti is sold, as part of the bondage system of rural India. It is not a post-colonial story, but a story, 'of the complicity ... of the power lines of local developers with the forces of global capital' (Spivak 1995: 198). The selling of bodies. Douloti's body is sold in a sexualised economy. Or rather, it is put on loan, but 'Bond-slaving loans are never re-paid' (Devi 1995: 76). As prostitute, as whore, her body is turned into a gleaming orifice, an object that can be valued through being consumed at the will of the user, 'who knows what Douloti ate, what she rubbed on her body. Her looks were so lusty, that's why she caught his eye' (Devi 1995: 51). Her body is consumed and violated, 'Douloti is bloodied many times all through the night' (Devi 1995: 58). Her body is turned into waste, 'The body hollow with tuberculosis, the sores of venereal disease, all over her frame, oozing evil-smelling pus, the whores come to hospital only to die' (Devi 1995: 91). The body, infected and infecting. The body, dying and dead. The subaltern woman? I read more.

Is not this where we must begin? Not with her body, which may be missing, may be unaccounted for, which we may miss, as we consume, as we read. This is not just about her body, but about other bodies, who are missing, but who haunt these pages. It is about other debts accrued, impossible to account for, here and now. How can we respond generously, if we do not respond to the circulation of bodies as debt, to the forms of exchange (capital, objects, images) that allow us to face up to distant others, which allow us to name them, her, Devi, Douloti, other others? Our ability to name, our acts of naming and being named, implicates us in the bloodied exchanges, the uses and the wasting of bodies, bodies that are already assimilated, that circulate within the economy as expendable goods.

And yet, how else to face her? Is to face her simply to face up to our responsibility for this legacy, our implication in the circulation of bodies as debt? Douloti's body is penetrated by the very forms of exchange which allow us to read her as text. How to read beyond this discourse of penetration, this brutality of unveiling? How to read her body? How to encounter her? How to be surprised by her, by this, by what makes this possible? Her body, in the end, oozes all over the place. It oozes all over the map of India, drawn lovingly on the floor, 'Filling the entire Indian peninsula from the Oceans to the Himalayas, here lies bonded-labour, spread eagled, Kamiya-whore' (Devi 1995: 93). There you are. There she is. And yet not there, not yet. For in this moment in which I read of where your body arrives, of what it might become, it then ceases to be your body. It becomes something that leaks beyond itself, a leaking which is also an infection. You leak beyond yourself, a leaking that is a response to the economies that allowed your body to be consumed and expelled, but which, as response, exceeds that expulsion, takes it over. I can't see the map beneath your body. But, at the very same time, I can't see you, as I face you, as I face this. It is an encounter with what is not yet possible, another future, another place, where you are missed, missed by this, or by that. I touch the pages. I am moved. Something gives.

It is only in facing up to you, that I miss your face. Something gives.

The possibility of something giving – not me or you – but something giving in the very encounter between a 'me' and a 'you', begins only with a recognition of the debts that are already accrued and which assimilate bodies, already recognised as strange or familiar, into economies of difference. But the question remains, how can we encounter an other in such a way, in a *better* way, that allows something to give?

Hearing and touch

In this section, I consider two forms of encounter – hearing and touch – in order to think about how we might respond to those others who are already recognised as strangers in a way that is both generous and responsible. Certainly, in Levinas's *Totality and Infinity*, as I discussed in the introduction to this chapter, the caress becomes one way of encountering 'the Other' which does not turn 'the Other' into an object, theme or thing: 'The caress does not *act*, does not grasp possibilities. The secret it forces does not inform it as an experience; it overwhelms the relation of the I with itself and with the non I' (1979: 259). The caress does not anticipate the other as an object that can be grasped, but animates the very relation of self and other, overwhelms it, such that it becomes impossible to distinguish where one body might begin and another might end. The overwhelming of the border involves secrecy; it involves a failure to communicate, where what passes between it is not disclosed, is not available to understanding or knowledge. In *Otherwise than Being*, the erotics of the caress is rethought in terms of proximity as exposure, a sensibility that constitutes the other's nearness to the self; its touching of the skin is a 'vulnerability, exposure to outrage, to wounding' which is also, 'sensibility on the surface of the skin' (Levinas 1991: 15).

There is a clear tension here between different ways of thinking about touch. Levinas begins with the caress as a particular kind of touch that undermines the opposition between presence and absence, insofar as it both approaches and does not approach what is there. At the same time, Levinas introduces this notion of exposure or, as I would put it, touch-ability, as the condition of signification or saying, as that which makes it possible to be for others, before being. The exposure of touching and being touched is the very proximity of the neighbour's approach, but a proximity that is not a presence (although, as proximity, nor is it an absence). This notion of the proximity of exposure, the very sensibility of the skin, allows Levinas to suggest that responsibility is an opening to others that *fails to grasp, fails to present the other, and yet is before the other, and for the other*.

By juxtaposing a particular modality of touch with the pre-ontological condition of exposure or touchability, Levinas's schema does not explicitly consider other forms of touch including those that seek to hold the other (such as the violence of the grasp, the shake or the beating) or to withdraw from the other (abjection). We can return to my discussion of skin and touch in Chapter 2. I suggested that we need an analysis of the skin, not as the pre-condition of exposure or touchability, but as the locus of social differentiation – the skin is touched differently by different others. An ethics of touch then is not simply about touching, or being touched by, the other. Rather, in touching an other we are, in that very moment, touching other 'touches' that have already affected 'the sensibility of the skin'. The skin functions to materialise the memory of these different touches (see Chapter 4); *the forms of the skin are a living history of this other's encounter with other others*. An ethics of touch is not, then, about naked skins that are exposed to each other in the present, even if that exposure does not lead to presence. An ethics of touch would fail to grasp this other *as* the other precisely insofar as it would recognise the impossibility of pure proximity to the other's skin given a prior history of encounters, which are not simply absent or simply present on the surface of the skin (= economies of touch).

In order to think through how an ethics of touch may 'touch' this other, I want to consider how touch involves 'communication'. By communication, I am not suggesting that touch involves a transparent movement from one to an other (where, for example, by touching you I might confirm my love), or that by touching, one can speak. Rather, thinking of speaking and hearing in terms of touch might allow us to challenge the very assumption that communication is about expression, or about the transparency of meaning, or pure exchange. Communication involves working with, 'that which fails to get across', or that which is necessarily secret. To hear, or to give the other a hearing, is to be moved by the other, such that one ceases to inhabit the same place. To think of hearing as touch is to consider that being open to hearing might not be a matter of listening to the other's voice: what moves (between) subjects, and hence what fails to move, might precisely be that which cannot be presented in the register of speech, or voicing.

What I am calling for in thinking about the intimacy of touch and hearing, or of particular forms of touch and hearing (both can involve the violence of assimilation) is a communicative ethics. By this I am not alluding to the work of Jürgen Habermas and other such scholars who have attempted to establish rules and procedures that will make communication as deliberative dialogue more possible (see Fraser 1989; Benhabib 1992). Rather, I want to think about a communicative ethics which can deal with, or even better work with, the very impossibility of communication as dialogue, as one voice simply speaking to, and being heard by, another. Iris Marion Young in her article, 'Asymmetrical Reciprocity: On Moral Respect, Wonder and Enlarged Thought' suggests that a communicative ethics must begin with a recognition of the asymmetry of self and other, hence departing from the work of Seyla Benhabib who argues, in line with Jürgen Habermas, that such an ethics must involve a relation of symmetry (1997: 340). Young develops this notion of asymmetry, by suggesting that a 'condition of our communication is that we acknowledge difference, interval and that others drag behind them shadows and histories, scars and traumas, that do not become present in our communication' (1997: 3).

Communication is not simply about the face to face, even if understood, in the Levinasian sense, as asymmetrical. For in the encounter in which something might be said or heard, there are always other encounters, other speech acts, scars and traumas, that remain unspoken, unvoiced, or not fully spoken or voiced. Particular modes of communication do not involve the rendering present of the other's voice, precisely because they open an unfinished, unheard history, which cannot be fully presented, even if it is not absent. Such an ethics of communication would allow what cannot be spoken or voiced in the present, *to be opened. or reopened*, as that which remains ungrasped and unrealised, as an approach that is always *yet to be taken*.

Young perceives the recognition of a time lag or interval as crucial to an ethics of communication – and with it, the recognition of distance, that which cannot be covered over, or filled in, by proximity. Pure proximity would constitute the violent fantasy of merger, rather than being, like Levinas's caress, that which approaches what might be there, without seeking to do so, and without ever arriving there. Young uses the example of 'going native' as a way of demonstrating the danger of assuming an absolute proximity. She suggests that the fantasy of 'going native' assumes that one can occupy the place of the other, and asks instead that 'we' keep our distance, and respect the boundary lines that have already been drawn as markers not only of territory, but of power. The other 'would prefer a stance of respectful distance in which whites acknowledge that they cannot reverse perspectives with Indians today, and thus must listen carefully across the distance' (Young 1997: 345). In Chapter 6, I also questioned the fantasy of 'going native' and more generally, 'becoming other', as a means by which the dominant subject can reassert his agency. The implication of such a critique is that 'proximity' (in acts of consumption, becoming or passing) can involve a technique for getting closer to the other in order to maintain a distance.

I do not think that 'listening carefully across the distance' can be the basis for an ethics of communication in the context of post-coloniality. There is a danger in assuming proximity *or* distance as the basis of an ethics. An ethics that assumes distance as its point of entry, fails to recognise the implication of the self in the encounter, and the responsibility the self has for the other to whom one is listening (as I argue in Chapter 8, we are 'in it'). An ethical communication is about a certain way of holding proximity and distance together: one gets close enough to others to be touched by that which cannot be simply got across. In such an encounter, 'one' does not stay in place, or one does not stay safely at a distance (there is no space which is not implicated in the encounter). It is through getting closer, rather than remaining at a distance, that the impossibility of pure proximity can be put to work, or made to work.

The question of testimonial speech – speech acts that are produced by witnesses of traumatic events – is of significance here. Jean-François Lyotard, in *The Differend*, points to an aporia in the very notion of testimonial speech, using the example of the Holocaust. In his powerful yet elusive writing, Lyotard suggests that a damage is a wrong accompanied by the loss of means to prove the damage (1989: 5). If one has witnessed the gas chambers, then one cannot testify, as one will be dead. If one testifies to what one witnessed in the gas chambers, then one was not a witness (for one would be dead), and one's testimony is false. Here, the mere fact of speaking about an injustice becomes that which injustice makes impossible: the other, who is wronged and damaged, not only does not, but cannot, speak. This certainly seems to correspond with Gayatri Spivak's consideration of the subaltern as the one who does not speak (1988). She later suggests, in an interview, that the event of speaking *as* a subaltern is impossible, in that one ceases to be a subaltern in the act of speaking as one (Spivak 1996: 289). However, at the same time, what Spivak emphasises, in a way that Lyotard does not, is that a testimonial ethics is not simply about speaking, but about *the conditions of possibility of hearing*.

I would argue that the injustice of Lyotard's aporia is a result of his fetishising of the mouth as the only organ through which injustice can be spoken. Instead, we need to consider the relationship between mouths and ears in the communication of injustice. As Robert Stam puts it, in his analysis of deconstruction and autobiography: 'the circuit from mouth to ear is also an *a priori* open or public thoroughfare, the messages sent along it take the form not so much of a sealed and esoteric letter but as a postcard for all to read' (1995: 78). It is the circuit between mouth and ear that demonstrates that testimony – and the communication of injustice – is not expressed or made present simply through speech, but is opened out in the very sociality of encounters, in the very relay of messages between mouths and ears, in the very 'more than one' and 'more than two' of the 'skin-to-skin'. The question then becomes: how can an ethics of communication bear witness to injustice and trauma without presuming that such witnessing is the presenting or ownership of 'the truth' (Felman 1992: 15), or that it is spoken through the organ of 'the mouth'?

The multiple ears required to hear what is not present as voice are those which will be touched by, or open to, that which cannot be got across, in 'the here' and 'the now' of the hearing. What cannot be got across, what resists pure communication, what makes ethics possible as an impossibility, cannot be found; it is not hidden in mouths that cannot speak. It is always yonder or approaching, elsewhere and otherwise to the immediacy of 'this encounter'. Such encounters always conceal as much as they reveal: they involve trauma, scars, wounds, and tears that are impossible to forget (they affect how we arrive or face each other, the encounter itself involves a form of remembering) *or* to present or to speak (they are not to be found in the mouth or on the skin of the one who is speaking or who remains silent). In my notion of ethical encounters, hearing does not take place in my ear, or in yours, but in between our mouths and our ears, in the very proximity and multiplicity of this encounter. What allows us to face each other (which again, in a strict sense, is economic) is also what allows us to move beyond the face, to hear and be touched by what one cannot grasp, as that which cannot be assimilated in a moment of recognition of either 'the Other' or the stranger.

The multiple ears that are required to 'hear' the other, without trans-forming this other into 'the Other' or 'the stranger', are ears that are alive to, or touched by, the sensations of other skins. Such sensations open this other to other others, who are not simply absent or present in the skin-to-skin of the encounter. An ethics that keeps alive the circuit between mouths, ears and skin is hence not about making her body present. It is the act of getting closer to this other's skin that prevents us from fleshing out her body *as* 'the stranger's body'.

Again, you come back to haunt me. Whose testimony am I reading? Sometimes I read with an expectation of the truth. I want you to tell me. I want to know. What happens next? What happens to her? Fiction or truth – it does not matter. You are telling me something. What are you saying? What can I hear?

But, no in this instance, you don't speak your resistance. Douloti, one named other. A fictional character in a short story, bound up as a collection. But your name, her name, carries weight; it is weighty, for me. It tells a story, here, now, to me and for me.

Amidst this violence, I ask, do you resist? In the story Douloti does not seem to resist. She does not join a political party and re-present herself like her uncle, whose talk of emancipation she finds difficult to understand. To him, she can only repeat the words, 'Bond-slavery loans are never re-paid' (Devi 1995: 76). She speaks these words softly. It must be like this. It must be like this, she says. She accepts her fate with sadness and with love. My tears, not hers, litter the pages. My sadness. The bloodied body. The pus.

If she does not speak her resistance, then how can we hear her? How can we listen out for her? How can we listen carefully? Have I got too close? The narrative moves me forward. Everywhere there are broken bodies. We begin with her father. His body is 'crooked and broken' (Devi 1995: 19). He takes the name of his crooked body; his body names him. They call him 'Crook Nagesia'. It is not that his body speaks the truth, or that the name finds him there, like that. But it bears witness to a certain truth, without possessing it. It not only carries the weight of an injustice, but *begins to take its shape*; the crooked form, the broken-ness, the scars of violence. From father to daughter. One bondage for another. Douloti's story – it is hers, I think – is told through the contracting forms of her fragile embodiment. Her body takes shape, changes shape. It begins as a 'body made of compassion' (Devi 1995: 47), and then it is reshaped by the very sexed bondage of slavery which uses it, expends it, kills it: 'If the body dries up she'll depart' (Devi 1995: 79).

Her resistance – is it spoken through the body? No – her body is not a transparent medium through which we can read a message and find our resolution. Her body ceases to be contained as body; it cannot be transformed from object to voice. It overwhelms the pages, as it becomes waste, a by-product of use and expenditure, filled with pus, a rotting carcass. The violence is communicated with and through her body, not as that which belongs to her (it is the very designation of body as property that allows it to be taken), but as that which leaks beyond her, as that which leaks into the world, as infection, as infecting; her 'tormented corpse … having vomited up all the blood in its desiccated lungs' (Devi 1995: 93). The pus leaks all over the page. The pus leaks on to my hands. I am infected by you. The touch of slime against paper. Skin and slime. Am I touching you?

To touch your body as the stranger's body, to love your body as the stranger's body, would be to forget how your body has taken shape, has taken the shape of the very violence of the labouring formations that have turned your body into waste. I cannot touch your body as the body of the stranger. Your body is already touched by other encounters; your skin weeps, not as you remember the violence, but as it remembers; it remembers it for you, a remembering that leaks beyond you, and into the flesh of the world. In touching you, in caressing your skin, I am also touching the scars that are a trace of the bloody violence of your consumption. I consume your consumption. And yet, in getting closer, I feel our skins touch, not as a coming together of two bodies, but as an insertion into a sociality in which we are not together, and yet we are close enough. My skin gets wet; it trembles with love.

This other presents itself as vomit, as violence spat out into the world. This other leaks as pus, as infection spreading outwards from a wound. This other fails to be contained in her skin. The fluids which seep across my hands are not simply from inside you; they are the trace of the encounters that have already violated you before the skin-to-skin of this reading could take place. The presentation of Douloti, who fails to be present as a body, as an object that can be grasped, as a theme that can be properly explored, as a name that has a referent, as a friend or a stranger we could recognise, demands my response and exceeds all possible response, leaving me with nowhere to stand, in this time, in this place: 'Today, on the fifteenth of August, Douloti has left no room at all in the India of people like Mohan for planting the standard of the Independence flag. What will Mohan do now? Douloti is all over India' (Devi 1995: 93). As her body metonymically leaks into other bodies, even the bodies of places and nations, there is nowhere left to stand, but on her, in her. It is the map, in some sense, that leads me to you: it is the names that litter the pages, that allow me to move between here and there. But now, having arrived, there is no map, no lesson in mapping, no topography of place. Standing in her body, which is no longer her body, this is where I find myself at, momentarily, before I turn the page to another story. She is missing, on and in the map. She fails to get across. Something gives.

8 Close encounters

Feminism and/in 'the globe'

30th of August, 1995

To begin with this date is to begin with an apparently individual or individuated subject. Rather an odd opening to a chapter you may think. A date? What is so individuated about a date? Dates are public; they announce the ordering of time as a series of (repeatable) events. Yet the public ordering of time makes sense in relation to the personal stories we create: 'On this date I ... Do you remember when we ... That is when you ... '. The relation between the public ordering of time and the (apparently) private reordering is determinate and unstable. The public ordering depends precisely on not 'belonging' to the individual subject (there must be consensus on how we measure our lives – these 'rules' must pre-exist individuation), and yet only makes sense through being inhabited, that is, through being given animation as life.

30th of August, 1995

So why does this date belong to me as an individual subject? I must make another announcement: this date is my birthday. Here is a date that I (feel like I) possess. It belongs to me. Indeed, it belongs only to me – birthdays are never shared as such. They are unliveable as shared.[1] The singularity of the personal pronoun – 'it is *my* birthday today' – conceals the unspeakable – that various others (whom I do not know) claim and possess this date as the indicator of their identity and origin. The birthday announces my presence as an event that both carries a trace of the past (30th of August 1969, this day was the day of my birth), and is in-the-present (today is my birth-day). 'Birth' and 'day' – here identity as self-presence constructs itself in relation to the temporal, of a 'then' which signals 'now'.

Although the privacy of the birthday appears as a form of self-possession (there I was, *here I am*), it becomes meaningful only through acts of recognition by others. Oh what a shame, to be alone on one's birthday. How fearful, how sad. Being alone on one's birthday becomes readable as a sign of loneliness, of a lack of friends and intimates. On this day/date, I receive presents and cards from friends and family. I have a party at my house in Lancaster and feel the anxiety and pleasure of the event taking place to celebrate my birthday – of being the 'reason' for this coming together. So the privacy of the birthday can take place only through the recognition we usually receive by those others we recognise as our friends. The date becomes liveable for me and them as my day.

So I dance around thinking, this is my day. And we take comfort in assuming that the feeling 'this is my day' is repeatable: it must be repeatable if we are to think of having a future. I am special, here and now. I will be special again. Birthdays convert the impersonality of dates into that which *must* belong to me. Birthdays confound the opposition between private and public, even as they become liveable through it.

August 30th, 1995

This date must repeat itself. It cannot be confined to my birthday even through the apparent individuation of my memory work. The workings of memory itself install my sense of self (my-self as the realm of privacy) by evoking what exceeds my life, what takes place through the very public order of remembering. For this day was the beginning of the UN conference for Women in Beijing. I remember thinking at the time how pleasurable it was to share my birthday with an event that may help create a space for international feminism. It was a thought deeply embedded with irony. My relation to this event which gave a form (forum) to international feminism was structured through the (fantastic) privacy of the 'birthday'. The irony is perhaps more instructive than it may appear on the surface. It may suggest that the very creation of a public space for international feminism emerges through *fantasies of how we 'belong' within this space*, of how we occupy an intimate, personal or even 'private' relationship to it.

August 30th, 1995

It is the day – the day the UN conference for women begins (and it is my birthday). I watch for news on the television, for images of 'international feminism' being created, being given a space. International feminism is, for me, a fantasy that is partially mediated through images of the UN conferences for Women. In the days before my birthday, I imagined all those women travelling and the difficulties of their movement in face of the restrictions on visas – the restrictions that were well documented in the mainstream British press as a sign of the impossibility of any democratic space being made possible within China.[2] The travelling, the movement from and to, the inbetween space which is no space, the stories that were narrated before the event could take place as such. I fantasised about all those women getting there. Those women not getting there.

So many fantasies, so many encounters. First, my encounter with the 'encounters' that constitute the impossible space of the conference. As an encounter, it involved proximity, not in the physical sense of 'getting closer', but as a fantasy of how I could be *in* the 'space' of international feminism, by having a connection *with* 'it'. And then, there are the encounters that my fantasy must miss, the encounters that my distance from the event cannot allow me to face. The event then signals a coming together which I have already missed, a missing which allows me to imagine a more private encounter (the 'sharing' of a special day). But if I had got closer in another way, if I had arrived, what would I be 'in'? Would I be in a space that we could call 'international feminism'?

This 'coming together' in one space involves an embodied dialogue – a speaking to each other that is at once 'face-to-face' and embedded in institutions. But does that institutional setting also define limits; setting out what can and cannot happen? Are these the only 'spaces' in which international feminism can take place? Are these 'the strange encounters' that constitute the value and impossibility of translating feminism across (national) spaces? I was unable to go to the conference. You know this already; I was constructing a different sort of event. So I imagined, fantasised about the chance meetings, the glances that were not legitimated in the 'proper events' of the conference. What chance meetings took place? What intimate moments became possible at lunch or over coffee? How does the singularity of these secret meetings[3] relate to the political process of forming coalitions?

Institutions cannot and do not fully 'colonise' spaces. The 'beyond' is always 'within' – the inside and outside don't fit together to form 'discrete spaces'. The 'face-to-face' encounters beyond the formalised spaces of the conference rooms or workshops are thus not within *or* outside institutions; they neither fully escape nor fully inhabit their limits. Indeed, the spatial dynamics of institutions took an interesting turn at Beijing. The division between the official and unofficial conferences (non-governmental organisations – NGOs) was secured by being set up in different spaces. Or, more specifically, the unofficial conference was relegated to the margins (Huairou) with stories of infectious diseases, of lesbian parades, and women stripping off in public spaces, establishing the danger of this event (as a danger to both public morality and health), and the 'need' to protect the centre (Beijing) from it.[4] The route between the two conferences was a difficult one to take, and it was one some were not allowed to take. So being there was not simply a matter of Being-There, of arriving in, or inhabiting, the institutional 'space' allocated to 'international feminism'.

So many encounters, so many forms of proximity that allow us to imagine the space in which international feminism might take place. My encounter, structured through the fantastic privacy of the birthday, was one that assumed a certain distance, a not being there. So I imagine those that were there, as those that had overcome this distance. But 'going there' was not 'being there': as a mode of encounter, the 'event' of the conference was itself fantastic, mediated by images of the event that were sent, through the globalised mediascape, across the world. Through the Internet, one's encounter with the event could be 'living', one could almost be there, despite not getting there. Such images, flashing on my screen, in the home in which I danced, came to stand for, or stand for, the globality of the event, as one that must be witnessed by absent friends. So the event, in some sense, did not happen: it was not in the present, as such. Its globality relied on images that alone could allow acts of witnessing the event which would confirm its 'global reach'. These images were relayed between women who were all, in some sense, missing from the event, and missing to each other. And yet 'we' belonged to the event; we confirmed it, as its absent witnesses, its addressees, its failed destination.

Significantly, then, the event, as the fantastic creation of 'international feminism' in which women became players on 'the global stage', required distance; the proximity of the encounters that allowed it to happen, which allowed women from different nations to face each other, required a certain 'not being there'. The face-to-face encounters within the impossible event, while they were enabled by the overcoming of physical distance, did not overcome distance as such. Getting closer does not, then, abolish the distance which installs the very necessity of the event of getting closer in the first place (the distance and division between the women who depart–arrive–depart–arrive ...). Getting closer, I watched the screen; it was the act of getting closer, in the living out of a certain distance, which allowed absent(ed) others to bear witness to 'the event'.

Thinking about the encounters of 'international feminism', and the way in which they complicate the relationship between proximity and distance, will be the task of this concluding chapter of *Strange Encounters*. I examine the kinds of encounters that are already taking place that construct 'global women', by examining the gendering of the international division of labour. I analyse how 'women' can become 'global agents' by reading closely the Beijing Platform for Action. Finally, I consider alternative ways in which feminism may move across spaces, to achieve an activism which is transnational, by revisiting the notion of community, as beyond the apparent intimacy of the face to face or the extimacy of the 'common' or the 'uncommon'. I suggest that feminism must encounter, not women who can be recognised as strangers or as friends, but the very encounters that already mediate the relationship between different women who, as distant others, are always close by. This chapter provides a way of thinking about how feminism involves strange encounters – ways of encountering what is already encountered – in order to engender ways of being and acting in the world that open the possibility of the distant in the near, the unassimilable in the already assimilated, and the surprising in the ordinary.

On being 'in-it': women and globality

Black and third world feminists have provided powerful critiques of the way in which Western feminism has defined the universal in terms of the West. Such universalist feminist approaches often proceed through producing 'third world women' as objects of knowledge. Chandra Talpade Mohanty suggests that the constitution of third world women as a homogenous group is a means by which Western feminists represent themselves as subjects of knowledge:

> a homogenous notion of the oppression of women as a group is assumed, which, in turn, produces the image of an 'average third world woman'. This average third world woman leads to an essentially truncated life based on her feminine gender (read: sexually constrained) and her being 'third world' (read: ignorant, poor, uneducated, tradition-bound, domestic, family-oriented, victimized etc.). This, I suggest, is in contrast to the (implicit) self-representation of Western women as educated, as modern, as having control over their own bodies and sexualities, and the freedom to make their own decisions.
>
> (Mohanty 1991: 56)

Mohanty examines the way in which Western feminists authorise themselves to speak of third world women, as if they are a singular group (in need of liberation), and hence tend to speak *for them*. Crucially, Mohanty demonstrates that the act of speaking of and for third world women involves a form of *self-representation*. Third world women come to define not simply what Western women are not (and hence what they are), but also what *they once were*, before feminism allowed Western women to be emancipated. Third world women become relegated to 'our' pre-history; they embody what 'we' were, before liberation by feminism and modernity. Or, borrowing Micheldo Rosaldo's terms, 'we' see 'them' as 'ourselves undressed' (cited in Mohanty 1991: 56). In such a narrative, black and 'third world' women are strangers to feminism, those who are already recognised as 'out of time' and hence 'out of place': their difference from Western women allows Western feminism to constitute itself, not only as the ideal and telos (what 'other' women should aspire to, so they can 'develop' into an image of 'us'), but also as the real ('we' can guarantee not only what the other is, but also what or who she can become).

One could argue that such a model of the relationship between Western feminism and women who inhabit spaces other than the West involves a refusal to encounter others at all: 'the other' is held in place as 'the stranger', as the object of Western feminist enquiry who is 'not (like) us (yet)' and whose difference serves only to confirm who 'we' are by defining who 'we' have become, or what we have overcome in relation to a past that is spatialised as the 'elsewhere' ('the third world'). The relationship between Western feminism and its other is one of narcissism, but a narcissism that is haunted by the spectre of difference: the other reflects back the image of what 'we once were', or even, 'what we might have been'.

The universalism of 'speaking for' the other, whose strangerness is only a sign of what might yet be (when 'she' might become part of 'our family'), is premised on fantasies of absolute proximity or absolute distance. On the one hand, the universalist rhetoric of some Western feminism involves a refusal to encounter, to get close enough to face the others; *it judges from afar by reading 'the other' as a sign of the universal.* Mohanty comments, for example, on how Western feminists have read 'the purdah' (veil) as a sign of women's oppression, and how this reading refuses to engage with the historically specific contexts in which the 'purdah' acquires meaning (1991: 67). There is no attempt to get close enough to see the contradictions and ambivalence which structure how the purdah comes to be lived – sometimes as a means for resistance – at different times and places. Likewise, Lama Unu Odeh argues that 'a veiled woman is neither this nor that. She could shift from one position to another' (1983: 55). The refusal to enter into a relationship with 'the veiled woman' is, for Odeh, a refusal to recognise the multiplicity of the veiled woman's subjectivity. The other becomes fixed as an object and sign precisely by a refusal to get closer, or to face that which cannot be assimilated into one's model of self or other.

However, universalism could also be read as a fantasy of proximity. For, at one level, reading the 'veiled woman' as an oppressed woman who is sexually controlled involves a fantasy that one can inhabit the place of the other, that one already knows what 'the other' means (and therefore needs). Or, to put it differently, the emphasis on the universal wrong of 'the purdah' (and the assumption of women's right as the right 'not to wear the veil'), involves the fantasy that one can 'get inside the skin of the other' (and speak for her). *This fantasy of proximity assumes that the language of universal rights has got 'close enough' to the truth of the other's (well) being.*

How can Western feminists respond to such a critique? Certainly, as I discussed in Chapter 3, the question of 'who speaks' has become extremely important within Western feminism, and has led to much caution about the perils of speaking on or for others (Yeatman 1993). One of the responses has been to remain silent (see Landry and Maclean 1996: 5). Gayatri Spivak provides us with a strong challenge to the pitfalls or even perversion of silence. She responds to those who refuse to speak because of their privilege in the following way: 'Why not develop a certain degree of rage against the history that has written such an abject script for you that you are silenced' (Spivak 1990: 62). Indeed silence, as a response to the feminist and post-colonial critiques of universalism, assumes that the best way to avoid speaking for others is to avoid speaking at all – it is hence a form of cultural relativism (I cannot speak of you, or to you, because you are different). Such a relativism also functions as a form of solipsism that confirms the privilege that it seeks to refuse (I can only speak about myself, or I can only speak about the impossibility of my speaking). I would argue that the perversion of remaining silent about those who do not inhabit the West, or even those who do not inhabit the West in the same way as privileged middle-class, white and heterosexual women (such as working-class, black and migrant women, and lesbian women in the West), can be associated with the universalism that inspired the very response of silence in the first place. It remains a form of speech based on taking 'me' or 'us' as the referent; it confirms the other's status as the stranger who is always and already marked by difference, and who hence cannot speak (my language).

The cultural relativism implicit in the response of silence can also involve a fantasy of distance premised on a refusal to encounter others beyond the category of 'the other' or 'the stranger'. Cultural relativism assumes distance and difference in order precisely not to take *responsibility* for that distance and difference. By assuming the one *already knows the difference*, the self and other relation is held in place. Such a politics whereby Western feminists simply refuse an encounter with those who inhabit places other than the West, or even other places within the West, does not move Western feminists into unlearning (beyond the unlearning of the right to speak), nor does it move others from their position as always already 'the strangers'.

The assumption of distance also involves a refusal to recognise the relationships of proximity between women who are differently located in the world. Western feminists are already in relationships with 'third world women' given our implication in an international division of labour – we do not *withdraw* from that implication by refusing the privilege of speech. We are, so to speak, right in it. The response of silence is hence perverse precisely insofar as it assumes *it is possible not to encounter those who are already recognised as strangers in the first place*. Women in different nation spaces, within a globalised economy of difference, cannot not encounter each other, what is at stake is *how*, rather than *whether*, the encounters take place.

What is needed here is a stronger sense of what it means to be 'in it', and how 'being in it' is the site of both differentiation and hierarchisation. In the first instance, we must refuse the temptation of understanding 'in-it-ness' as simply a matter of speech. As I argued in Chapter 2, following Gayatri Spivak, the emphasis on the question, 'who speaks?' has led to a concealment of the material relationships of labour and production that allow for the very possibility of speaking and hearing. Before we can ask the question of how and whether we can speak, or how we do speak, we must attend to the way in which encounters already take place in the organisation and spatialisation of labour. As M. Jacqui Alexander and Chandra Talpade Mohanty have argued, the international division of labour is not simply a question of the differentiation of tasks within the global, but the constitution of subjects as *subjected to* that global differentiation: 'An international division of labour is central to the establishment, consolidation, and maintenance of the current world order: global assembly lines are as much about the production of people as they are about "providing jobs" or making profit' (1997: 5). The production of people in the international division of labour also involves the production of spaces: spaces, as well as people, are utilised for *differential production* and capital accumulation (Alexander and Mohanty 1997: 5).

The international division of labour produces, not simply 'people' and 'spaces' but gendered subjects, and gendered spaces. For example, Maria Mies in her classic study of the lacemakers of Narsapur in India, 'illustrates how women bear the impact of the development process in countries where poor peasant and tribal societies are being "integrated" into an international division of labour under the dictates of capital accumulation' (Mohanty 1997: 12). Capital accumulation relies on traditional and gendered notions of work in order to constitute subjects who can meet the needs of transnational capital (Ong 1987, Mies 1986). We have a shift in the spatialisation of the gendered division of labour, as women move from domestic spaces to international spaces of casual and poorly paid work (Mitter 1986).

The gendering of the international division of labour involves an encounter between women as they are differentially constituted in and around 'the globe'. Indeed, the relationship between first world consumption and third world production is gendered. Encounters hence already take place between women as consumers and women as workers within different spaces in the globe. Although the complexity of the relationship between production and consumption in globalisation cannot be understood in terms of a simple formula of first world consumption and third world production, forms of hierarchisation and differentiation clearly take place *between* first and third world nations, as well as *within* them (for example, in class stratification, or the differentiation of 'home' from migrant workers). What I want to consider is how the *movement* of commodities – including knowledges and technologies – already mediates an encounter between Western women as 'consumer-citizens' and third world women as workers.

Such a relationship is concealed by the commodity fetishism that I discussed in Chapter 6. Commodities are cut off from their histories of production and, in Marx's terms, 'appear as autonomous figures endowed with a life of their own' (1976: 164). What is cut off through commodity fetishism is, precisely, the encounters that already take place between women as they are differentially constituted in relationship to the globe. The signs of work that are missing in the polished surfaces of the commodity (see McClintock 1995: 219) include the exploited labour of many women in the third world. The assumption that 'we' in the West can *not* encounter women who live 'elsewhere' hence repeats this fetishism, and conceals the signs of (her) labour.

Certainly, as I argued in Chapter 6, commodity fetishism can become displaced onto what I have called 'stranger fetishism', where the commodity is assumed to 'contain' the difference that the Western consumer can 'have'. It is important to supplement my analysis in this chapter with a reflection on the gendering of stranger fetishism. One extremely powerful example of the displacement between commodity and stranger fetishism is The Body

Shop. This multinational cosmetics company, owned by Anita Roddick, clearly defines itself as a form of global and environmental activism that refuses to fetishise the commodity. In a recent issue of The Body Shop's Magazine, *The Naked Body*, Western consumers are not only told how their products are produced, but are shown that this production gives women workers in the third world 'a better deal'. In an article on 'raw materials', the product 'Aloe Vera Body Lotion' is advertised not by addressing the Western woman consumer, and who she might seek to become through the commodity, but by giving a history of how the commodity itself is produced, and who has produced it: 'The butter is produced from the fruit of the wild shea tree that grows in abundance across the savannah. ... Traditionally, it is the women who gather the fruits and make the shea butter. ... Ghanaian women have always used it to protect the skin' (Body Shop International 1999: 23).

While the value of the commodity is measured through the association between it and an authentic and traditional difference (that is clearly gendered), the article then tells the consumer how the 'new' or 'modern' forms of production have allowed The Body Shop to 'help' Ghanaian women:

> In the Tamale region of Northern Ghana, women from 10 villages have joined together to form the Tungteiya Shea Butter Association, from which The Body Shop buys shea butter. The women receive a fair price as part of the Body Shop Community Trade programme and, importantly, are paid on the spot. The butter is then shipped to Holland for further refining and finally arrives in the UK, where it is used to make several products including The Body Shop Rich Cleansing Cream, Vitamin E Eye Cream, Vitamin E Hand & Nail Treatment and Aloe Vera Body Lotion.
>
> (Body Shop International 1994:23)

The product is advertised by telling a history of its production, a history that allows the consumer, if you like, to face the distant others, women workers in Ghana. But as a facing, this encounter is highly mediated, and dependent on forms of concealment. The difference of the product is not only collapsed into 'their tradition', but is then reconstituted as 'our modernity' (the product is refined in Europe), and as our benevolence (by becoming a little more like them, by using this product, we are not appropriating their skins, but we are saving their skins). This narrative (in which appropriation is read as a form of redemption) allows the consumer to align herself with the product and the company as 'helping Ghanaian women'. The narrative repeats the universalist feminist one, in which the Western feminist sees herself as saving the skins of her sisters in the third world. The apparent non-encounter of universalist Western feminism, in which the women in the third world allow Western feminists to define themselves, conceals more brutal forms of encounter based, not only on the reduction of third world difference, but also on the appropriation of third world women's labour.

This encounter as an appropriation, not only of the difference of third world women as tradition, but also of her labour, is clearly expressed in the *Body Shop Book*.[5] Here, Anita Roddick is presented in the narrative, as a white woman whose travels have allowed the constitution of a global femininity:

> I'd been around the world and seen how women in other countries cared for themselves. The skin of Tahitian women looked pretty good for all their butter massages. And fresh pineapple seemed to get skin clean and clear in Sri Lanka. Could the successful traditions of other cultures develop new products back in England? I found something very interesting about ingredients that had been used by human beings for hundreds and thousands of years. And they certainly made good stories to pass along to customers.
>
> (Body Shop International 1994: 9)

The difference of other cultures is first tied to the skin of other women, and then associated with tradition and history. The making of the product is narrated as the appropriation of their skin as a sign of a shared history, and as 'the matter' that can be transformed into 'our present' through the telling of (origin) stories. The difference of these other skins is then negated by the assumption that women share the same skin; care for the skin becomes a sign of universal femininity (see Stacey forthcoming; Ahmed 1998b).

Within this narrative of difference and universality, Anita Roddick becomes a figure of the white woman missionary. Her agency becomes a gift to the third world; she gives their tradition value, and allows them to enter the universal. At the same time, that gift is a form of appropriation; she takes from their tradition the ingredients of a global femininity, one which has already *refined* their difference into a commodity. Through this narrative, Western women as consumers come to embody global femininity: by taking their skins, not only can we 'save their skins', but we can also give that skin a universal value. In this way, the production of Western women as consumers involves a form of global nomadic citizenship (see Chapter 4), predicated on the ability to inhabit the globe, by travelling within it, and 'finding' differences that are always elsewhere. As Caren Kaplan puts it, 'there is no part of the world that is seemingly unreachable – Anita Roddick has been literally *everywhere*' (1995: 59). This nomadic form of global citizenship involves converting local traditions (found in or on 'their skins'), into the very modernity and globality of the commodity form. Becoming 'like her' is a narrative of 'saving her skin': as such 'becoming like her' translates swiftly into 'her becoming like us'. The narrative implies that she will be saved through the conversion of tradition into the modernity promised by the commodity itself. The doubling between these narratives of becoming collapses into the image of 'global woman': not only do we acquire her 'authenticity', but she acquires our 'modernity', leading to the substantiation of an idealised and hybrid femininity based on the care of skin.

Such narratives involve modes of encounter that suggest the proximity of women in different spaces within a globalised economy of difference. But being 'in it' clearly does not mean we are 'in it' in the same way. The close encounters that I have discussed in this section involve both differentiation and hierarchisation in the very production of the signifier, 'global woman'. If being 'in it' is the site of difference and antagonism, then both universalist and cultural relativist responses to difference – speaking for or silence – fail to recognise how encounters between women in 'the globe' already mediate not only, in some sense, what is already said, in the very constitution of gendered subjects through differentiated labour and consumption, but also what it is possible to say.

Women as global agents

How can women encounter each other differently, given that such encounters are already mediated by the divisions of labour and consumption that position women in different parts of the world in relationships of antagonism? In this section, I look more closely at the representations of 'women' within and around the UN conference, as one imaginary and material space in which feminist activism is given a global dimension.[6] Partly, we need to examine the rhetoric that surrounded the event, that made claims on behalf of the event, and that constituted the event itself as the 'globalisation' of feminism. We could analyse, for example, the rhetoric used by Hilary Clinton in her opening speech in the conference, a speech that is available on the Internet. Her speech which is *about* how women are in some sense *already* global agents was, in terms of its distribution and hence consumption, dependent upon a globalised mediascape to confirm its object. Her speech produces the very subject category (women as global actors, woman as global actor) that it is supposedly about. What is evident from Hilary Clinton's speech is that 'women', as subject category, comes to measure, or be the measure of, the level of social advancement of different nations:

> What we are learning about the world is that, if women are healthy and educated, their families will flourish. If women are free from violence their families will flourish. If women have a chance to work and earn as full and equal partners in society, their families will flourish.
>
> (1995)[7]

What is striking about this statement, is the use of 'their families' as means of closing the gap between the concerns of women and the concerns of and for international politics. That is, Hilary Clinton suggests, without reference to either nation or globe, that women's rights secure the flourishing of families and hence, by implication, the advancement of the family of 'the nation' and 'the globe' as a 'family of nations'. Women become global actors precisely insofar as they are relegated into the familial space at the very same time as that space becomes the imagined form of the globe itself.

In this public address, Clinton constitutes women as actors on a global stage by appealing to what women share or have in common: 'At this very moment, as we sit here, women around the world are giving birth, raising children, washing clothes, cleaning houses, planting crops, working on assembly lines, running companies, and running countries' (1995). What is listed is a series of acts that women 'around the world' are doing, or are even doing together, at the very same moment. The list begins with the acts most commonly used to bind women together as mothers (child-birth and child-care) and then moves towards acts normally associated with men as 'leaders' of nations. By positing women as leaders of nations through this metonymic chain, Clinton implies that women become global actors precisely through an *extension* of the activities within the home: women as mothers, reproduce not only children, but also nations, while women as housewives and carers, manage not only domestic space, but also global space. Significantly then, women enter international politics by *being themselves*, a narrative which collapses the boundary line (always tenuously drawn) between their private space and public space, and between the local and the global, through reference to very traditional notions of what women already contribute to the (re)production of the familial and social order.

Clinton's address uses the 'we' as a way of articulating the common concerns of women around the world, whether as mothers, within the 'private' space of the family, or as mother figures, within the 'public' space of the nation. At the same time, Clinton uses the 'I' as a way of signalling her own mobility in reaching these other women, usually hidden from the 'eye' of international politics: 'I have met new mothers in Jojakarat, Indonesia, who come together regularly in their village to discuss nutrition, family planning, and baby care. ... I have met women in South Africa who helped lead the struggle to end apartheid and are now helping build a new democracy.' It is the encounter between the mobility of the white Western woman, who moves across and between private and public spaces, as well as between nations, and those 'women' whom she speaks of, that is striking here. Some women are afforded agency within the global, through relegating other women into 'local' spaces, *at the very same time as that relegation is concealed under the signifier of 'global women'*. Clinton's 'I' can assert itself, by naming the encounters she had with women, who inhabit the 'localised' spaces of the family, community and nation, in the very process of articulating what it is 'we' *already* have in common (in the work that we do).

The globe becomes a fetish precisely through being imaged as 'women'. Women-as-globe is only possible as an image by concealing the work that needs to be done to make it possible: it is the encounters, the meetings, between the white Western woman, and the women in other spaces, which allow her 'I' to become 'global' by claiming their activities as 'her own'. The constitution of women as global agents clearly involves a universalism predicated on a prior act of differentiation: 'we' as women are (making) the globe, by translating the work 'they' do within families, communities, and nations into an 'I' that speaks.

We can consider how the very documentation produced by the UN conference for women in Beijing participated in the constitution of 'women' as global agents. The document, 'Platform for Action', needs to be thought of as an effect of multiple encounters, including those that took place between the participants who were present (and absent) at the conference (see my opening comments in this chapter), and those that are already at stake in the gendering of the international division of labour. At the same time, however, we need to think of the Platform as making encounters possible, that is, as producing its own subject, and as having its own effects. Like all public documents, in which subjects are defined as 'having' rights, we have the transformation of a performative into a constative: the document itself produces the very subjects that it claims to re-present (see Derrida 1986: 10). However, that moment of production is only possible given a prior history of encountering, which allows certain subjects to be faced, at the moment they are constituted, as such.

The Platform for Action certainly takes for granted the subject status of 'women' through the following dictum: women's rights are human rights. It seeks to 'ensure the full implementation of the human rights of women and of the girl child as inalienable, integral and indivisible part of all human rights' (Declaration 9). Such subject status is afforded through a discourse of potentiality: women, in some sense, must become subjects with rights by realising their full potential, a realisation that requires, paradoxically, that they already have the rights that they do not yet have (the document presupposes that women are subjects by implying they are *not yet subjects*, that they have yet to 'become' what they 'are'). Advancement and development is deemed possible, only by advancing and developing women, such that they become women and human, at one and the same time: 'The empowerment and advancement of women, including the right to freedom of thought, conscience, religion and belief, thus contributing to the moral, ethical, spiritual and intellectual needs of women and men, individually or in community with others and thereby guaranteeing them the possibility of realising their full potential in society' (Declaration 12). The realisation of 'their potential' is allowed by collapsing a universal discourse of advancement or development (which assumes the primacy of the individual who has rights and freedoms guaranteed under law) into the advancement and development of women as such. Women both measure the advancement of the human, and themselves need to be advanced, so that they can become human.

While the declaration constitutes women as subjects insofar as they are potentially human, the documentation differentiates between women, according to their advancement: by implication, *some women are defined as more advanced than others*. The call for advancement is also about bringing some women into the category of 'women' and (implicitly) other women into the category of 'human': 'to improve the effectiveness of anti-poverty programmes directed towards the poorest and most disadvantaged groups of women, such as rural and indigenous women, female heads of households, young women and older women, refugees and migrant women and women with disabilities' (Declaration 60 a). Throughout the document, there are repeated references to these various categories of 'other women'. By listing these different groups of women who are 'more oppressed', the document seeks to differentiate between women and complicate any simple positing of 'women' as a global or homogenous group, bound together in a shared oppression. What is then posited is a generalised category of 'other women' against an implicit category of women who are 'less disadvantaged' and, in the terms of the document (which conflates disadvantage with under-development) are more advanced. The grouping together of various forms of otherness does an enormous amount of work in the document: it allows the positing of 'woman' as global agent, by defining her against women who have yet to advance or to develop into women. This notion of undeveloped women as a *symptom* of underdevelopment in general confirms the human-woman agent – the individual who has autonomy, rights and freedom – as the proper telos or goal of globalised feminism. Even if collective agencies are named as contributors to the emancipation of women, the narrative of globalisation assumes the primacy of an individual – who is both gendered as woman and ungendered as human[8] – and whose potential, when realised, becomes a sign of global advancement and development.

The assumption that the aim of global feminism is to enable individuals to realise their potential (to find a future that is already present(ed) as their nature – in the discourse of potentiality one's becoming is determined by one's being) is hence linked to the ideal of development which equates development with modernity. Throughout, the document calls for women to be given access to modernity, understood in terms of 'resources', that is, in terms of the transformation of land and 'nature' into both capital and technology: 'We are determined to: ensure women's equal access to economic resources including land, credit, science and technology, vocational training, information, communication and markets, as a means to further the advancement and empowerment of women and girls' (Declaration 36). The term 'economic resources' functions as a way of gathering together a diverse range of value-laden activities: what is significant is that access becomes access to the networks of exchange, and the flow of capital within the globalised economy. As I have already suggested, following Alexander and Mohanty, globalisation needs to be understood in terms of the constitution of subjects and spaces through the differentiation and spatialisation of forms of labour. We can also consider the networks of exchange and flows of capital as spatial forms of subject-constitution: for example, the accumulation of third world debt and first world profit under the banner of development produces subjects with differing degrees of entitlement and agency, both within and between nation spaces. Within the narrative of advancement as access to resources, advancement becomes a means of fulfilling one's debt to modernity, or of becoming modern as an acquisition of debt.[9] Indeed, implicit in this narrative of access, is that the acquisition of debt is what enables the constitution of others into subjects in the global space.

Gayatri Spivak provides us with a powerful critique of how women's emancipation is coded as access to global telecommunications as such (forthcoming). As she demonstrates, this process involves the transformation of the heterogeneity of indigenous knowledges into property. In such narratives, these technologies function not simply as symbols of, *but the very material* of Western modernity: by having 'it', women will become 'it'. That is, they will become modern and realise their potential (they will hence become themselves – become selves – through modernity). Modernity becomes a sign of what is missing for these 'other women', for what makes them 'other than women'. The United Nations itself, as an organisation that is premised on neutrality, but which is based on notions of individual autonomy, democracy and civil society that are ideologically inflected, constitutes itself as a necessary element, not only in the development of women, but also in the very constitution of women as (global) subjects (see Kabeer 1995). In other words, the well-being of 'all women' and the constitution of women as actors in the globe, is assumed to be a measure of the degree to which women are 'brought' into modernity by global agencies. Although it would not be correct to say that the feminist critique of development is totally missing from this narrative – the emphasis is on giving agency to women in grass roots communities – the transparency of those institutions that are already global in reach is clearly affirmed (they are presented as 'giving' women 'the globe', rather than occupying and regulating 'the globe'). Such global institutions are presented as the necessary condition for the 'development of women' insofar as they provide the mechanism which enables the individual to be 'translated' into the global, and constituted as a global subject.

The conflation of individual development and global development is tied up with the notion of generation: the document defines itself as about *allowing women to grow up*. The relationship between the signifiers of 'girl' and 'woman' is hence significant: 'The girl child of today is the woman of tomorrow. The skills, ideas and energy of the girl child are vital for the full attainment of the goals of equality, development and peace. For the girl child to develop her full potential she needs to be nurtured in an enabling environment' (Declaration 39). The temporality of this narrative is important: growing up becomes a measure of global development. The life course of the girl child becomes a metaphor for the life course of 'the globe' itself. In this way, the fulfilment of the girl's potential marks the course or trajectory of the globalisation of feminism.

The document comes to represent itself as 'the making of a new genera-tion': 'It will be crucial for the international community to demonstrate a new commitment to the future – a commitment to inspiring a new generation of women and men to work together for a more just society' (Declaration 40). Self-making becomes global-making through the positing of a 'new generation'; they will be the agents, even the *foundation*, of a new and better community in which 'home' becomes 'the globe' and 'the globe' becomes 'home'. This generation, positing by the Document as founda-tional, is hence a symptom of the future: it is the girl and boy who will remake the international community *in their own image*, that is, through an embodiment of their potential, an embodiment of what has not yet taken form, but which takes their form. The document is premised on an elided heterosexuality: the making of a new generation confirms the significance of the heterosexual couple to the international community. The absence of any reference to sexuality – and in particular to lesbians – within the document suggests that the new 'international community' will be reproduced through the normalising of a (supposedly egalitarian) heterosexuality. The new generation of global agents will be (re)produced from, or even through, the legislation of the heterosexual family as the proper 'form' of the international community.

The document, in 'making a new generation', involves forms of legisla-tion which define global citizenship and agency in terms of the heterosexual couple and the heteronormative family, which also becomes the proper goal of global feminist activism. It constitutes 'women' as global agents insofar as 'women' allow the reconstitution of this familial form, as long as women *give birth to* the very forms which measure her advancement in terms of the reproduction of the (hu)man. The work of women is, in some sense, to (re)produce the family as the image of the 'healthy world'. Advancement for women – which throughout the document is represented through an overcoming of the vulnerability of the girl child (as well as other forms of 'under-developed womanhood') – by fulfilling one's debt to modernity, or one's duty to modernise, is here an advancement of the family into a form of global nomadic citizenship, which despite its emphasis on movement and the overcoming of boundaries, remains predicated on traditional forms of social differentiation.

Transnational feminist communities

The document, of course, must be translated into local contexts and transformed into action. Given its significance as a framework for action, where the question of gender is posed, after all, as a matter of international political concern, the document names a number of actors; it names those who will act upon it (it acts, in part then, by naming the actors). Actors that are named include, 'all actors of civil society, particularly women's groups and networks and other non-governmental organizations and community-based organizations' (Declaration 20), as well as 'Governments and the international community' (Declaration 21). As a form of writing that defines itself as a 'platform' for action, then, the document opens up a gap between writing and action, a gap that brings into play a range of actors who have not necessarily authorised the writing, but who have been authorised by it. This authorisation itself differentiates between the actors who are named as such by the document: we have to consider not only who is the 'we' that writes the text, but also who signed it – 'the Governments' who represent 'their people' – and hence who authorised it through the proper names of the signatory (see Derrida 1986).

As I have suggested, the constitution of women as global actors involves forms of differentiation, where various 'other' women are named as yet to fulfil their debt to modernity. The ideal, then, of the document is the *becoming women of all women*: it is the development of all women into modern individuals, who are able to reproduce not only the family, but the globe as a familial space. In such a model, women who are marked as different to those women who are already 'modernised' must be brought into the international community. As a form of encounter, this both reproduces the gendering of the international division of labour (where third world women become a sign of tradition that is converted into modernity through the appropriation of that tradition as commodity), as it makes that division the very foundation for a new international community. As such, 'third world women' become those who are already recognised as out of time with the making of a new community, and who can only be brought into time, through entering the modernity promised as the family of the nations (the strangers whose future will be an entry into, and an affirmation of, the inclusivity of the modern and democratic 'we' of the globe).

However, I do not want to suggest that an alternative approach would simply be to welcome those who are already recognised as strangers *as strangers*: such a narrative would repeat the forms of fetishism which allow the concealment of third world women's labour (her difference would then be authenticated as that which is prior to – or resists – assimilation). Rather, we need to recognise the forms of assimilation that already constitute 'other others' in terms of difference (differences which will then be *refined* into what we have in common). In order to do this, we cannot simply overcome the encounters that already assimilate others in a globalised economy of difference. We need a politics that works with what is already assimilated, for example, which accepts that the encounters implicit in the gendering of the international division of labour already mediate how it is possible for women to encounter other women in different nation spaces at all.

Transnational feminist activism must begin, then, with a recognition of the relationship between the local and the global as a site of differentiation, as well as contradiction (Lowe and Lloyd 1997: 15). To begin to link up local sites of feminist activity in a way that is transnational involves recognising how local and transnational processes are already linked in the uneven and contradictory globalisation of capitalist modernity. As a result, transnational feminism becomes possible only when we find the critical resources to activate these (already constituted, but unstable) links between women, in different sites within the globalised economy, in a way which avoids assuming equivalence (Grewal and Kaplan 1994: 19). Or, as Alexander and Mohanty put it, 'we also need to understand the local in relation to larger, cross-national purposes. This would require a corresponding shift in the conception of political organising and mobilization across borders' (1997: xix).

If transnational feminism involves crossing national borders, then we need to consider how it may do so in a way that does not simply reaffirm the border-crossings that are already taking place in global capitalism. I would suggest that we need to think of feminist transnational activism as a way of *(re)encountering what is already encountered*, in the very crossing of national and regional borders. We need to ask: how can feminism be translated across national spaces in a way that works with the very gap between the writing of 'women' as global actors, and forms of action or collective activism? It is where the document fails to translate – where it fails to constitute women as subjects within and subjects of 'the globe' – that an alternative form of transnational feminist activism might become possible. As a result, we can begin to think of transnational feminism as that which necessarily works with the very failure of such encounters to translate into forms of 'being' or 'acting' in the world. Such an emphasis on failure is certainly about recognising how the forms of appropriation of third world women's labour do not fully hold her in place. An encounter premised on the failure of appropriation (gendered global capitalism as a form of 'eating her up') is one that emphasises how 'she' is constituted by, and yet not fully grasped by, such forms of appropriation. But how could such re-encounters, which 'put to work' the failure of the encounters that are already in place, be 'made to work'?

In her preface to Mahasweta Devi's *Imaginary Maps* that I discussed in Chapter 7, Gayatri Spivak discusses the relationship between face-to-face encounters and collective activism in terms of supplementation, calling for 'a collective struggle *supplemented* by the impossibility of full ethical engagement' (Spivak 1995: xxv). She suggests that a collective activism which does not involve face-to-face encounters with others will fail. Such encounters, based on a proximity that does not allow merger, benevolence or knowledge (in other words, that does not overcome distance) involve work: they involve 'painstaking labour'. This work is differentiated from anthropological knowledge: it is not field work (see Chapter 3). Rather, as a form of encounter, it involves getting closer to others in order to occupy or inhabit the distance between us. Such encounters must supplement collective activism precisely because they prevent 'us' assuming we can gain 'access' to the difference of those others whom the networks and flows of global capitalism allow us to recognise as strangers, as out of time with, and out of place in, the 'global community'. At the same time, we cannot assume that the distance or difference 'belongs' to her.

Such a model suggests the intimacy of the political and the ethical as ways of achieving 'better' relationship to others. The relationship between the face to face and the collective needs to be thought beyond the terms of supplementation. The face-to-face encounters or secret meetings discussed by Spivak do not involve the presumption of 'privacy' – these meetings are secret only in the sense that they do not involve the revelation of the other's 'truth'. However, she is also talking about meetings as involving encounters between two people (not 'the self' and 'the other', but this person and that person), which can only happen, 'when the respondents inhabit something like normality' (Spivak 1995: xxv). The meetings that do not reveal, but conceal, are not simply about two people facing each other; rather, such meetings, insofar as they are face to face, are *forms of* (and not supplements to) collective activism, but a collectivity understood in different terms, beyond the reification of the social group. In this sense, meetings are never private; they are not withdrawn from the multiplicity of public spaces (where there are always more than one or two others to be faced). They involve, in the proximity and distance of facing, an engagement with other others. The meeting is singular – it is with 'this other' – and yet also collective – *'this other' brings with her other others.* In getting together, and speaking to each other, we are also opening up a space in which other others can be encountered, even if they are not yet faced.

So, for example, the act of speaking to an other within the improper spaces in the UN conference should not be seen as separate from the collective work done within the conference, and its making of 'women as global agents'. Rather, it is such meetings that both allowed that making to occur (concealed behind the generic 'we' of the document) and, if named or declared, would represent what *does not make up* the category of 'global women'. The constitution of the subject-category 'global women' depends on the erasure or concealment of these close encounters from the document itself. Or, to put it differently, close encounters work with what is *missing from or in the formation of collectives* (they hence cannot take place without or within the forming of collectives).

Thinking of the face-to-face encounter as collective in its very singularity is about developing a different understanding of collective politics in which alliances are always formed insofar as they are *yet to be formed*. Alliances are not guaranteed by the pre-existing form of a social group or community, where that form is understood as commonality (a community of friends) or uncommonality (a community of strangers). The collective then is not simply about what 'we' have in common – or what 'we' do not have in common. Collectivities are formed through the *very work that we need to do* in order to get closer to others, without simply repeating the appropriation of 'them' as labour, or as a sign of difference. Collectivity then is intimately tied to the secrecy of the encounter: it is not about proximity or distance, but a getting closer which accepts the distance, and puts it to work.

What I am calling for, against either universalism or cultural relativism, is politics that is premised on closer encounters, on encounters with those who are other than 'the other' or 'the stranger' ('ourselves undressed'). Such a politics assumes that 'action' and 'activism' cannot be separated out from other forms of work: whether that work is about the differentiation of tasks (globalisation as labour), ways of speaking (to others, with others), and even ways of being in the world. This approach to activism assumes an intimate relationship between action and writing (for example, in the very constitution of 'platforms for action') and it also assumes an intimate relationship between ontology and politics (between being and acting). Thinking about how we might work with, and speak to, others, or how we may inhabit the world *with* others, involves imagining a different form of political community, one that moves beyond the opposition between common and uncommon, between friends and strangers, or between sameness and difference.

Such a politics based on encounters between other others is one bound up with responsibility – with recognising that (labouring) relations between others are always constitutive of the possibility of either speaking or not speaking. Beginning from an 'in-it-ness', a politics of encountering gets closer in order to allow the differences between us, as differences that involve power and antagonism, to make a difference to the very encounter itself. The differences between us necessitate the dialogue, rather than disallow it – a dialogue must take place, precisely *because* we don't speak the same language.

It is the work that needs to be done to get closer to others in a way that does not appropriate their labour as 'my labour', or their talk as 'my talk', that makes possible a different form of collective politics. The 'we' of such a collective politics is what must be worked for, rather than being the foundation of our collective work. In the very 'painstaking labour' of getting closer, of speaking *to* each other, and of working *for* each other, we also get closer to 'other others'. In such acts of alignment (rather than merger), we can reshape the very bodily form of the community, as a community that is yet to come.

One encounters, one has a close encounter, where something happens that is surprising, and where 'we' establish an alliance through the very process of being unsettled by that which is not yet. This is not a community of strangers or friends. It is a community, rather, where we are surprised by those who are already assimilated as strangers in a globalised economy of difference (the spatialisation of labour). In other words, a close encounter is always a strange encounter, where something fails to be revealed. Through strange encounters, transnational feminist communities may be formed by working with what fails to be made into a collective identity (such as 'global woman'), that is, by remaking *what it is that we may yet have in common.*

Notes

Introduction

1 See Chapter 6 for a further exploration of the relationship between commodity fetishism and stranger fetishism.

2 Indeed, my reading of fetishism in terms of the transformation of fantasy into figures brings Marx into dialogue with Freud. We could argue that commodity fetishism involves, not only the displacement of material labour onto objects, but also a process of projection, whereby a fantasy is 'pushed out' and given an external form, as something 'out there'. I am reading stranger fetishism through Marx rather than Freud as I think that Marx's model of what is concealed in the processes of fetishisation (the substitution of the commodity which henceforth becomes an 'enigmatic' object) is more appropriate to my own analysis. While Marx emphasises the material relationships of labour as that which is concealed, and determining in the very act of concealment, Freud's model privileges the phallus, as the lack which is concealed; a lack which is determining of a psychic economy based on having and not having the phallus (Freud 1963: 153–155). The social and material relations of labour can be investigated more fully through the Marxian model: such relations of labour are both determining and yet, by being concealed through processes of fetishisation (the commodity object is 'cut off' and put in their place), those relations cannot simply be accessed as the real. In some sense, the relations of labour are determining *in the very process of displacement and substitution*: they determine insofar as they fail to be revealed within the commodity form. Through re-reading Marx's model of commodity fetishism, we can understand how histories are material (or materialise) as determining, precisely insofar as they cannot be fully revealed in the present. See Anne McClintock's analysis of the limits of a psychoanalytical model of fetishism for social history (1995: 183–184). Despite these limits, my approach to stranger fetishism also depends upon many of the intra- and inter-psychic processes (recognition, projection, identification) that were introduced through the corpus of Freud's work.

3 I would argue that much recent critical theory is deeply invested in figures, such as the figure of the migrant or the nomad (see Chapter 4) and that this investment constitutes a form of fetishism that conceals histories of determination and forms of difference.

4 Following Bauman (1995), Diken does differentiate between different 'types' of strangers, including those that are welcomed (such as tourists) and those that are not welcomed (such as immigrants) (1998: 132). However, this is inadequate: it assumes the category of *an undifferentiated stranger* and then introduces differences as *secondary*, as merely a matter of type. My model of stranger fetish-

ism suggests that such differences are concealed by the very assumption that there is an undifferentiated or unspecified stranger, in the first place.

5 Although I will be examining a few of the critiques of post-colonial theory and criticism, I do not have the time here to do justice to the complexity of the debates. Please see Hall (1996) and Moore-Gilbert (1997) for excellent analyses of the recent critiques of post-colonialism.

6 To talk even of decolonisation is inappropriate in the case of settler colonies like Australia, New Zealand, the United States and Canada. In these cases, the colonisers or invaders did not leave, and no real dismantling of the forms of colonialism has taken place. Although there are significant differences in the recognition of native title in each case, they remain nation-states based on invasion and the appropriation of Indigenous peoples and their land.

7 In this work, I hence name post-coloniality as an impossible context: a context that does not properly explain all the encounters I discuss, but allows me to investigate some *partial sites of determination*. In some instances, then, colonialism is not even my proper object. Rather, this work itself is that which is *in* post-coloniality (in the sense that it is what comes out of it): it was made possible by my own encounters with post-colonialism as it has come into existence as a body of theoretical knowledge. Although this work comes from my own encounter with post-colonialism, *post-coloniality is not a time or space one can simply inhabit*. As a result, post-coloniality is a partial and failed naming of the work itself.

8 I have in an earlier paper been critical of Bhabha's analysis of hybridity for its failure to attend to how hybridity can be recuperated into a discourse of racial purity and its over-emphasis on the transgressive aspects of hybridisation (Ahmed 1999b). However, this critique is not the same as the critique of Bhabha offered by Ahmad and Dirlik, who suggest that Bhabha emphasises hybridity at the expense of an analysis of power (Ahmad 1995: 13; Dirlik 1998: 656). This is an unjust reading. Bhabha's model of hybridity is explicitly linked to power, insofar as it is produced by the very forms of interpellation required by colonial subjectification.

9 Of course, naming Gayatri Spivak as a post-colonial critic has been made problematic by her most recent book, *A Critique of Postcolonial Reason*, which describes her transition from post-colonial theory to transnational cultural studies, and which provides a strong critique of how post-colonialism has appropriated the Native Informant's position (1999: ix). Spivak's critique is quite different from those offered by Dirlik, Juan and Ahmad, who all read post-colonial work as symptomatic of global capitalism. I would read Spivak's critique as an internal one, in that it responds to the contested nature of post-colonialism as a body of work that does tend to invoke too easily the category of 'the other' (for a critique of the use of this category, see Chapter 7). Although I would define this book as having 'come out of' my engagement with post-colonial work, I also have criticisms of other post-colonial writers. I have left the word, 'post-coloniality' in my title, to make clear that this is the terrain where I am, although exactly what 'this terrain' is will always be disputed, and even though I may myself be disputing how others have constituted the terrain. In response to Spivak's critique, I certainly do not position myself as *the other* or the subaltern (rather, I talk of how my own travels are linked to occupying a position of privilege by using the category of 'global nomadic citizenship'); I hence challenge what has been called by some 'postcolonial ventriloquism' (Juan 1998: 8).

10 Such a consideration of the ways in which local encounters with difference are linked to the structuration of global capitalism may allow us to critique the work of Dirlik (1997). His argument that post-colonial theory privileges the

local at the expense of the structural and general, leads to his own privileging of the structural and general at the expense of the local. His suggestion that 'globalized capitalism' is 'the totality within which local cultural encounters take place' (Dirlik 1997: 9) is in danger of reifying the forms of globality itself, and of making 'it' appear as if it comes from nowhere. I want to argue that the global is itself an effect of local encounters, as well as affecting those encounters. My concern with how the local and the global become mutually determined (and are hence not fully determined) is a direct critique of both localism and what we can call theoretical globalism.

1 Recognising strangers

1 To the extent that I am challenging the assumed opposition between strange and familiar (and also in Chapter 4, between home and away), I am following Freud, whose model of the uncanny emphasises how the strange leads back to the familiar. He also suggests that homely (*das Heimliche*) and unhomely (*das Unheimliche*) are intimately linked (Freud 1964: 225–226). However, Freud explains this intimacy of apparent opposites through a model of repression: 'this uncanny is in reality nothing new or alien, but something which is familiar and old established in the mind and which has become alienated from it only through a process of repression' (1964: 241). In contrast, I am seeking to explain the familiarity of the stranger by considering the *production* rather than repression of that which is strange: the stranger is produced as an effect of recognition and as a category of knowledge (see Chapter 2), and is henceforth familiar in its very strangerness. When we look out 'for strangers' we already know what we are looking for.

2 In Chapter 2, I consider how the recognition of strangers involves an economy of touch, as well as a visual economy. We can also note here that recognition has become an important part of political struggle – marginalised groups struggle to be recognised, or *to be seen*, by mainstream politics, which is also a struggle against forms of misrecognition (Taylor 1994; Fraser 1997). A key debate has emerged within feminism on the limits of the politics of recognition (see also Brown 1995; Skeggs 1999). Although I can't enter these debates here, my analysis of how recognition operates as a visual economy in everyday life and social encounters between others might suggest some limits to a politics of recognition, although it might also suggest the difficulties of simply overcoming recognition. In Chapter 6, I complicate this model of recognition as 'seeing the difference' by considering the implications of the structural possibility that the difference might not be seeable as the subject may be passing as it 'passes through' the community.

3 For a discussion of the relationship between migration and strangers see Chapter 4. Here, I argue that migration does not allow us to relativise the condition of strangerness.

4 Alene Branton, secretary to the steering committee of the National Neighbourhood Watch Association in the UK, is reported to have said, 'We were set up to be the eyes and ears of the police. We never expected to be the feet as well' (Bennetto 1995).

5 He contrasts the modern proximity of strangers with 'primitive cultures' where strangers are more at a distance.

6 I also consider the relationship between dwelling and movement in chapters 4 and 8 where I develop the notion of 'global nomadic citizenship'.

7 Importantly, stranger danger discourse attempts to define the stranger as anybody we don't know; it seeks to contest what I have called the recognisability of strangers, and the assumption that 'strangers' only look a certain way. As James

Brewer puts it, 'Who are the bad guys? How can you recognise them before its too late? ... What do the bad guys look like? They look like *YOU*' (1994: 15, 17). What this reveals, despite itself, is precisely the ways in which strangers are already recognised as looking unlike 'YOU': the discourse of stranger danger seeks to contest the very familiarity of strangers, but can only do so, by first confirming that familiarity, and the 'common-sense' assumption that danger is posed only by certain bodies, who are marked by their difference from the everyday of the neighbourhood.

2 Embodying strangers

1 Feminist critiques of Merleau-Ponty have drawn attention to how his approach to embodiment has been based around an elided masculinity (Irigaray 1993; Young 1990). What I want to suggest is that the failure to address (sexual) difference is structural to his model of inter-embodiment as a generalised 'sharing between bodies'. Difference is here not what is already marked on bodies (such as male or female bodies), but is what is constituted through the very forms of inter-embodiment, or bodily exchange, that Merleau-Ponty draws our attention to, in his powerful descriptions of his own bodily dwelling.
2 In Chapter 6, I further complicate this analysis by examining how bodies can take shape through the recognition of 'the strange' as assimilable. In the desire to assimilate that which has already been recognised as strange, there is also a desire to get closer to 'the stranger's body', or even to inhabit that body. I demonstrate that such a desire for proximity does not fully expand the contours of the *body-at-home* to incorporate the stranger's body: what is confirmed is precisely the difference between the one who is the stranger, who becomes reduced to the body, and the one who *temporarily* becomes or passes as the stranger, by moving through the body.
3 This idea of expanding and contracting skins is further developed in Chapter 4, where I consider how migration involves skin sensations and skin memories.

3 Knowing strangers

1 There is an intimate relationship assumed here between 'foe' and stranger. In Latin, the word for 'stranger' was the same as the word for 'enemy' (Walzer 1989: 32). This conflation of stranger and enemy survives powerfully in the stranger danger discourses discussed in the previous chapter. However, the broader argument of this book is that the identification of stranger as a friend still relies on the same discursive mechanisms (which I have theorised as 'stranger fetishism') as the identification of the stranger as an enemy. In this chapter, the stranger is known again precisely as the one who is different from 'us', yet also familiar in that difference. The accumulation of knowledge about strangers hence functions to establish an epistemic community.
2 See also Chapter 8 for a further exploration of these issues.
3 I have put 'co-author' in quotation marks because it is this description of Topsy Napurrula Nelson's contribution to the article that is precisely in dispute. Huggins *et al.* suggest that naming Nelson as co-author rather than chief informant involves an appropriation of her voice, while Bell argues that naming her as chief informant rather than co-author would involve a denial of her voice.
4 This letter was eventually published in 1991, with the following names: Jackie Huggins, Jo Willmot, Isabel Tarrago, Kathy Willetts, Liz Bond, Lillian Holt, Eleanor Bourke, Maryann Bin-Salik, Pat Fowell, Joann Schmider, Valerie Craige and Linda McBride-Levi. It was printed along with another response from Diane Bell (who always seems to be given the last word) and an editorial which

clearly 'sides' with Bell against the dissenting Indigenous women. As a reader, I found this editorial extremely dismissive in its refusal to even recognise the substance of Huggins *et al.*'s critique about race and/in feminism. The editorial simply implies that the Indigenous women are betraying feminism with the following statement: 'we find it deplorable that speaking out about rape still means paying a price – even in *feminist* circles' (Klein 1991: 505–506). See Aileen Moreton-Robinson (forthcoming) for a fuller account of what was and is at stake for Indigenous women who questioned Bell's authority to speak.

5   Hence it is not surprising that in Bell's more recent ethnography she links her work to the 'postmodern turn in anthropology', though she also describes postmodern work as 'jargon-ridden, elitist and morally vacuous' (1998: 30).

6   One of the problems of considering the debate in terms of 'who speaks' is that it allows others to trivialise the issue of representation. Take the dialogue between Larbalestier and Bell that took place in the *Anthropological Forum*. Larbalestier claims that the problem with the original article is not so much 'what is said', but the 'shaping of the speech' (1990: 146). Bell responds to this by reading 'the shaping of the speech' as simply a matter of form or aesthetics: 'Were I undertaking an analysis of say, an epic poem, I might find it helpful, but Napurrula and I were trying to tell you (the reader) that Aboriginal women and girls were being raped' (Bell 1990: 163). Of course, by paying attention to the shaping of the speech, Larbalestier is actually talking about the *institutional conditions* which make speech acts possible, and which affect the form that the speech acts take. My attempt to move the terrain from the question of 'who speaks' to 'who knows' – and from the question of otherness to strangerness – is an attempt to show that the issues involved in speech acts are not trivial, but substantive, and that they can involve issues of violence.

7   Joy Hendrey emphasises the problems and risks attached to the development of friendships within the field. The relationship, in her case, increased her knowledge at the expense of friendship (Hendrey 1992: 173). Alternatively, you could argue that the increase of knowledge takes place *through* her friendship (see also Hastrup 1995: 2–4).

8   For an exploration of the relationship between 'being strange' and 'becoming strange' in consumerism see Chapter 6.

9   As Annette Hamilton argues, the picture presented by Bell of the Indigenous women tends to locate them in the past, rather than 'as political actors in the contemporary scene' (1986: 14). This contributes to a representation of 'them' as 'being' rather than 'becoming', as having 'an' identity which can be known and interpreted through ethnographic translation. I consider Diane Bell's later ethnography, *Ngarrindjeri Wurruwarrin*, quite different in this respect. Not only is there more attention to the partiality of her own perspective throughout the text (the I doesn't insert itself, only then to disappear), but you get a sense of the complexity of the relationship of the past and the present, as well as the impossibility of grasping the truth of the Ngarrindjeri women in the ethnographic document, given the ways in which their stories interweave. Of course, in this text, Bell is also responding to the Hindmarsh Island Royal Commission in 1995 and the failure of the Ngarrindjeri women's land claim in South Australia. Doesn't this remind us that ethnographic knowledges are necessary for social justice, that Indigenous peoples need anthropologists to help them to reclaim the land that has been stolen? In the opening prologue, Bell implies that better ethnography would have led to a just resolution in the Hindmarsh Island case (1998: 35). At times, she almost mourns the absence of anthropologists in past encounters between white peoples and Indigenous peoples (Bell 1998: 154). The implication of centring such a regretful narrative on the absence of anthropologists, is that anthropologists (at least good ones) would

have provided the necessary witnesses to establish the truth of Indigenous oral testimonies. While I can certainly recognise the good political sense of this argument, I would also point to the injustice that is already at stake in the very rule of law that requires that oral testimonies be translated into anthropological truths before they can be given a proper hearing. That is, the position of anthropologists as proper witnesses as well as translators (translating Indigenous knowledges into documents that are admissible to the Law) is linked to injustice rather than the realisation of social justice. This does not mean that anthropologists should stop representing Indigenous peoples in land claims. Of course, it does not – we have to work within the pragmatic constraints that are enforced by the common law, as it unfolds through its legal decisions and judgements. We have to fight for justice in particular cases, even if there is an injustice in the very way we have to fight for justice. As we work within these constraints, we need to think more critically about what would be the necessary conditions for an-other justice.

4 Home and away: narratives of migration and estrangement

1　As I argued in the introduction, stranger fetishism operates precisely as a fetishism of figures. The figure comes to have a 'life of its own' by being cut off from the histories of its determination which I have theorised in terms of strange encounters (suggesting that the history of its determination, also involves the failure of its determination).

2　Although I offer here a strong critique of Braidotti's use of 'the nomad' as a figure, I am otherwise very sympathetic to her theoretical and political commitment to explore the difficulties and contradictions of subjectivity and community.

3　To define free choice against force is certainly to beg a lot of important questions about the social conditions that make some movements possible and others impossible. On the one hand, you can consider the refugee as the one who is forced to move due to situations of extreme persecution. However, to conclude from this that migrants make free choices is to assume that force only operates in this way. The constraints to choice do not just impose on the body from the outside, but are constitutive of subjects in the first place. The whole notion of 'choosing' requires a more proper dismantling in its very presupposition of an autonomous subject who can be detached from the social relations in which it is embedded.

4　In a similar vein, we can contest the opposition between local and transnational (see Chapter 8). It is problematic to define the local in terms of fixity, and the transnational in terms of movement. As Lata Mani has argued, 'the local' is not a fixed point, but involves a temporality of struggle (1989: 5). Caren Kaplan also suggests that we should view the local in terms of movement and multiplicity rather than stasis and singularity (1998: 168). Likewise, I am suggesting that 'home' needs to be theorised in terms of movement as well as attachment. That is, we need to avoid 'locating' movement in what is 'away' from 'home'.

5 Multiculturalism and the proximity of strangers

1　This is the major category used to define ethnic difference. Clearly, this is quite important as it makes language the key register of difference. Given the role of the English language in disseminating national culture (one of the explicit 'limits of multiculturalism'), as well as the way in which such a definition conceals, not only race, but also ethnicity, the use of the category has strategic effects. For a discussion of the effects of the category see Jupp 1996: 9–12.

2 For example, in the context of Native Title, Aboriginal people's land claims must be accommodated within the Law that historically has been linked to their historical dispossession. In Elizabeth Povinelli's excellent discussion of multiculturalism and Indigenous citizenship, she argues that, 'In the liberal imagination, the state apparatuses, as well as its law, principles of governance, and national attitudes, need only to be *adjusted* to accommodate others: they do not need to experience the fundamental alterity of, in this case, Indigenous discourse, desires and practices' (1998: 581).

3 See Ghassan Hage's analysis of multiculturalism as cultural enrichment. In his reading, the multicultural national subject (who is structured around a fantastic whiteness) 'mixes' the 'ethnic stew' and claims agency in the very act of allowing others to co-exist, in order to be enriched by them (1998: 118–121). See also my discussion of multiculturalism and food in Chapter 6.

4 The One Nation party entered the political stage with the election of Pauline Hanson as an Independent Candidate to the House of Representatives in March 1996. She since lost her seat in 1998, although One Nation remains vocal as a political force. As an extreme right and populist party, One Nation is both a response to the particular struggles over nationhood in Australia, and can be situated in relation to the emergence of other monocultural agendas in right-wing opposition politics, particularly in the United States.

5 For an analysis of the role of shame in discourses around reconciliation see Povinelli (1998) and Probyn (forthcoming). For an analysis of the limits of tolerance within multiculturalism see Hage (1998: 85–86) and Ang (1996: 38–40).

6 This account of the origins of multiculturalism does name different racial and ethnic groups. However, what it does is juxtapose them: it simply places them alongside each other as contributors to Australian multiculturalism. Such an uncritical juxtaposition works to conceal the differences in the position of Indigenous peoples and migrants in relationship to white settler groups. Part of the problem in the more recent report is the equation of Indigenous issues and immigration through the inclusive language of multiculturalism.

7 This notion of hospitality is investigated further in Chapter 7, where I attempt to theorise a form of hospitality that does not rely on stranger fetishism.

6 Going strange, going native

1 I am indebted to my student Jane Huntley, whose wonderful essay on Boots's '*Global Collection*', not only made me aware of the significance of the *Global Collection*, but also inspired these opening comments. Boots is a nationwide pharmacy and superstore in the United Kingdom. The *Global Collection* is a range of cosmetic products which is marketed as coming from different regions of the world.

2 The title of this chapter points to an instructive paradox. A classical opposition is, of course, between natives and strangers. But as I argued in my reading of anthropological ethnographies (Chapter 3), the 'native' is associated with the state of 'being a stranger', while the anthropologist (who is apparently away from home) is the one who 'becomes a stranger' (rather than *is* one) by transforming that being into knowledge. As such, 'going native', as a nineteenth-century fantasy (see Low 1996), slides easily into a narrative of 'going strange'.

3 In the case of the hair treatment, the caption reads that, 'Oshima, Japan, is the traditional source of material camellia extract.' In other words, the selling of the commodity fixes difference through telling a story of origins. We must refuse to

participate in the narrative by assuming the object itself has come 'from there'. Rather, we must ask, how does the object become consumed through the imaginary construction of 'there'. Globalisation must be understood, not only in terms of actual global interchange or interconnectedness and the crossing of borders, but also as doing the work of the imaginative construction (and with it, regulation) of places and spaces.

4 As I suggested in Chapter 5, a multicultural Australia is constructed through the normalisation of whiteness; it is the white national subject who decides which 'others' can be 'welcomed into' the nation. We can think of Australian multiculturalism as involving the production of 'hybridised whiteness': the white nation is transformed by the process of incorporating non-white others, but a transformation that does not question the *already* white constitution of the face of the nation. Indeed, as I suggest later in this chapter, whiteness is linked with becoming rather than being: it is linked precisely with its own ability to 'undo itself' through getting closer to others. The hybridisation of whiteness is one way in which it is constituted as pliable, and as 'on the move', rather than fixed.

5 For a close and critical reading of this text see Chapter 3 of my book, *Differences that Matter* (1998a). For a reading of Deleuze and Guattari's becoming in relationship to *Dances with Wolves* see Ahmed 1999a.

6 The privileging of becoming can be related to the privileging of migration and nomadism in critical theory (Chambers 1994: 4). See Chapter 4 for a critique of the assumption that migrancy and nomadism are always transgressive of identity thinking.

7 For a more extended discussion of passing see Ahmed (1999b).

8 I have written extensively about this event, which involves other aspects that I cannot mention here. It was this event that first inspired me to think about strange encounters as a way of theorising how subjects are both fixed and unfixed in regimes of difference. When I was first working on this project, I had intended to introduce this book by discussing this encounter, which was very significant in mobilising me, politically, as a young person. However, the encounter kept cropping up in all my other writing. I felt it was time to leave it behind or, as it turns out, to prevent it from 'centring' my writing (so it does crop up, but not until Chapter 6). There are always other encounters at stake. Memory work can be thought of in terms of returning to such 'unsettling encounters' that one may have in 'public life' (Goffman 1972); those moments when one is faced by others (especially others that have a relationship to the law such as parents, teachers or the police) in such a way that one is 'moved from one's place'. I think memory work in critical writing is crucial precisely as a way of *re-encountering these encounters*. This is why the encounter discussed by Audre Lorde in *Sister Outsider*, between herself as a child and a white woman on a train, is so powerful, as a form of personal, intellectual and political work (see Chapter 2).

9 Please see my analysis of skin fetishism in Chapter 2 and my consideration of the relationship between migration, memory and skin in Chapter 4.

10 This recalls my discussion in Chapter 5 of the multicultural demand that the different appearance of strangers must conceal and reveal 'a native heart'.

11 There is an interesting gendered dimension to the narratives of passing for black as a white subject. In the stories of white women who pass, the emphasis is very much on their sympathy and involvement with others. In the story of the white man who passes in *Black Like Me*, the emphasis is on his ability to observe the reactions of others from a distance. Here, white femininity and white masculinity are reconstituted through passing in a way that conserves, not only the privilege of whiteness, but also traditional forms of gender differentiation.

7 Ethical encounters: the other, others and strangers

1 To be fair to Bauman, this follows from Levinas's own critique of Heidegger's notion of *Mitsein* – with-ness – as ontological (insofar as it presupposes that one *is* before one is *with* others), against which Levinas contrasts for-ness, as ethical (before being). I would argue that 'with-ness' could be theorised as pre-ontological, that is, before one 'is' one is 'with'. In other words, with-ness could be theorised as prior to being, an approach that would place sociality – with-ness – and ethics – for-ness – together.

2 In *Differences that Matter* (1998a), I also make this mistake. Although I associate particularity with the general (the particular other is located in a broader set of social relations), I do imply that a particular other (the subaltern woman) is missing from Levinas, and hence I fetishise her particularity. My attempt here is to find another way of making the particularity of 'differences' matter in ethics.

3 Derrida, in his later work on Levinas, deconstructs the opposition between host and guest:

> the *hôte* who receives (the host), the one who welcomes the invited or re-ceived *hôte* (the guest), the welcoming *hôte* who considers himself the owner of the place, is in truth a *hôte* received in his own home. He re-ceives the hospitality that he offers *in* his own home; he receives it *from* his own home – which in the end does not belong to him. The *hôte* as host is a guest.
>
> (1999: 41)

This understanding of the host as guest also involves a deconstruction of the native/stranger opposition: the natives are also the strangers, estranged from the very home that receives them. Returning to my argument in Chapter 5, you could argue that multicultural hospitality, in which 'white Australians' are positioned as 'the natives', is premised on the mastery of the host, as the one who will or will not welcome the guest/stranger. As I argued, the notion of 'welcoming the strangers' is premised on the same mastery as the notion of 'expelling them' – in both cases, the encounter with 'the strangers' becomes a means by which the 'we' asserts itself as *willing*, even if that 'we' is touched differently by the difference that is assumed to belong to 'the strangers'. We can now also see that the mastery implicit in multicultural hospitality (a hospitality which is not very hospitable) relies also on concealing the fact that the 'nation/home' is not 'ours to give', but gives to us. An ethics and politics beyond multicultural hospitality requires that we give up the notion that the home is 'ours to give'. In this sense, 'we are all guests', relying on the hospitality of others. While this is extremely suggestive, we must be careful to recognise that the power to give remains with the national subject (in this case, the white Australian subject) and that any ethics or politics of hospitality must recognise the power that *already* exists *to allow some guests to act as hosts* (the transformation of guests into hosts has material effects: it involves an economy of difference). In other words, even if no subjects have the intrinsic 'right' to be hosts, some subjects have the power to be hosts. This means that even if we are all guests, *we are not all guests in the same way*. We need to consider colonialism in terms of the historical injustice of the transformation of guests into hosts before we can ask the question of what would be a better form of hospitality.

8 Close encounters: feminism and/in 'the globe'

1 Or, alternatively, the event of discovering a 'shared birthday' often comes to be felt as a 'special bond'.

2 For example, see the report by Graham Hutchings and Christopher Munnion, 'Hilary should stick to the US, says Beijing', *The Daily Telegraph*, 8 September 1995.

3 I am alluding here to Spivak's notion of secret encounters with the subaltern woman through which she articulates an understanding of ethical singularity in the context of the global. See Chapter 7 for an elaboration of Spivak's ethics of singularity.

4 See the report by Graham Hutchings (1995). Hutchings comments: 'Taxi drivers are said to have been told not to accept fare from women in a state of undress, and to eject female passengers if they try and strip off inside the cab'. See also the report by James Pringle (1995). Pringle comments on the use of insect repellents 'in case the city's mosquitoes pick up AIDS'. The links between the construction of sexuality (sexual excess) and disease were important in establishing the danger of 'foreign women' to the public health and morality of the city. There was particular attention to the 'dangers' of prostitutes and lesbians.

5 I am indebted to Marta Herrero and Jackie Stacey for sharing with me their work on The Body Shop.

6 For a discussion of the use of rights discourse in and around the conference see Chapter 1 of my book *Differences that Matter*, and Sum (forthcoming).

7 Thanks to Ngai-Ling Sum whose chapter in our edited book, *Transformations* (forthcoming) brought this speech to my attention.

8 The document maintains this contradiction throughout, at times talking about women as differentiated subjects and elsewhere using gender-neutral language, or adding 'and men'. This contradiction represents the tension between the neo-liberal agenda of the document – with its emphasis on the individual as an autonomous subject, whose potential is guaranteed by freedom from social relations in which it is embedded – and the feminist concern with gender as a site of social differentiation. See my discussion of the relationship between feminism and multiculturalism in Chapter 5 for a teasing out of some of these tensions.

9 This is not just about third world debt – for example, as my reading of Devi's story in Chapter 7 demonstrated, debts for subaltern subjects can be accrued through local developers who have an alliance with global capital (see Spivak 1995: 198). A fuller investigation of the relationship between subject constitution and debt is required – such an investigation would no doubt draw on the legacy of Marxist theory.

References

Agar, M. (1980) *The Professional Stranger: An Informal Introduction to Ethnography*, New York: Academic Press.

Ahmad, A. (1992) *In Theory: Classes. Nations. Literatures*, London: Verso.

—— (1995) 'The Politics of Literary Post-Coloniality', *Race and Class* 36, 3: 1–20.

Ahmad, R. and Gupta, R. (eds) (1994) *Flaming Spirit: Stories from the Asian Women's Writing Collective*, London: Virago Press.

Ahmed, S. (1998a) *Differences that Matter: Feminist Theory and Postmodernism*, Cambridge: Cambridge University Press.

—— (1998b) 'Tanning the Body: Skin, Colour and Tanning', *New Formations* 34: 27–42.

—— (1999a) 'Phantasies of Becoming (the Other)', *European Journal of Cultural Studies* 2, 1: 47–63.

—— (1999b) ' "She'll Wake up One of These Days and Find She's Turned into a Nigger": Passing Through Hybridity', *Theory. Culture and Society* 16, 2: 87–106.

Alexander, M.J. and Mohanty, C.T. (1997) 'Introduction: Genealogies, Legacies and Movements' in M.J. Alexander and C.T. Mohanty (eds) *Feminist Genealogies. Colonial Legacies. Democratic Futures*, New York: Routledge.

Althusser, L. (1971) *Lenin and Philosophy and Other Essays*, trans. B. Brewster, London: New Left Books.

Anderson, B. (1983) *Imagined Communities: Reflections on the Origin and Spread of Nationalism*, London: Verso.

Anderson, E. (1990) *Streetwise: Race. Class and Change in an Urban Community*, Chicago: University of Chicago Press.

Ang, I. (1996) 'The Curse of the Smile: Ambivalence and the "Asian" Woman in Australian Multiculturalism', *Feminist Review* 52: 36–49.

Asad, T. (ed.) (1973) *Anthropology and the Colonial Encounter*, London: Ithaca Press.

—— (1986) 'The Concept of Cultural Translation in British Social Anthropology' in J. Clifford and G.E. Marcus (eds) *Writing Culture: The Poetics and Politics of Ethno-graphy*, Cambridge: Cambridge University Press.

Australian Council on Population and Ethnic Affairs (1982) *Multiculturalism for All Australians: Our Developing Nationhood*, Canberra, Australia.

Australian Law Reform Commission (1991) 'Multiculturalism: Criminal Law', Discussion Paper 48. Sydney, Australia.

Bailyn, B. and Morgan, P.D. (1991) *Strangers Within the Realm: Cultural Margins of the First British Empire*, Chapel Hill: University of North Carolina Press.

Balibar, E. (1991) 'Is There a "Neo-Racism"?' in E. Balibar and I. Wallerstein (eds) *Race, Nation and Class: Ambiguous Identities*, London: Verso.

Bauman, Z. (1993) *Postmodern Ethics*, Oxford: Blackwell.

—— (1995) *Life in Fragments: Essays in Postmodern Morality*, Oxford: Blackwell.

—— (1997) 'The Making and Unmaking of Strangers' in P. Werbner and T. Modood (eds) *Debating Cultural Hybridity: Multi-Cultural Identities and the Politics of Anti-Racism*, London: Zed Books.

Bell, D. (1983) *Daughters of the Dreaming*, St Leonards, NSW: Allen and Unwin.

—— (1990) 'A Reply from Diane Bell', *Anthropological Forum* 6, 2: 158–165.

—— (1991a) 'Intraracial Rape Revisited: On Forging a Feminist Future Beyond Factions and Identity Politics', *Women's Studies International Forum* 14, 5: 385–412.

—— (1991b) 'Letter to the Editor', *Women's Studies International Forum* 14, 5: 507–513.

—— (1993) ' "Yes Virginia, There is a Feminist Ethnography": Reflections from 3 Australian Fields' in D. Bell, P. Caplan and W.J. Karim (eds) *Gendered Fields: Women, Men and Ethnography*, London: Routledge.

—— (1996) 'White Women Can't Speak?' in Sue Wilkinson and Celia Kitzinger (eds) *Representing the Other: A Feminism and Psychology Reader*, London: Sage.

—— (1998) *Ngarrindjeri Wurruwarrin; A World That Is, Was, and Will Be*, North Melbourne: Spinifex Press.

Bell, D. and Nelson, T.N. (1989) 'Speaking about Rape is Everyone's Business', *Women's Studies International Forum* 12, 4: 403–416.

Benhabib, S. (1992) *Situating the Self: Gender, Community and Postmodernism in Contemporary Ethics*, Cambridge: Polity Press.

Bennetto, J. (1995) 'Alert After Jewish Graves Desecrated', *The Independent*, 3 June.

Bhabha, H. (1994) *The Location of Culture*, London: Routledge.

Bhachu, P. (1996) 'The Multiple Landscapes of Transnational Asian Women in the Diaspora' in V. Amit-Talai and C. Knowles (eds) *Re-Situating Identities: The Politics of Race, Ethnicity and Culture*, Ontoria: Broadview Press.

Biddle, J. (1997) 'Shame', *Australian Feminist Studies* 2, 6: 222–239.

Blanchot, M. (1993) *The Infinite Conversation*, trans. S. Hanson, Minneapolis: University of Minnesota Press.

—— (1986) *The Writing of the Disaster*, trans. A. Smock, Lincoln: University of Nebraska Press.

Body Shop International PLC (1994) *The Body Shop Book: Skin, Hair and Body Care*, London: Little Brown Company.

—— (1999) *The Naked Body*, Spring Edition.

Bordo, S. (1993) *Unbearable Weight: Feminism, Western Culture and the Body*, University of Berkeley: California Press.

Bottomley, G. (1992) *From Another Place: Migration and the Politics of Culture*, Cambridge: Cambridge University Press.

Brah, A. (1996) *Cartographies of Diaspora: Contesting Identities*, London: Routledge.

Braidotti, R. (1994) *Nomadic Subjects: Embodiment and Sexual Difference in Contemporary Feminist Theory*, New York: Columbia University Press.

Brewer, J.D. (1994) *The Danger from Strangers: Confronting the Threat of Assault*, New York: Insight Books.

Brinks, E. (1995) ' "Who's Been in my Closet?": Mimetic Identification and the Psychosis of Class Transvestism in *Single White Female*' in S.E. Case, P. Brett and S.L.

Foster (eds) *Cruising the Performative: Interventions into the Representation of Ethnicity, Nationality and Sexuality*, Bloomington: Indiana University Press.

Brown, W. (1995) *States of Injury: Power and Freedom in Late Modernity*, Princeton: Princeton University Press.

Buijs, G. (1993) 'Introduction' in G. Buijs (ed.) *Migrant Women: Crossing Boundaries and Changing Identities*, Oxford: Berg.

Butler, J. (1993) *Bodies that Matter: On the Discursive Limits of 'Sex'*, London: Routledge.

Cataldi, S. (1993) *Emotion, Depth and the Flesh: A Study of Sensitive Space*, New York: State University of New York Press.

Chambers, I. (1994) *Migrancy, Culture, Identity*, London: Routledge.

Clifford, J. (1986) 'Partial Truths' in J. Clifford and G.E. Marcus (eds) *Writing Culture: The Poetics and Politics of Ethno-graphy*, Cambridge: Cambridge University Press.

Clinton, H. (1995) 'Remarks for the United Nations: Fourth World Conference on Women', Beijing, China, 5 September. www. whitehouse.gov/ White House/EOP/First lady/9-5-95.html

Cohen, R. (1994) *Frontiers of Identity: The British and the Others*, London: Longman.

Cornell, D. (1992) *The Philosophy of the Limit*, London: Routledge.

Crapanzano, V. (1986) 'Hermes' Dilemma: The Masking of Subversion in Ethnographic Description' in J. Clifford and G.E. Marcus (eds) *Writing Culture: The Poetics and Politics of Ethno-graphy*, Cambridge: Cambridge University Press.

Crenson, M.A. (1983) *Neighborhood Politics*, Cambridge, MA: Harvard University Press.

Critchley, S. (1992) *The Ethics of Deconstruction: Derrida and Levinas*, London: Routledge.

Davis, C. (1996) *Levinas: An Introduction*, Cambridge: Polity Press.

de Certeau, M. (1986) *Heterologies: Discourse on the Other*, Manchester: Manchester University Press.

Deleuze, G. and Guattari, F. (1992) *A Thousand Plateaus: Capitalism and Schizophrenia*, trans. B. Massumi, London: Athlone Press.

Department of Immigration and Multicultural Affairs (1989) *National Agenda for a Multicultural Australia*, www.immi.gov.au/multicultural/toc.htm

Department of Immigration and Multicultural Affairs (1997) *Multicultural Australia: The Way Forward*, www.immi.gov.au/multicultural/macpaper.htm

Derrida, J. (1978) *Writing and Difference*, trans. A. Bass, Chicago: University of Chicago Press.

—— (1986) 'Declarations of Independence', *New Political Science* 15: 7–15.

—— (1988) *The Ear of the Other: Otobiography, Transference, Translation*, trans. P. Kamuf, Lincoln: University of Nebraska Press.

—— (1992) *Given Time: 1 Counterfeit Money*, trans. P. Kamuf, Chicago: University of Chicago Press.

—— (1993) *Aporias*, trans. T. Dutoit, Stanford: Stanford University Press.

—— (1995) *Politics of Friendship*, trans. G. Collins, London: Verso.

—— (1999) *Adieu to Emmanuel Levinas*, trans. P.A. Brault and M. Naas, Stanford: Stanford University Press.

Devi, M. (1995) 'Douloti the Bountiful' in *Imaginary Maps*, trans. G.C. Spivak, New York: Routledge.

Dhingra, L. (1994) ' La Vie en Rose' in K. Pullinger (ed.) *Border Lines: Stories of Exile and Home*, New York: Serpent's Tail.

Diken, B. (1998) *Strangers, Ambivalence and Social Theory*, Aldershot: Ashgate.

Dillon, M. (1999) 'The Sovereign and the Stranger' in J. Edkins, N. Persram and V. Pin-Fat (eds) *Sovereignty and Subjectivity*, Boulder, CO: Lynne Rienner Publishers.

Diprose, R. (1994) *The Bodies of Women: Ethics, Embodiment and Sexual Difference*, London: Routledge.

—— (1996) 'Giving Corporeality Against The Law', *Australian Feminist Studies* 11, 24: 253–262.

Dirlik, A. (1997) *The Postcolonial Aura: Third World Criticism in the Age of Global Capitalism*, Boulder, CO: Westview Press.

Doel, M. (1995) 'Bodies Without Organs: Schizoanalysis and Deconstruction' in S. Pile and N. Thrift (eds) *Mapping the Subject: Geographies of Cultural Transformation*, London: Routledge.

Douglas, M. (1994) *Purity and Danger: An Analysis of the Concepts of Pollution and Taboo*, London: Routledge.

Fabian, J. (1992) *Time and the Work of Anthropology: Critical Essays 1971–1991*, Switzerland: Harwood Academic Publishers.

Fanon, F. (1975) *Black Skin, White Masks*, trans. C.L. Markmann, London: Paladin.

Featherstone, M. (1990) *Global Culture: Nationalism, Globalization and Modernity*, London: Sage.

Féher, F. and Heller, A. (1994) 'Naturalisation or "Culturalisation"?' in R. Bauböck (ed.) *From Aliens to Citizens: Redefining the Status of Immigrants in Europe*, New York: Avebury Press.

Felman, S. (1992) 'Education and Crisis, or the Vicissitudes of Teaching' in S. Felman and D. Laub (eds) *Testimony: Crises of Witnessing in Literature, Psychoanalysis and History*, London: Routledge.

Foucault, M. (1975) *Discipline and Punish: The Birth of the Prison*, trans. A. Sheridan, New York: Pantheon Books.

Fraser, N. (1989) *Unruly Practices: Power, Discourse and Gender in Contemporary Social Theory*, Cambridge: Polity Press.

—— (1997) *Justice Interruptus: Critical Reflections on the 'PostSocialist' Condition*, New York: Routledge.

Freud, S. (1963) 'Three Essays on the Theory of Sexuality' in *The Standard Edition of the Complete Psychological Works of Freud*, vol. VII, trans. J. Strachey, London: The Hogarth Press.

—— (1964) 'The Uncanny' in *The Standard Edition of the Complete Psychological Works of Freud*, vol. XVII, trans, J. Strachey, London: The Hogarth Press.

Frow, J. and Morris, M. (1993) 'Introduction' in J. Frow and M. Morris (eds) *Australian Cultural Studies: A Reader*, St Leonards: Allen and Unwin.

Ganguly, K. (1992) 'Migrant Identities, Personal Memory and the Construction of Self', *Cultural Studies* 6: 27–51.

Garber, M. (1992) *Vested Interests: Cross-Dressing and Cultural Anxiety*, London: Routledge.

Gatens, M. (1991) 'Corporeal Representation in/and The Body Politic' in R. Diprose and R. Ferrel (eds) *Cartographies: Poststructuralism and the Mapping of Bodies and Spaces*, St Leonards: Allen and Unwin.

—— (1996) *Imaginary Bodies: Ethics, Power and Corporeality*, London: Routledge.

Gilman, S. (1985) *Difference and Pathology: Stereotypes of Sexuality, Race and Madness*, Ithaca: Cornell University Press.

Giroux, H. (1994) *Disturbing Pleasures*, London: Routledge.

Goffman, E. (1972) *Relations in Public: Microstudies of the Public Order*, New York: Harper and Row.

—— (1984) *Stigma: Notes on the Management of Spoiled Identity*, Harmondsworth: Pelican Books.

Goldberg, D.T. (1994) 'Introduction: Multicultural Conditions' in D.T. Goldberg (ed.) *Multiculturalism*, Oxford: Blackwell.

Goldman, A.H. (1995) 'Comparative Identities: Exile in the Writings of Frantz Fanon and W.E.B. Du Bois' in M.G. Henderson (ed.) *Borders, Boundaries and Frames: Essays in Cultural Criticism and Cultural Studies*, London: Routledge.

Greenblatt, S. (1993) 'Introduction' in S.J. Greenblatt (ed.) *New World Encounters*, Berkeley: University of California Press.

Grewal, I. and Kaplan, C. (1994) 'Introduction' in I. Grewal and C. Kaplan (eds) *Scattered Hegemonies: Postmodernity and Transnational Feminist Practices*, Minneapolis: University of Minnesota Press.

Griffin, J.H. (1970) *Black Like Me*, London: Panther Modern Society.

Grosz, E. (1994) *Volatile Bodies: Towards a Corporeal Feminism*, London: Routledge.

Grosz, E. and Probyn, E. (eds) (1995) *Sexy Bodies: The Strange Carnalities of Feminism*, London: Routledge.

Gunew, S. (1994) *Framing Marginality: Multicultural Literary Studies*, Ringwood, Victoria: Penguin.

Hage, G. (1998) *White Nation: Fantasies of White Supremacy in a Multicultural Society*, Annandale, NSW: Pluto Press.

Hall, S. (1996) 'When was the "Post-Colonial?":Thinking at the Limit' in I. Chambers and L. Curti (eds) *The Post-Colonial Question: Common Skies. Divided Horizons*, London: Routledge.

Hallman, H.W. (1984) *Neighborhoods: Their Place in Urban Life*, Beverley Hills: Sage Publications.

Hamilton, A. (1986) 'Daughters of the Imaginary', *Canberra Anthropology* 9, 2: 1–25.

Hanson, P. (1997) *The Truth*, Ipswich, Queensland: n.p.

Hastrup, K. (1995) *A Passage to Anthropology: Between Experience and Theory*, London: Routledge.

Hendrey, J. (1992) 'The Paradox of Friendship in the Field' in J. Okely and H. Callaway (eds) *Anthropology and Autobiography*, London: Routledge.

Hill, D.M. (1994) *Citizens and Cities: Urban Policy in the 1990s*, Hemel Hempstead: Harvester Wheatsheaf.

Hilpern, K. (1997) 'Child Protection: Law and the Lynch Mob', *The Guardian* 19 February.

Home Office (1992) *Welcome to Neighbourhood Watch*: Great Britain.

—— (1997) *Welcome to Neighbourhood Watch*: Great Britain.

hooks, b. (1992) 'Eating the Other' in *Black Looks: Race and Representation*, London: Turnaround.

Horton, J. (1993) 'Liberalism, Multiculturalism and Tolerance' in J. Horton (ed.) *Liberalism, Multiculturalism and Toleration*, Houndmills: Macmillan.

Huggins, J. (1994) 'A Contemporary View of Aboriginal Women's Relationship to the White Women's Movement' in N. Grieve and A. Burns (eds) *Australian Women: Contemporary Feminist Thought*, Oxford: Oxford University Press.

Huggins, J. *et al.* (1991) 'Letter to the Editor', *Women's Studies International Forum* 14, 5: 507–513.

Hulme, P. (1986) *Colonial Encounters: Europe and the Native Caribbean, 1492–1797*, London: Routledge.

Hutchings, G. (1995) 'Chinese Tell Conference Cab Drivers the Naked Truth', *The Daily Telegraph* 23 August.

Hutchings, G. and Munnion, C. (1995) 'Hilary Should Stick to the US, says Beijing', *The Daily Telegraph* 8 September.

Ifekwunigwe, J.O. (1997) 'Diaspora's Daughters, Africa's Orphans?: On Lineage, Authenticity and "Mixed-Race" Identity' in H. Mirza (ed.) *Black British Feminism*, London: Routledge.

Inglis, C. (1997) 'Asian Immigration, Multiculturalism and National Identity in Australia' in G. Rystad (ed.) *Encountering Strangers: Responses and Consequences*, Lund University Press.

Irigaray, L. (1993) *An Ethics of Sexual Difference*, trans. C. Burke and K. Munton, Ithaca: Cornell University Press.

Jackson, A. (ed.) (1987) *Anthropology at Home*, London: Tavistock Publishers.

Jayasuriya, L. (1997) *Immigration and Multiculturalism in Australia: Selected Essays*, Nedlands, Western Australia: University of Western Australia Press.

Jupp, J. (1996) *Understanding Australian Multiculturalism*, Canberra: Australian Government Publishing Service.

Kabeer, N. (1995) *Reversed Realities: Gender Hierarchies in Development Thought*, London: Verso.

Kaplan, C. (1995) 'A World Without Borders: The Body Shop's Transnational Geographies', *Social Text* 13, 2: 45–66.

—— (1998) *Questions of Travel: Postmodern Discourses of Displacement*, Durham: Duke University Press.

Karim, W.J. (1993) 'Epilogue: The "Nativised" Self and the Native' in D. Bell, P. Caplan and W.J. Karim (eds) *Gendered Fields: Women, Men and Ethnography*, London: Routledge.

Klein, R. (1991) 'Editorial', *Women's Studies International Forum* 14, 5: 505–506.

Kristeva, J. (1982) *Powers of Horror: An Essay on Abjection*, trans. L.S. Roudiez, New York: Columbia University Press.

—— (1991) *Strangers to Ourselves*, trans. L.S. Roudiez, Hemel Hempstead: Harvester Wheatsheaf.

Lacan, J. (1977) *Écrits: A Selection*, trans. A. Sheridan London: Tavistock Publications.

Lancashire Constabulary (1996) *Operation Streetwise Workbook*, England: The Hillgate Group.

Landry, D. and MacLean, G. (1996) 'Introduction: Reading Spivak' in D. Landry and G. Maclean (eds) *The Spivak Reader Selected Works*, London: Routledge.

Larbalestier, J. (1990) 'The Politics of Representation: Australian Aboriginal Women and Feminism', *Anthropological Forum* 6, 2: 143–157.

Levinas, E. (1979) *Totality and Infinity: An Essay on Exteriority*, trans. A. Lingis, The Hague: M. Nijhoff Publishers.

—— (1985) *Ethics and Infinity: Conversations with Philippe Wemoi*, trans. R.A. Cohen, Pittsburgh: Duquesne University Press.

—— (1987) *Time and the Other: And Additional Essays*, trans. R.A. Cohen, Pittsburgh, PA: Duquesne University Press.

—— (1991) *Otherwise than Being or Beyond Essence*, trans. A. Lingis, Dordrecht: Kluwer Academic Publishers.

Lienhardt, R.G. (1956) 'Mode of Thought' in E.E. Evans-Pritchard *et al.* (eds) *The Institutions of Primitive Society*, Oxford: Blackwell.

Lofland, L.H. (1973) *A World of Strangers: Order and Action in Urban Public Space*, New York: Basic Books.

Lorde, A. (1984) *Sister Outsider: Essays and Speeches*, Freedom, California: The Crossing Press.

Low, G.C.-L. (1996) *White Skins, Black Masks: Representation and Colonialism*, London: Routledge.

Lowe, L. (1996) *Immigrant Acts: On Asian American Cultural Politics*, Durham: Duke University Press.

Lowe, L. and Lloyd, D. (1997) 'Introduction' in L. Lowe and D. Lloyd (eds) *The Politics of Culture in the Shadow of Capital*, Durham: Duke University Press.

Lucashenko, M. (1994) 'No Other Truth? Aboriginal Women and Australian Feminism', *Social Alternatives* 12, 4: 21–24.

Lyotard, J.-F. (1989) *The Differend: Phrases in Dispute*, trans. G. Van Den Abbeele, Manchester: Manchester University Press.

Mani, L. (1989) 'Multiple Mediations: Feminist Scholarship in the Age of Multinational Reception', *Inscriptions* 5, 1–24.

Martin, E. (1995) *Flexible Bodies: Tracking Immunity in American Culture from the Days of Polio to the Age of Aids*, Boston, MA: Beacon Press.

Marx, K. (1976) *Capital: Volume 1*, Harmondsworth: Penguin Books.

McBeth, S. (1993) 'Myths of Objectivity and the Collaborative Process in Life History Research' in C.B. Brettell (ed.) *When They Read What We Write: The Politics of Ethnography*, Westport: Bergin and Garvey.

McClintock, A. (1992).'The Angel of Progress: Pitfalls of the Term "Post-Colonialism"', *Social Text* 32, 33: 84–99.

—— (1995) *Imperial Leather: Race, Gender and Sexuality in the Colonial Context*, London: Routledge.

McCaig, N.M. (1996) 'Understanding Global Nomads' in C.D. Smith (ed.) *Strangers at Home: Essays on the Long term Impact of Living Overseas and Coming 'Home' to a Strange Land*, New York: Aletheia Publications.

McGrane, B. (1989) *Beyond Anthropology: Society and the Other*, New York: Columbia University Press.

Meer, A. (1994) 'Rain' in R. Ahmad and R. Gupta (eds) (1994) *Flaming Spirit: Stories from the Asian Women's Writing Collective*, London: Virago Press.

Merleau-Ponty, M. (1968) *The Visible and the Invisible*, trans. A. Lingis, Illinois: Northwestern University Press.

Merry, S.E. (1981) *Urban Danger: Life in a Neighborhood of Strangers*, Philadelphia: Temple University Press.

Mies, M. (1986) *Patriarchy and Accumulation on a World Scale: Women in the International Division of Labour*, London: Zed Press.

Mitter, S. (1986) *Common Fate, Common Bond: Women in the Global Economy*, London: Pluto Press.

Mohanty, C.T. (1991) 'Under Western Eyes: Feminism and Colonial Discourse' in C.T. Mohanty, A. Russo and L. Torres (eds) *Third World Women and the Politics of Feminism*, Bloomington: Indiana University Press.

—— (1997) 'Women Workers and Capitalist Scripts: Ideologies of Domination, Common Interests and the Politics of Solidarity' in M.J. Alexander and C.T. Mohanty (eds) *Feminist Genealogies, Colonial Legacies, Democratic Futures*, London: Routledge.

Moore-Gilbert, B. (1997) *Postcolonial Theory: Contexts, Practices, Politics*, London: Verso.

Moreton-Robinson, A. (1998) 'When the Object Speaks, A Postcolonial Encounter: Anthropological Representations and Aboriginal Women's Self-Presentations', *Discourse: Studies in the Cultural Politics of Education* 19, 3: 275–289.

—— (forthcoming) 'Tiddas Talkin Up to the White Woman: When Huggins *et al.* took on Bell' in M. Grossman, P. Morrissey and D. Cuthbert (eds) *Black Lines: Contemporary Critical Writing by Indigenous Australians*, Melbourne: Melbourne University Press.

Morris, D.J. and Hess, K. (1975) *Neighborhood Power: The New Localism*, Boston: Beacon Press.

Morris, J. (ed.) (1996) *Encounters with Strangers: Feminism and Disability*, London: Women's Press.

Mullen, H. (1994) 'Optic White: Blackness and the Production of Whiteness', *Diacritics* 24, 2–4: 71–89.

Nancy, J.-L. (1994) 'Corpus' in J.F. MacCannell and L. Zakarin (eds) *Thinking Bodies*, Stanford: Stanford University Press.

Narayan, U. (1997) *Dislocating Cultures: Identities, Traditions and Third-World Feminisms*, New York: Routledge.

Nelson, T.N. (1990) 'Letter to the Editor', *Women's Studies International Forum* 14, 5: 507.

O'Barr, W.A. (1994) *Culture and the Ad: Exploring Otherness in the World of Advertising*, Boulder, CO: Westview Press.

Odeh, L.U. (1983) 'Post-Colonial Feminism and the Veil', *Feminist Review* 43: 26–37.

Okely, J. (1992) 'Anthropology and Autobiography: Participatory Experience and Embodied Knowledge' in J. Okely and H. Callaway (eds) *Anthropology and Autobiography*, London: Routledge.

Ong, A. (1987) *Spirits of Resistance and Capitalist Discipline: Factory Women in Malaysia*, Albany: State University of New York Press.

O'Sullivan, J. (1997) 'In the Name of the Children', *The Independent*, 28 March.

Parry, B. (1987) 'Problems in Current Theories of Colonial Discourse', *Oxford Literary Review* 9: 27–58.

Pels, D. (1999) 'Privileged Nomads: On the Strangeness of Intellectuals and the Intellectuality of Strangers', *Theory, Culture and Society* 16, 1: 63–86.

Persram, N. (1996) 'In My Father's House are Many Mansions: The Nation and Postcolonial Desire' in H. Mirza (ed.) *Black British Feminism*, London: Routledge.

Peters, J.D. (1999) 'Exile, Nomadism and Diaspora: The Stakes of Mobility in the Western Canon' in H. Naficy (ed.) *Home, Exile, Homeland: Film, Media and the Politics of Place*, London: Routledge.

Plato (1970) *The Republic*, trans. D. Lee, Harmondsworth: Penguin.

Povinelli, E. (1998) 'The State of Shame: Australian Multiculturalism and the Crisis of Indigenous Citizenship', *Critical Inquiry* 24: 575–610.

Powdermaker, H. (1966) *Stranger and Friend: The Way of an Anthropologist*, London: W.W. Norton and Co.

Pratt, M.L. (1986) 'Fieldwork in Common Places' in J. Clifford and G.E. Marcus (eds) *Writing Culture: The Poetics and Politics of Ethnography*, Cambridge: University of Cambridge Press.

—— (1992) *Imperial Eyes: Travel Writing and Transculturation*, London: Routledge.

Pringle, J. (1995) '8 foreigners flock to China for women's forum', *The Times* 30 August.

Probyn, E. (1996) *Outside Belongings*, London: Routledge.

—— (forthcoming) 'Shaming Theory, Thinking Disconnections: Feminism and Reconciliation' in S. Ahmed, J. Kilby, C. Lury, M. McNeil and B. Skeggs (eds) *Transformations: Thinking Through Feminism*, London: Routledge.

Rich, A.C. (1986) *Blood. Bread and Poetry: Selected Prose, 1979–1985*, New York: WW Norton.

Robertson, G. *et al.* (eds) (1994) *Travellers' Tales: Narratives of Home and Displacement*, London: Routledge.

Rystad, G. (ed.) (1997) *Encountering Strangers: Responses and Consequences*, Lund: Lund University Press.

Said, E. (1978) *Orientalism*, London: Routledge and Kegan Paul.

—— (1990) 'Reflections on Exile' in R. Ferguson, M. Gewer, T. Minh-Ha and C. West (eds) *Out There: Marginalization and Contemporary Culture*, New York: New Museum of Contemporary Art.

San Juan, E. (1998) *Beyond Postcolonial Theory*, New York: St Martin's Press.

Sarup, M. (1994) 'Home and Identity' in G. Robertson *et al.* (eds) *Travellers' Tales: Narratives of Home and Displacement*, London: Routledge.

Schilder, P. (1970) *The Image and Appearance of the Human Body*, New York: International Universities Press.

Schutz, A. (1944) 'The Stranger: An Essay in Social Psychology', *American Journal of Sociology* 46: 499–507.

Scougal, D.A.Y. (1996) 'Letter: A Man's Home or His Prison', *The Independent* 6 January.

Seaman, P.A. (1996) 'Rediscovering a Sense of Place' in C.D. Smith (ed.) *Strangers at Home: Essays on the Long Term Impact of Living Overseas and Coming 'Home' to a Strange Land*, New York: Aletheia Publications.

Shohat, E. (1992) 'Notes on the "Post-Colonial" ', *Social Text* 31, 32: 99–113.

Shohat, E. and Stam, R. (1994) *Unthinking Eurocentrism: Multiculturalism and the Media*, London: Routledge.

Sibley, D. (1995) *Geographies of Exclusion: Society and Difference in the West*, London: Routledge.

Simmel, G. (1971) *On Individuality and Social Forms*, D.M. Levine (ed.), Chicago: University of Chicago Press.

Skeggs, B. (1999) 'Matter out of Place: Visibility and Sexualities in Leisure Spaces', *Leisure Studies* 18: 213–232.

Smith, A. (1974) *The Body*, Harmondsworth: Penguin Books.

Spivak, G.C. (1988) 'Can the Subaltern Speak?' in C. Nelson and L. Grossberg (eds) *Marxism and the Interpretation of Culture*, Urbana: University of Illinois Press.

—— (1990) *The Post-Colonial Critic: Interviews, Strategies, Dialogues*, ed. S. Harasym, London: Routledge.

—— (1995) Translator's preface and afterword in *Imaginary Maps*, London: Routledge.

—— (1996) *The Spivak Reader*, D. Landry and G. Maclean (eds), London: Routledge.

—— (1999) *A Critique of Postcolonial Reason: Toward a History of the Vanishing Present*, Cambridge, MA: Harvard University Press.

—— (forthcoming) 'Claiming Transformation: Travel Notes' in S. Ahmed, J. Kilby, C. Lury, M. McNeil and B. Skeggs (eds) *Transformations: Thinking Through Feminism*, London: Routledge.

Stacey, Jackie (forthcoming) 'The Global Within: The Embodiment of Health in Contemporary Culture' in S. Franklin, C. Lury and J. Stacey, *Global Nature, Global Culture*, London: Sage.

Stacey, Judith (1988) 'Can There be a Feminist Ethnography?', *Women's Studies International Forum* 11, 1: 21–27.

Stallybrass, P. and White, A. (1986) *The Politics and Poetics of Transgression*, London: Methuen.

Stam, R. (1995) *Derrida and Autobiography*, Cambridge: Cambridge University Press.

Stanko, E.A. (1990) *Everyday Violence: How Women and Men Experience Sexual and Physical Danger*, London: Pandora.

—— (1997) 'Safety Talk: Conceptualising Women's Risk Assessment as a "Technology of the Soul" ', *Theoretical Criminology* 1, 4: 479–499.

Stockton, K. (1994) 'Bodies and God: Poststructuralist Feminists Return to the Fold of Spiritual Materialism' in M. Ferguson and J. Wicke (eds) *Feminism and Postmodernism*, Durham: Duke University Press.

Stratton, J. (1998) *Race Daze: Australia in Identity Crisis*, Annandale, NSW: Pluto Press.

Stratton, J. and Ang, I. (1994) 'Multicultural Imagined Communities: Cultural Difference and National Identity in Australia and USA', *Continuum: The Australian Journal of Media and Culture* 9, 2: 124–158.

Sum, N. (forthcoming) 'From Politics of Identity to Politics of Complexity: A Possible Research Agenda for Feminist Politics/Movements Across Time and Space' in S. Ahmed, J. Kilby, C. Lury, M. McNeil and B. Skeggs (eds) *Transformations: Thinking Through Feminism*, London: Routledge.

Sunderland, P.L. (1997) ' "You May Not Know It, But I'm Black": White Women's Self- Identification as Black', *Ethnos* 62, 1–2: 32–58.

Taylor, C. (1994) 'The Politics of Recognition' in D.T. Goldberg (ed.) *Multiculturalism: A Critical Reader*, Oxford: Blackwell.

Todorov, T. (1984) *The Conquest of America: The Question of the Other*, New York: Harper Colophon Books.

Trouillot, M. (1991) 'Anthropology and the Savage Slot: The Poetics and Politics of Otherness' in R. Fox (ed.) *Recapturing Anthropology: Working in the Present*, New Mexico: School of American Research Press.

Twine, F.W. (1996) 'Brown Skinned White Girls: Class, Culture and the Construction of White Identity in Suburban Communities', *Gender, Place and Culture* 3, 2: 205–224.

Tyler, C.A. (1994) 'Passing: Narcissism, Identity and Difference', *Differences* 6: 212–248.

United Nations (1995) 'Report of the Fourth World Conference on Women', www.undp.org/fwcw/fwcw2.htm

Vasseleu, C. (1998) *Textures of Light: Vision and Touch in Irigaray, Levinas and Merleau-Ponty*, London: Routledge.

Visweswaran, K. (1994) *Fictions of Feminist Ethnography*, Minneapolis: University of Minnesota Press.

Walzer, M. (1989) *Spheres of Justice: A Defence of Pluralism and Equality*, Oxford: Blackwell.

Weiss, G. (1999) *Body Images: Embodiment as Intercorporeality*, London: Routledge.

Werbner, P. (1996) 'Essentialising the Other: A Critical Response' in T. Ranger, Y. Samad and O. Stuart (eds) *Culture, Identity and Politics: Ethnic Minorities in Britain*, Avebury: Aldershot.

Willett, C. (1995) *Maternal Ethics and Other Slave Moralities*, London: Routledge.

Wyschogrod, E. (1998) *An Ethics of Remembering: History, Heterology and the Nameless Others*, Chicago: University of Chicago Press.

Yeatman, A. (1993) 'Voice and Representation in the Politics of Difference' in S. Gunew and A. Yeatman (eds) *Feminism and the Politics of Difference*, St Leonards: Allen and Unwin.

Young, A. (1996) *Imagining Crime: Textual Outlaws and Criminal Conversations*, London: Sage.

Young, I.M. (1990) *Throwing Like a Girl and Other Essays in Feminist Philosophy and Social Theory*, Bloomington: Indiana University Press.

—— (1997) 'Asymmetrical Reciprocity: On Moral Respect, Wonder and Enlarged Thought', *Constellations* 3, 3: 340–358.

Young, L. (1996) *Fear of the Dark: 'Race', Gender and Sexuality in the Cinema*, London: Routledge.

Index

abjection: alien 2;
incorporation/expulsion 54; Kristeva
51, 52; silencing 166–7
Aboriginal people: *see* Indigenous people
activism 178–9
Agar, Michael 59–60, 61, 125
Ahmad, Aijaz 10, 12, 13, 83, 183n8,
183n9
Ahmad, R. 94
Ahmed, Sara 23, 61, 142, 170;
Differences that Matter 142; stopped by
police 128–9
Alexander, M. Jacqui 167, 168, 174–5,
178
aliens 1–3
Althusser, Louis 22–3
Anderson, Benedict 97–8
Anderson, Elijah 22, 23, 27, 33–4
Ang, Ien 97, 104, 112
anthropology 57–60, 63–4, 186n5
anti-poverty 174
Asad, Talal 57, 58
Asian migrants 79, 93
Asian Women's Writing Collective 79,
93–4
assimilation 106–7, 113, 119, 124
Australia: Department of Immigration
and Multicultural Affairs 102; fusion
cooking 118; identity 96–7, 105–6,
108–9; migration 90;
multiculturalism 16, 95, 102–10,
188n2; racism 63; *see also* Bell,
Diane

Australian Council on Population and
Ethnic Affairs 95
Australian Law Commission 109
autobiography 67–8, 189n8

Bailyn, B. 11
Balibar, E. 117, 132
Bauman, Zygmunt x, 4, 24, 101, 143
becoming 189n6; confrontation 121;
mediation 122; narrative 122, 123,
124–5; other 119
becoming native: assimilation 124;
boundaries 156–7; fantasy 132,
156–7, 188n2; hybridity 121; white
man 120; *see also* passing for black
Beijing Conference for Women: *see* UN,
Beijing Conference
being-at-home 86–7, 88, 91
Bell, Diane: co-authorship 63, 185n3;
Daughters of the Dreaming 67–70, 74;
Indigenous women 186–7n9;
knowing strangers 67; and Nelson
64–5, 71–2; rape 61–2; speaking for
61–2, 186n6
belonging 99–100, 127
Benhabib, Seyla 156
Benjamin, W. 58, 59
Bennetto, J. 31
Bhabha, Homi 129, 183n8
Bhachu, Parminder 90
Biddle, Jennifer 45
birthdays 161–2
black feminist literature 127

CPSIA information can be obtained
at www.ICGtesting.com
Printed in the USA
FFOW04n0140010817
38242FF